My Very Last Possession

My Very Last Possession

And Other Stories by
Pak Wansŏ

Translated by
Chun Kyung-Ja et al.

AN EAST GATE BOOK

M.E. Sharpe
Armonk, New York
London, England

An East Gate Book

Copyright © 1999 by M. E. Sharpe, Inc.

Library of Congress Cataloging-in-Publication Data

Pak, Wan-sŏ, 1931–
My very last possession and other stories by Pak Wansŏ /
translated and edited by Kyung-Ja Chun.
p.   cm.
"An East gate book."
ISBN 0-7656-0428-0 (hc. : alk. paper).—ISBN 0-7656-0429-9 (pbk. : alk. paper)
1. Pak, Wan-sŏ, 1931– . —Translations into English.   I. Chun,
Kyung-Ja, 1945–   II. Title.
PL992.62.W34A26   1998
895.7′34—dc21   99-10681
CIP

Printed in the United States of America

BM (c)   10   9   8   7   6   5   4   3   2
BM (p)   10   9   8   7   6   5   4   3

Contents

Introduction

This collection comprises ten stories by Pak Wansŏ, one of Korea's most respected and widely read contemporary writers. The author belongs to the generation born in the 1930s when the Korean people suffered under the heel of Japanese colonial rule. She was born in 1931 near Kaesŏng, just north of the 38th parallel, which has divided the two Koreas since 1945. In 1934 her father died and her widowed mother moved to Seoul with her older brother, leaving her in the care of grandparents and an uncle for four years. From 1938 to 1945 she attended schools in Seoul. As a teenager she was directly affected by the tragic division of Korea: her family relocated permanently to Seoul, unable to return to their home in the Communist north.

As a young woman the author survived the savagery and pandemonium of the Korean War. Just weeks before the war broke out on June 25, 1950, Pak was admitted to the nation's best college, Seoul National University, an indication of great intellectual potential that was to be borne out by her career as a writer, which began almost twenty years later. The war not only interrupted her education, but took the lives of her older brother and uncle, forcing Pak to work to support her family. During the war, she took a job in the U.S. Eighth Army PX, and her experiences during this period were to resurface decades later in several short stories. In 1953 she married Ho Yŏngjin, and the marriage lasted thirty-five years, until her husband's death in 1988.

From the late 1950s and into the present, Korea has undergone rapid and far-reaching social and economic change. The people of Korea have endured repressive military dictatorship and chronic political instability as they struggled to overcome poverty. Pak Wansŏ's realistic prose holds up a mirror to the lives of ordinary Koreans in the course of their "industrial revolution," an era of merciless dislocation and wrenching transformation. Her first novel, *The Naked Tree*, was published in 1970, when Pak was almost thirty-nine years old. Despite her late start, she has since been a prolific author, publishing more than ten novels and scores of short stories and novellas. She has been awarded several prestigious literary prizes.

Over the last three decades, changes have been more conspicuous than continuities in many domains of Korean life, but certain values that for Koreans constitute their distinctive identity have been tenaciously preserved, both for good and for ill. The popularity of Pak Wansŏ's fiction is based on her intelligence and her compassion in grappling with themes of deep significance to her readers. First and foremost, Pak concerns herself with the fate of the family in Korea. A distinctive aspect of Korea's Confucian cultural heritage is the stress placed on the institution of the family. In traditional agrarian Korea, personal morality, social prestige, economic welfare, political order, and legal obligation all centered on family bonds. The Confucian ideal of filial piety served not just as a paradigm for harmonious family relations, but as a master metaphor for the hierarchies of social status, for patriarchal structures of political authority, and for gender-based demarcations of public and private realms of life. What gives universal appeal to Pak's work is her depiction of the moral dilemmas of Korean family life: The family can be a fortress of altruistic love in a merciless world and a sanctuary from which worldly achievements can be launched, but at the same time it can be a prison in which injustice and suffering are reproduced and surrender to outmoded prejudices is demanded.

With the advent of "modernization," the centrality of the family in Korean life has undergone radical changes. The emergence of a capitalist, market-based society in Korea has occasioned rapid urbanization and a concomitant demographic shift: More households are nuclear families and fewer are extended families. Women have entered the workforce in vast numbers and in ever more diverse roles. Going against the grain of Confucian tradition, the system of higher education gradually has been opened to women, but little progress has been made in curtailing male domination of the state bureaucracies, the business world, the universities, and the learned professions. Despite emergence of "progressive" rhetoric espousing equality of opportunity, and despite recent legislation purporting to protect the rights of women, gender discrimination remains pervasive in contemporary Korea.

Another set of significant changes has stemmed from Korean government initiatives to control population growth in one of the world's most densely populated nations: The average size of Korean nuclear families has dramatically diminished since the 1960s. Given this trend, care for the elderly has become a prominent issue with profound moral, economic, and political dimensions. Unlike the wealthier countries of the West, the south Korean government never has made adequate provisions for the welfare of the aged in the form of social insurance, subsidized housing, or the like. Such responsibility has fallen primarily on relatives. In four of the stories in this collection, Pak uses the unhappy condition of the aged as a prism through which to ponder erosion of family values.

Beyond the stresses attributable to rapid industrialization, the integrity of the Korean family — and by extension the Korean nation itself — has been assailed by civil war, by large-scale emigration, and by violent political upheavals. One story is devoted to a family painfully split apart during the Korean War. Another depicts a family fragmented by overseas emigration, a case typifying the diaspora that has scattered millions of Koreans to the far corners of the world — from Japan to Uzbekistan to California — in this century. A third story centers on a mother whose only son was killed during a police crackdown on a political demonstration.

The ways in which Pak's characters resolve their very personal dilemmas express the human reality of traumatic choices that too often are distorted by self-deception. At the same time, these stories exemplify patterns of an epic-scale drama — the often tragic and yet sometimes absurdly comic drama that is modern Korean life. Without spoiling the stories for readers by disclosing too much of their content, a brief sketch of some of the themes addressed in this collection may serve to indicate the richness of the literary world of Pak Wansŏ.

The opening story, "She Knows, I Know and Heaven Knows" (1984), focuses on the vulnerability of innocence in modern society, where naive trust in traditional values exposes the unsuspecting to cruel exploitation. A wealthy, sophisticated couple employs a poor widow to be a surrogate wife and nurse for the husband's elderly father, effectively purchasing the wife's release from the traditional duties of a daughter-in-law. The emptiness of filial piety and the hypocrisy of sham rituals are underscored by the greed of the nouveau riche couple, whose preoccupation with appearances does not keep them from viciously defrauding a social inferior. On the one hand, modernization seems to be responsible for loss of conscience, yet, on the other hand, implicit nostalgia for a simpler society based on trust has a certain ambivalence: Is such nostalgia itself self-deception?

In "Butterfly of Illusion" (1995), Pak Wansŏ approaches the predicament of the elderly from another perspective, comparing a painfully isolated old widow with another social outcast, a woman who from girlhood has been condemned to loneliness by a selfish mother who pushed her into becoming a Buddhist fortune-teller. The old widow's memory is failing, and she feels unwelcome at home, as she is shifted from daughter to son and back again. Repeatedly she flees a dehumanizing captivity by wandering off, seeking to escape into the past. Her well-meaning daughter, a working woman with duties to her children and husband, is confused by the subconscious resentments that plague her. The old widow and the fortune-teller end up creating an improbable refuge of reciprocated kindness within a cold and uncaring universe.

The Korean diaspora is at issue in "Farewell at Kimpo" (1974). Who or what is responsible for the mass emigration of Koreans that split up so many families? In this story, an old woman who has seen three of her four children emigrate is preparing to depart for America to spend her last years with her daughter. Inflated hopes of a better life in America are exposed as wishful thinking, driven by economic desperation rather than by well-informed choice. The illiterate old woman has no clear picture of the world. She does not even grasp until the last minute that she is being expelled from the only world she knows. In showing the sorts of conflicts emigration created for thousands of Korean families in the 1960s and 1970s, Pak once again reveals pathologies of conventional family values.

The fourth story, "Mr. Hong's Medals" (1983), uses the tragedy of a family divided by the Korean War to dramatize how Confucian ritualism can detach social convention from authentic concern for relatives. The basic irony here is that preservation of "the family" as an abstraction — a lineage to be preserved at all costs — leads directly to the destruction of a flesh-and-blood family. The ingratitude of an adopted son makes filial piety into a self-caricature, an empty gesture. Mr. Hong, eager for praise for discharging an abstract duty, takes a perverse pride in sacrificing the welfare of his own wife and son. The accolades he lusts after are tainted by inarticulate guilt at having abandoned his family. The beneficiary of his sacrifice, the nephew he adopts as his son, finally abandons his dying uncle, treating him as a mere economic burden. The old, ideal family structure has been doubly destroyed: first, by the division of the country and, second, by the ruthlessness of modern life.

The institution of marriage comes under searching reflection in "Thus Ended My Days of Watching Over the House" (1978). This story, set during the period of military dictatorship, depicts the crisis experienced by the wife of a professor whose husband has been summoned for interrogation by the secret police. On one level, it is about the indirect victims, the families, of persons persecuted by a dictatorship which converted higher education into a system of indoctrination and surveillance. On a deeper level, however, the story concerns the painful superficiality of many marriages in a society that has confined women to the private sphere while leading men to "shield" their wives from public affairs. The woman's husband treats her like an infant, telling her not to worry while he is away, and yet he expects her blind support. She sees herself as a powerless sleepwalker. Depending on what happens to her husband, her life could be destroyed, too. The form of marriage has no substance: Socially she is an appendage of her husband, but she knows almost nothing about her husband's activities. Within the household, she is a mere instrument through which he can discharge his obligations as family head. She must carry on in his absence, looking after her mother-in-law and trapped in a web of relations, while unable to affect her own fate.

For the first time in her life the woman thinks for herself about her life: she has been "terrorized" as much as her husband, but her fear is primarily caused by the uncertainty of being left at the mercy of unknown forces. Bonsai trees prized by the professor are allowed by the wife to shrivel and die while her husband is away. The unnaturally stunted growth of bonsai is a powerful symbol for Pak Wansŏ: it stands for the way many Korean women have been stunted by the patronizing, dismissive attitudes of their husbands, and also for the distortions of education under a dictatorship that required teachers to spy on their own students. Just as Korea itself was suffocated and oppressed under Japanese colonial rule, in more recent times women and the young have had their plasticity and creativity deformed by a system that demands obedience without question, and that subordinates liberty to order.

Black comedy animates the subtext of "A Certain Barbarity" (1976), in which a social-climbing family in a poor neighborhood exhibits a combustible blend of greed and gullibility. The corrupting influence of economic modernization is embodied in the tragic flaw of this hapless household: To be envied by the neighbors is so intoxicating that the protagonists bankrupt themselves to create an illusion of wealth while they are being fleeced by a relative who turns out to be a despicable con man. The cyclical justice of karma brings their downfall, but the reader is left wondering whether this family is an aberration, or whether they typify something pervasive in modern Korean society. It is no accident that the flaunting of wealth in this story takes the form of mimicry of the Japanese style of conspicuous consumption. Envy of Japanese wealth in Korea is coupled with condemnation of Japan's historic crimes against the Korean people — the sardonic comments of the narrator in "A Certain Barbarity" can be fully appreciated only if this double-edged attitude is kept in mind.

The author puts her familiarity with the American military post exchanges in Korea to good use in "Encounter at the Airport" (1978). This story recounts the ingenuity of Korean women employed in the American PXs, for whom desperate economic straits led to an amazing versatility in defeating U.S. countermeasures against the black market. The unforgettable heroine is an indefatigable master of disguise, as well as an exemplary free spirit uncowed by the men she encounters, whether military commanders or her useless American husband. Comical scenes are interlaced with realistic anecdotes that depict the often uncomprehending attitude the American military has displayed toward the Korean people during almost fifty years of American military presence in Korea.

"Granny Flowers in Those Heartless Days" (1978) is probably Pak Wansŏ's best-known piece of short fiction. The story comprises two separate parables, each set in a rural village during the Korean War and each featuring an enigmatic old "granny" as protagonist. Traditionally, in Korean society, elders are given power and responsibility over the young. In each of these villages the men are off at war and the oldest woman is a matriarch, responsible for all the women in the extended family of the village. The two heroines are almost superhuman in their virtue: one exemplifies courage, and the second compassion. In a way, the two old grannies are eccentric "sages." They have important lessons to teach men, who are too easily consumed by warlike "virtues" — a foolish and self-destructive "bravery" devoid of compassion.

Another of Pak's well-known and frequently anthologized works is "Three Days in That Autumn" (1980), a jarringly realistic story chronicling the psychological breakdown of a female physician who has spent her entire work life as an abortionist. In this narrative, the author evokes the hellish yet eerily coherent "life-world" constructed by the main character, whose entire life has been shaped by the trauma of being raped during the Korean War. This repressed memory, heightened by the doctor's dissonant feelings toward her dead father, resurfaces in a catastrophic way as she counts down the last three days to her long-planned retirement. Accumulated guilt over having performed so many abortions, terminating the unwanted pregnancies not only of prostitutes but of frivolous middle-class housewives, drives the woman to the edge of madness. The story is an eloquent condemnation of an anomic society in which the hidden consequences of rampant hypocrisy are seldom publicly addressed.

The final story included here, "My Very Last Possession" (1994), takes the form of a lengthy monologue, a one-sided telephone conversation. The narrator is a woman whose only son was killed in the course of police suppression of a student protest demonstration. Though it is not clear whether the son was a dissident or only an innocent bystander, the mother's bereavement makes her into a symbol of opposition to the undemocratic government. An entirely unpolitical woman suddenly faces a transformed world, in which some of her relatives and old friends are uncomfortable with her newfound notoriety and her association with "radical" causes.

The author artfully contrasts the two coexisting worlds in which this woman finds herself. In the "old" world, appearance, stability, and ritual reign. In the "new" world, what matters is truth, overcoming injustice, and responding to violence. The mother's acquaintances keep their distance from her, claiming they do it to spare her pain, but she knows that they actually are afraid to associate with a politicized person. Against the historical background of the June 1987 democratization movement, when the death of innocent students mobilized Korean society as a whole against the military dictatorship, this story expresses the complex ways in which ordinary citizens, women as well as men, become politically active when government grows oppressive. The pain of a mother who has lost her only son is universally understandable, but when the death is senseless, people are outraged and demand changes to prevent recurrence of such abuses. An ordinary family, detached from the "big picture" of political strife, can be suddenly lifted up and thrown into the eye of the storm. On one of its levels, thus, "My Very Last Possession" is a critique of political violence, a recapitulation of the troubles Korea endured during the 1980s in the course of moving toward democracy.

My Very Last Possession

She Knows, I Know, and Heaven Knows

"**B**y the way, where's our bereaved widow? Could it be she's off somewhere stricken with grief?"

"Stricken? She's too busy planning the rest of her life, I'll bet. I hear she's not your average nice old lady."

"What a disgrace. Couldn't she at least wait for the full three days of mourning to pass? I mean, it's not like they're going to toss her into the street right away."

"Couldn't agree more. I don't even ask for the full three days — if she would just act the part of the dignified widow until the funeral tomorrow, the family at least could save face . . . "

"How can you expect a person with no sense of human decency to behave like a human? From the very first I saw the sort she was. Jintae's mom pretends to be such a sly fox, but her slyness turned out to be in vain, or else she was hoodwinked when she brought that old bag lady home. What was she thinking?"

"At least she wasn't a real bag lady, they say. Used to be a street peddler — you know, selling odds and ends out of a basket — out by the Sŏngnam Moran Market."

"It wasn't Sŏngnam, it was under Chamsil Overpass. She sold vegetables there."

"No, no. Chamsil's right, but not under the Overpass. Jintae's mom happened on her near the Saemaul Market — she was peddling elastic belts and stockings from bundles spread on the sidewalk."

"Whatever you say, I know best what that old lady was when she came into this house. Let me tell you, she wasn't far from being a bag lady. Her hair was a rat's nest; her back salted with grime; and she let off a sour, rotten odor that stung your nose. She had enough black filth under her fingernails and toenails to make a brick of charcoal and then some."

"Oh, come off it. Really?"

The women cackled. They were all friends of Jintae's mother — the woman of the house and wife of the late sir's eldest son. Some were old classmates from her schooldays, others were friends from her savings pool and the flower-arrangement club, and there were a couple of neighbors as well. Ever since her old father-in-law passed away, they had been streaming in and out of the house under the pretext of helping out, talking up a storm and often laughing loudly. The day before, their voices at least had been lowered and their laughter muffled, but by this time they at times seemed to forget that the household was in mourning.

"Won't they be upset if we laugh so loudly?"

"Why not laugh? He lived a long life. A cheerful wake is in order."

"Jintae's mom, you know, she just couldn't hold out."

"What do you mean?"

"It's not even three years since she brought that old lady in. If only she had toughed it out somehow and cared for the old sir herself, think how pure and worthy she'd be feeling now. Then it could have been a cheerful funeral, all right."

"Somebody else's three years may seem short to you, but how would you like to look after a widower father-in-law, paralyzed by a stroke, for three long years? And don't they say: 'Even the worst wife is better than the best child'? Jintae's mother did her daughterly duty by getting that old lady for him."

"Yeah, such devoted daughters-in-law are few and far between, I suppose. All day yesterday she wept such bitter tears, and today, she's still laid up back there, refusing to eat. What good are those daughters of his, anyway? They just sit there with their mouths clamped tight and pretend to choke back their sobs. As if we couldn't read anything from those dry, blank eyes of theirs. Daughters are useless and sons are no better. It's the daughters-in-law who really care and serve you till your dying day."

"By the way, we should at least warm up some milk for Jintae's mom. Filial devotion is all well and good, but she's so worn out from the fast."

"Good idea. Let's take her some milk and soup. People say that down through the ages there's never been a woman on god's green earth who followed her departed father-in-law to the other side, but Jintae's mom . . . what a fool."

The ladies flocked in a drove toward the bedroom where Jintae's mother lay ill, leaving the kitchen empty. The old woman, Sŏngnamdaek, who all this time had been lurking hunched and still in an alcove beside the kitchen, now cracked the door and peeked in.

"Those busybodies go everywhere in a gang," she muttered, tut-tutting to herself.

The kitchen, cleared at last of those women who were better at flapping their mouths than doing any useful work, or even realizing what needed to be done, was a mess. On each of the four burners on the stove something was furiously boiling away. Half-trimmed scallions lay strewn all over the kitchen floor, along with a chunk of radish and a mateless slipper. The doorway was half-blocked by a lacquered table, and from the mess on top of it one couldn't tell whether the table was in process of being set or cleared.

Considering the indignities she had endured the day before, Sŏngnamdaek knew she should pretend not to have noticed anything. Still, she tiptoed quietly out into the kitchen, and lowered the heat on the stove to keep the soup from boiling over. On another burner, all the water had boiled off from the pork. She poked it with a chopstick and, judging it done, turned off the gas. Some fish stew was simmering nicely — she had a spoonful. A bit on the bland side, but soothing going down. Her mistake, however, was to have opened her mouth for a taste. All at once, the hunger demon reared his ugly head inside Sŏngnamdaek, and her insides started writhing like a coiled-up dragon, ready to scream in protest. Since the prior morning when the old sir died, she had had nothing at all that could properly be called food. The so-called wife of the deceased could not very well be stuffing her face when the daughter-in-law was observing a mourning fast. But, actually, back in the room where Jintae's mother was laid up there was no shortage of nourishment: milk, pine nut porridge, yogurt, ginseng tea, even health tonic drinks; but not a soul cared to tend to the needs of the widow. Not only had they banished her from the kitchen, but nobody summoned her at mealtimes; nor had it occurred to anyone to send a meal to her room.

The kitchen was a paradise of food. Just the leftovers on the lacquered table — pork chops, filets of fish, steamed vegetables, stew, rice doused in soup — made a handsome repast for a hungry stomach. Those ostensibly cultivated ladies would soon sweep all of this into the garbage in the name of hygiene — the mere thought of it made Sŏngnamdaek's heart sink. She was about to down a slice of pork wrapped in *kimchi** when the word "disgrace" popped into her mind. Reflexively, her hand pulled back. Over three long years of caring for the old sir, she had heard that word all too often from Jintae's mother: "Please don't disgrace our family."

Sŏngnamdaek was not comfortable except in a simple box skirt belted at the waist with a cloth sash. She could not stand to cover her bare feet with socks or hose except in the depths of winter. A big eater, all she needed was nothing fancier than stale *kimchi* or miso soup to feel that rice tasted like honey. Her big voice clanged like a bell, and years of balancing heavy loads on her head had left her with the habit of wagging her behind furiously whenever she walked. If she heard a peddler out in the alley she had to rush outside and look over his wares, even when she had nothing to buy. Each sentence out of her mouth ended with a curse, and she felt positively nauseous if she dropped the curse. Such were some of Sŏngnamdaek's nasty habits.

That this rough-hewn woman had been ground and polished into the semblance of a quiet, at-ease mistress of a normal household was due mainly to the icy admonitions Jintae's mother had constantly given her about not shaming the family. But the metamorphosis also was a testimony to Sŏngnamdaek's powers of perseverance — she could endure even the worst sessions of torture. Whenever her patience wavered, she thought about the one-bedroom apartment that had been promised to her. She had not been able to afford to give her son a proper education, so he had turned out to be a common laborer. With a few years of tenacity, she would be in a position to give him his own apartment — something he could never buy on his own, not even with his entire life savings. The thought of this was enough to send Sŏngnamdaek into a blissful state, even to make her wriggle her behind in her sleep.

That she had a son, a daughter-in-law, and a grandson of her own — all this was her secret. She had not foreseen that her life would take this strange turn, but she had long pretended to be a luckless widow

---

Kimchi: A staple of nearly every Korean meal, if only in the form of a sidedish, usually consisting of napa cabbage pickled with salt, cayenne pepper, and garlic.

living on her own, fearing people would condemn her son for letting his poor mother lead such a hard life. Jintae's mother was very preoccupied with seeing to it that none of Sŏngnamdaek's unseemly habits tarnished the family reputation, yet not once had she asked about her past. She seemed to bear an almost instinctive disgust for the past of a lowly woman like Sŏngnamdaek. The older woman could tell as much from the remark Jintae's mom used to add without fail whenever she was pleading for propriety for the sake of her family,

"Grandma Sŏngnamdaek, can't you please do something about that habit of swiveling when you walk, as if you're running from the guards with a heavy basket of vegetables on your head? Aren't you embarrassed? I haven't told anybody you have a background like that. Every time you show your true colors, it makes me feel like fainting, after all the trouble I've gone through to hide your origins even from my husband and the children. Don't you see, if you'd just stop advertising what you are, would it be so hard to impersonate a seemly old housewife?"

Sŏngnamdaek had heard those pleas often enough, but starting yesterday those friends of Jintae's mother had taken to gossiping about her past under their breath and then today they had raised their voices as if they wanted her to overhear. Had Jintae's mother, so prim and proper in her cold way, spilled the beans as soon as her father-in-law passed away? Or had she done that long ago, keeping up a facade for Sŏngnamdaek alone? Sŏngnamdaek, who was rather dull-witted, was at a loss to figure out the matter. In truth, she did not feel particularly betrayed or ashamed that her past had been revealed. Hers had been a sad and weary lot, of course, and she had spent more days being chased about with a load on her head than hawking her wares while sitting comfortably on the sidewalk, but she was sure of one thing: she had done nothing dishonest, nothing serious enough that she deserved to be chased. In the next life, she often told herself, the ones punished would be those market guards, the bullies who made life hell for peddlers, not the peddlers themselves. Sŏngnamdaek felt none of the mortification that drove Jintae's mother to draw a cloak of secrecy over her "mother-in-law's" past.

"Let them chatter and cackle to their hearts' content. There's nobody alive who won't let off some dust when shaken, but I've done nothing that's so bad."

Sŏngnamdaek had nerves of steel and was not at all gutless, but she was of no mind to berate Jintae's mother's circle of friends for mocking her in that malicious way. "If they are so interested in whether I worked at the Sŏngnam Market, Chamsil Overpass, or the Saemaul Market, they'll die from shock when they hear my neck was strong enough to lug a thousand cloves of garlic around on my head," she told herself. She even felt enough at ease to have a laugh at their expense.

Maybe Sŏngnamdaek was inclined to excuse the busybodies because she herself was beginning to have serious doubts about Jintae's mother. After making such a fuss about hiding Sŏngnamdaek's background, something she hadn't even asked to have hidden, it was unspeakably two-faced for Jintae's mom to have revealed the story behind her back like that. Still more outrageous had been her abrupt change of character.

Early the previous morning, as the old sir met his end, his daughter-in-law's exhibition of grief had degenerated into an uproar. Her husband, by custom the chief mourner, and their two children, Jintae and Jinsuk, had their hands so full trying to console her and deal with her hysterical laments that they barely managed to look after the practical affairs of the deceased. Sŏngnamdaek had been left alone to tend to the corpse, making sure the old sir was indeed dead. She straightened out his arms and legs, folding his hands together over his stomach and placing his feet side by side. She then propped his head up squarely on the pillow, and covered him with a single-layer quilt. She also took one of the dead man's shirts out from the wardrobe, recalling it would be used later when invoking the spirit of the deceased. These steps were about all Sŏngnamdaek recalled from her experience with funeral rites, but she did know it was Jintae's mother's place, not hers, to leave off with the wailing and tend to the funeral arrangements.

All the same, the sudden liberation from looking after the old sir's needs left Sŏngnamdaek feeling so empty that she felt real tears well up in her eyes. After sobbing quietly for a few minutes, she started looking for something to do, and so began to cook the funeral meal. She washed the rice and was about to turn on the gas stove when Jintae's mother, having finished her raucous laments, emerged into the kitchen. Sounding not at all like someone who moments before had been weeping, Jintae's mother interrogated her in a most hostile tone, asking, "Just what do you think you're doing there?"

"Getting the funeral meal started. By the way, you should hurry and contact all the people you need to notify. Don't worry about things here in the kitchen. I think the first invocation of the spirit of the deceased is supposed to be done by someone who hasn't seen the corpse. But, oh, I guess the undertakers take care of that, too, nowadays."

"Sŏngnamdaek, get back to your room this minute! Just where do you think you are? How dare you tell me what to do!"

Venom dripped from her eyes as well as her voice. Sŏngnamdaek was dumbstruck as if she'd been knocked over the head. While the old sir was alive, Jintae's mother had taken care always to call her "Grandma Sŏngnamdaek." That was the name by which she was addressed by everyone in the family — not only Jintae's mother, but his father and the children as well as the aunts. As a matter of fact, she had not been very fond of that form of address. It was not what originally had been promised.

Back when Jintae's mother had first brought Sŏngnamdaek into the house, she had not brought her in merely as a servant to care for her father-in-law, but as a stepmother. She had sworn she'd treat her in every respect like a mother-in-law, and had repeated over and over that her father-in-law's one-bedroom apartment would belong to Sŏngnamdaek after he died. The time Sŏngnamdaek had spent living with the old sir in that apartment had been relatively happy. He'd had a stroke and one side of his body was affected, but he still could walk with support. His appetite was good and he had a kind heart. At first, she was put off by the way he kept nagging her about saving money, but soon she realized that he only did it because he wanted to set aside something for her future from the small monthly allowance his daughter-in-law gave him.

After Sŏngnamdaek and the old sir lived for two years on their own, the old sir suffered a second stroke and collapsed into a near-coma. From that point Sŏngnamdaek had the task of cleaning up after his bodily functions. Once things reached this stage, Jintae's mother had brought the old man back to live in his son's house, saying it was her duty as a daughter-in-law to do more to care for him. So Sŏngnamdaek was forced to accompany the old sir and to leave behind the apartment where she'd grown comfortable. As far as she could recall, Jintae's mother had never called her "mother" when they had lived apart, and once the households were merged she was disappointed at first to be addressed as "Grandma Sŏngnamdaek," though soon she got used to it. Sometimes she thought that "Granny" would sound warmer, but not even once had she voiced a wish for that name to be used. Sŏngnamdaek was not that greedy; she had never dared to imagine that

Jintae's mother, someone with her lofty, ladylike qualities, would be on daughter-in-law terms with her. Maybe that was why her anger at the patronizing attitude of the younger woman didn't last. Still, she thought it a shame that Jintae's mother lacked the patience to wait until after the old sir passed away and accounts were settled before beginning to sever their ties. Settling accounts meant, of course, transferring title to the one-bedroom apartment to Sŏngnamdaek.

Alerted that the friends of Jintae's mother were about to come back into the kitchen, Sŏngnamdaek scurried back to her room to hide. She left in such a hurry that all she took with her to eat was a radish. She peeled it as well as she could with her nails, and started chomping on it. The taste was on the stale side and, once down, the radish gnawed at her insides, making them burn and smart.

Of all the afflictions in the world, hunger has to be the worst, but Sŏngnamdaek couldn't even finish the radish, thinking of the old sir. Quietly she told herself: "When my real husband, the one I rubbed skin with and whose son I bore, passed away, I was still so young. People called me hard-hearted when I shed not a single tear, terrified though I was by the future I faced, all alone with a baby to feed. Now, what a spectacle I am, crying like this! Sure, my tears may come cheaper these days when my stomach's full, but my dead husband would be hurt if he could see me crying for another man." She mopped her eyes with the hem of her skirt.

While living with the old sir on their own, Sŏngnamdaek had shown him devotion and respect, making him whatever meals he wanted. To begin with, his appetite had been hearty enough; and perhaps the eating also assuaged the boredom of an old man with nothing to do. He ate a lot but nagged her at times about the amount they were spending on food. The old sir seemed unaware that his daughter-in-law had promised her the apartment when he was gone, and so he was eager to give Sŏngnamdaek what he could set aside of the money from their allowance. Once she understood this, she hadn't minded his nagging. Even after his second stroke and their move to the son's house, the old sir's appetite hadn't diminished. Jintae's mother, however, never let him have more than a half-bowl of rice or a half-portion of noodles. How pitiless and unfeeling her voice was when she came into the kitchen as lunch was being readied, lifting the knife to chop the block of instant noodles in half, putting one part back in the wrapper and saying, "Here, make lunch for father." Served such a small portion, the old sir was silent but despair shone in his eyes. Lying back as Sŏngnamdaek fed him curly strands of noodles, he kept glancing back and forth from her face to the bowl as it grew emptier and emptier. Thinking again of the misery and reproach in those eyes made Sŏngnamdaek feel the fear of heaven — how could she sleep peacefully on stormy nights?

But what could she have done? She turned excuses over in her mind, unsure whether they were meant for herself or for heaven. Truly, there was nothing she could have done. Jintae's mother only allowed her into the kitchen to boil the allotted half-package of noodles; she even had a lock installed on the refrigerator. Sŏngnamdaek herself could eat all she wanted, but the housemaid always ate with her, there in the kitchen, so she had no chance to put anything aside to take to the old sir.

"It's for your sake, Grandma Sŏngnamdaek. If you feed him all he wants, think what'll happen. It all goes in one end and right out the other end. How will you clean up the mess? You'll spend hours doing laundry."

Whenever Sŏngnamdaek beseeched her to give the old sir more to eat, Jintae's mother always claimed to be doing what was best for her. But the old man's excrement was not much less for his being fed smaller portions. It's no exaggeration to say that Sŏngnamdaek's days and nights were spent digging her way out from under cascades of crap and urine. Trousers, underwear, diapers — he soiled garments at an alarming pace, and groaned with discomfort whenever she changed and cleaned him. Frequently she had thanked God for that marvelous invention, the washing machine.

As time passed, the old sir grew more and more emaciated. That once fine figure of a man shrank until his ribs showed, his knees were like gnarls on a tree limb stripped of bark, and his shriveled calves clung to the bones. To Sŏngnamdaek, it seemed that he had not so much died as withered away.

While the old sir was still alive, Jintae's mother had not let Sŏngnamdaek into the kitchen except to eat, and now that he was dead, Jintae's father had shooed her out of the room where the deceased was laid out. The coffin had been left in the room where he passed away, and so naturally she had thought she should stay with him there. But the son of the old sir had coldly ordered her to leave and stay out of sight, saying it would not do for the guests to run into her. What had he meant by "it would not do," she wondered. Had the order come from Jintae's mother, she would have objected, but she was a bit intimidated by the man of the house and had let herself be banished. She had not been allowed to attend the dressing of the body for the funeral or its placement in the coffin, even though she had been looking after that very body for years, washing excrement from it day in and day out. After the coffin arrived, she sneaked a peek at it over the shoulders of strangers. It was enormous, with mother-of-pearl inlays, and you could see your face reflected in the lacquered wood. The sheer size and opulence of the coffin reinforced her feeling that the old man had withered away instead of dying. She imagined the coffin was empty, that he had gone on shrinking and shrinking until in the end he vanished.

The women had returned to the kitchen. They gossiped for a time about Jintae's mother, praising her but also expressing doubts about the devotion she demonstrated through her histrionic grieving over her father-in-law's death. But soon their conversation took a peculiar turn.

"Hey, ever thought about this?" One women said, giggling.

"What?"

"The mere idea of it makes me burst out laughing, I swear, even in my sleep."

"What? What's so hysterically funny? You're squirming like a mute who's seen something she shouldn't have."

"Well, that woman, Sŏngnamdaek or whatever she's called, do you think she ever slept with the old man?"

"Slept with him? Aah, aah, naughty girl, the things you think about!"

"Well, I confess I've wondered myself. Back when they lived by themselves in that apartment, the old sir was still a fine figure of a man, wasn't he? Sturdy and vigorous, I'll bet he could've done it every night."

"Vigorous? Give me a break. He'd had a stroke already by that time. One arm and leg were wobbly, you know, limp."

"Doesn't mean the middle leg was limp, too. Did you see it with your own eyes, did you?"

"Ow, filthy mind you have! When you get started, my mouth gets a little foul, too. Should steer clear of the likes of you, I guess."

"So don't then. No matter how prim and proper you pretend to be, your husband is leading the pack upstairs in telling dirty jokes."

"How'd you find out?"

"I was carrying food up — think I don't have ears?"

"You're a fool if you can't even tolerate a few jokes in a house in mourning. I bet your husband is holding a campaign meeting, eh?"

"My husband's gambling. Mouth shut and eyes lit."

"Hmph. I wish him luck. He'll add a tidy sum to his campaign war chest."

"Those two always fight whenever they meet, it doesn't matter where. Enough of that already, let's get back to the main issue."

"The main issue? What was that?"

"You know, whether or not the missus slept with the mister."

"Correction, could or could not."

"Think she would've stuck around this long if she couldn't?"

"How old is she anyway? Doubt she remarried looking for that."

"I don't know her exact age, but she's healthy enough and so uncouth."

"Don't know about health, but what's being uncouth got to do with lust?"

"Everything. Vulgarity means simplicity, and the simpler you are, the more you rely on things like that to get some pleasure out of life."

"There's something to what you say, I guess. You know my husband? He quit his job and got his M.A. and Ph.D. late, then barely landed a professorship at a no-name provincial college. Now, not only is his hair gray, he can't do it, either. I'm busy myself, what with charity work for this and that group, and I have a lot on my mind, so I haven't had much of an urge in that department."

"Look here. Think about your age and my age. It's not because you are particularly refined or anything. It's just time, that's all."

"So you're saying that at our age we're already at the end of the road in that respect?"

"That's right. Why? Feel sorry? We're from an era that grew up too fast and got old too soon, don't you think?"

"Well, it sounds grand, talking about our 'era' and all. Being such prematurely aged matrons yourselves, why dwell on unseemly matters between the missus and the old sir, who after all was no spring chicken himself?"

"I have my reasons. I guess you haven't heard the sordid story from Jintae's mother?"

"What story?"

"Well . . . "

The woman's voice faded and instead she burst out laughing, the sort of voluptuous laugh indicating a lewd imagination at play.

"Are you teasing me? Hurry up and tell it."

"I heard this from Jintae's mother. Seems the old lady was no ordinary pickle. When the old sir got to the point of shitting and pissing on himself, she got pretty self-important in her own mind. Guess she thought there was nobody else to clean up after him. And when he soiled himself, she used to bring several basins full of water into the room — it's good, of course, to have him washed thoroughly and all, but Jintae's mother sometimes thought the washing was taking too long. So she peeked in, and there the old lady was, endlessly massaging him down there."

"Oh, God! How obscene!"

"Gross! Ugh!"

The ladies nearly doubled over as they let out shrill squeals like little girls.

Lord, what despicable creatures. They must've raised children themselves, so they should know what work it is to change a boy's diaper, much worse than a girl's. How could they concoct such vile stories about their elders? Old Sŏngnamdaek's teeth were chattering with indignation. Washing the old sir clean of his own smeared excrement after he'd been sitting in it was a task unfit for a human, and it required no ordinary patience and strength of stomach to remove the filth from the old man's lower parts, so shrunken with age that little but wrinkles remained. More than once she'd been tempted to do a cursory job of washing him, especially when he was soiling himself so often, but she told herself that it wouldn't be right to do things halfway and still expect the apartment to be hers; that would be to reveal the heart of a thief and heaven would punish her for it. So she'd shaken off her nausea time and again to perform her duties with a thoroughness nobody could fault.

More strongly than what she felt about the silly chatterboxes in the kitchen, Sŏngnamdaek felt outrage toward Jintae's mother for portraying things in such a light. She shuddered all over like a dog doused with dishwater.

"I knew it would be like that."

"What?"

"Can't you tell from the way the old lady walks? She wags her hips so blatantly like this when she walks, you know."

The woman apparently was mimicking the way she walked. Sŏngnamdaek could hear gasps and cackles of laughter. As she sat in her room almost quaking, the sound of that laughter was like a flame mercilessly burning her.

"I can't even imitate it."

"Yeah, with your rear end, it won't even be close."

"Anyway, you all have seen what I'm talking about, right? A walk like that is a sure sign that she's still very lively in that department."

What had led Sŏngnamdaek to decide to take on caring for the old sir was, of course, the bait of the apartment thrown in front of her by Jintae's mother. At first glance, she had seen that the old sir had lost his capacities as a male. However much she coveted the apartment, she did not want to do that in her old age. Though widowed very young, Sŏngnamdaek had always been so burdened with worries over how she was going to survive and raise her son that she'd never had much leisure to think about men physically. She had developed a very strong phobia about sex. If the old sir had turned out to be demanding in that regard, against her expectation, she would have fled in a hurry, even if she'd been promised not just an apartment but the whole building. Thankfully, he had treated her like a trusted friend, and she had no fears whatever about facing her long dead husband in the next world. No matter what lies others might tell, she believed her late husband would know she had been his alone.

"Well, at any rate, I feel sorry for the old lady in more ways than one."

"She must have gotten some enjoyment out of it, at least in the beginning."

"Really, how much pleasure could she have had? Hobbled by his stroke, the old sir could never have been a match for those strong, swiveling hips of hers."

"Come to think of it, the old sir must have had a hard time, too."

"Think he shortened his life by taking too lively a wife? Without her demands he might have survived several more years, at least."

"That old man lived long enough. And with his last years as hot as they must've been, what did he have to regret? Jintae's mother should be free at long last to live, shouldn't she? You all can't understand — after all, you never had to live with your in-laws."

"True. I guess you're right. But Sŏngnamdaek wouldn't be trying to hang around as a mother-in-law by any chance, would she?"

"I don't think so. Look how she made herself scarce as soon as the old man croaked. She doesn't show her face in the kitchen or in the funeral chamber, as though it's all somebody else's business."

"Do you think they recorded the marriage in the family register?"

"Register Sŏngnamdaek? What a crazy idea! Jintae's mother wasn't born yesterday, why sow seeds of future trouble, wouldn't you say?"

"Well, then, I guess they can just give her some cash and send her away."

"About the money, seems Sŏngnamdaek was shrewder than Jintae's mother. When the old folks were living by themselves in that small apartment, she took just as much for living expenses as they used for the big house, and even then she whined and whimpered every month as if she was being short-changed. Jintae's mother would go over there and find there was never enough to eat, it was impossible. Where did all that money go, then? They lived like that for over two years, and so Sŏngnamdaek must have put away a fortune for herself. Even so, the old sir was always asking for more money to give to her, even if it was only a few coins, and he kept on holding his hand out to his daughter-in-law. Old they might have been, but I guess a married couple is still a married couple. Many times I heard Jintae's mother complain about him doing that."

"Do you think he really had to rely on his son and daughter-in-law for all his spending? I mean, he used to do well enough for himself when he was younger."

"I think he deeded almost all his property to his son. Maybe he felt bad giving up everything; he kept that little apartment in his name, and look what good use he made of it as a love nest in his last years. Lived just like newlyweds there. Anyway, shouldn't hand over everything to your children while you're still alive, I guess."

"I suppose then that the apartment is the only thing the old sir had left to pass along."

"Jintae's mother said she sold it some time back. When the old man moved back into the house after his second stroke, she went ahead and unloaded it. It looked like he'd have no occasion to live there again, and even if they'd kept it, it wasn't such a valuable asset. She did well to sell it, if you ask me. It wasn't that big a thing, but a lot of annoyances can come up, you know, with the legal succession and taxes and the like."

The apartment sold? My apartment? Who had the right to sell my apartment? How in the world could such a thing happen?

Sŏngnamdaek sprang to her feet. She meant to run straight to Jintae's mother and confront her. She clenched and unclenched her fists, itching to grab that woman by her smooth white neck and shake her silly. Sŏngnamdaek didn't know which way to turn. When she thought of those vicious rumormongers in the other room, her feet froze. She shuddered with loathing of the voices encircling her from just outside the door. "I must confront her. Of course I have to confront her. Do they think I'll cower on my belly like a corpse out of fear for the likes of them?" She stood there pawing the air, trying to face things squarely but terrified about what might be mere rumors. As she mustered her courage, the voices started up again outside her door.

"Miri's mother, are you going out for some rice cakes? Shall we order a few kilos?"

"Don't be silly, nobody eats so many rice cakes these days. And if you phone in the order, they'll deliver. Wait, that fish is for tomorrow. Put it aside. If we leave it out here, it'll be gone before you know it. Why don't you put some steamed pork out on the table? What, all gone again? What appetites! I think we might need to go ahead and use tomorrow's vegetables."

"Is it really necessary to make this much food, I mean, after all, we're just going to a crematorium, not to a burial ceremony."

"Naturally. Can't send guests home on empty stomachs, whether from a cemetery or a crematorium."

"Didn't the old sir even prepare a tomb site for himself during that long life of his? Think how much face his children will lose — getting their father cremated!"

"If you want to be buried, cemeteries are convenient enough these days, even if you didn't buy a grave plot in advance. It's not that he couldn't; he didn't want to be buried. Seems the old sir left instructions to cremate his body. You know, his first wife, the mother-in-law, died when Jintae's family was still living in America, and I hear the old sir had a bad time of it, getting through the whole business with only his daughters around. He was obstinate about having the old lady cremated. In the years to come, he said, there wouldn't be any descendants who cared to look after the ancestors' graves. The daughters couldn't stop him and he had his way, but he kept on dwelling on it, apparently. He said there'd be no joy for him being buried underground all alone, and that he absolutely didn't want to be buried. Guess he told himself that since the wife became smoke, he ought to be cremated himself in order to meet her in the next world. Granted, it doesn't seem dutiful of the children to cremate their father, but don't you think they have an obligation to respect his wishes?"

Sŏngnamdaek sank silently to the floor. As she listened to those faint voices, seemingly very far away, she felt the vindictive rage draining out of her. And when all her resolve had drained away, she felt wretchedly limp and powerless like a deflated balloon. That the old sir had wanted to be cremated and expressed such as his dying wish was an out-and-out lie. It was true that he'd insisted upon cremation for his first wife, but he'd told her that he'd done so out of anger at his son, who'd mortally offended him by refusing to return from America at the news of his mother's death. Jintae's father had made do with a phone call and dispatch of some condolence money. The old sir had never hidden the cherished love he'd shared with his late wife, and often he had complained to Sŏngnamdaek that it tore him up inside whenever he thought about the flames engulfing her in the crematorium. He'd even said: "When I'm gone, I'm going to call my wife's wandering spirit into my tomb, beg her forgiveness, comfort her, and make up for my having wronged her." Hearing the old man recount his guilty nightmares — of his wife in agony with her face ablaze or jumping about in burning robes — Sŏngnamdaek knew how deeply he regretted in his heart of hearts having chosen to have her cremated. That such a man would expressly ask to be cremated was the height of absurdity. What's more, from the day he suffered his second stroke until he died, he was never lucid enough to express a dying wish in any case. Hadn't she herself been the one who'd alerted the family to his approaching death?

But if she spoke the truth about this now, who would believe her? Those busybodies had her marked as a simpleton, and perhaps she was, but even to someone so simple the whole story was by this time becoming crystal clear. Finally, Sŏngnamdaek grasped the clever conspiracy that had been laid, and realized that all the family had played their roles, while she was kept in the dark. That same plan was even now being carried out, and it was designed to obliterate without a trace the man who, only days before, had been the patriarch of the house, filling it with his wild cries and with the atrocious stench of his excrement. And how easy for Jintae's mother to deny that the promise to Sŏngnamdaek had ever been made! Sŏngnamdaek grew dizzy and fell to the floor as if someone had kicked her down. She felt she was being pulled into the ruthless gears of a diabolical machine, in a diabolical scheme which expunged from existence whatever did not serve its own evil ends. Perhaps she had surrendered too readily to the inevitable; she still felt the numbness of betrayal, but with that numbness came a certain release from the pain.

Sŏngnamdaek slept well that night. The next day, she changed into a white mourning dress and, without asking permission from anyone, got into the hearse. Jintae's mother was still observing her fast, and was the focus of the attention and heartfelt sympathy of all the guests. Friends solemnly supported the weak daughter-in-law on each side. They were chattering glibly about taking her to the hospital for an injection to fend off a double funeral, but Jintae's mother, ever so dignified, shook her head and climbed into the hearse. Here and there the guests whispered about her, some marveling at the devotion of such an exemplary daughter-in-law, and other staring blank-faced as if at an actress's dramatic performance. Even during the funeral, all eyes were on Jintae's mother, not on the deceased. Her sisters-in-law outdid themselves by throwing themselves on the coffin and wailing loudly, but her position as the star was unassailable. Her face white as a sheet, she collapsed onto her husband's lap like a white handkerchief, creating yet another commotion. Jintae's father must have felt she'd hammed it up a little too much this time, for he felt it necessary to explain.

"She served father devotedly with all her heart and soul, and the shock of losing him was more than she could bear. Is it any wonder that she collapsed from the fatigue? She had to tend to his incontinence for more than ten months, and you know how obsessed with cleanliness she is? She never does anything halfway. Can you imagine how much she suffered?"

Upon hearing this, people were affected even more deeply and they exerted themselves to the utmost, jawing her praises. Sŏngnamdaek felt so ashamed that her face burned. Knowing she was the only authentic "article" in the entire funeral procession, she felt edgy and out of place. Fearful lest her authenticity be revealed, she made herself as small as possible by curling up and concentrating on the passing scenes outside the window. Squalid buildings not worth a second glance; a dull-looking man standing idly, another walking purposefully with his wits about him; somebody pursuing a bus and doggedly trying to jump aboard; a motorbike zigzagging through traffic, bearing a load piled perilously high behind the rider; a panhandler showing off leg stumps like truncated lotus roots; a woman with a load balanced on her head; a man lugging an A-frame on his back ... how long since she'd witnessed such vistas of real humanity. As if famished in spirit, she took them in with ravenous eyes.

The crematorium complex was composed of two main buildings,

besides some small annexes housing toilets, vending machines, and so on. The crematorium itself could be identified by its towering chimney. The interior of the crematorium was a dark and chilling gray, making it seem to be a realm entirely apart from the bright spring day outside. Corpses were queued up to wait their turns. From time to time a simple religious rite was performed, but there was nothing special to mark the room as a crematorium except for the five iron doors stretching across one wall through which the coffins were loaded to be incinerated. The atmosphere was one of desolation, and a breeze blew through the place as if it were an unfinished structure unfit for human use.

On a parallel with the crematorium and facing it was the other main building, which contained a cafeteria and a waiting room. The two buildings were joined by a concrete walkway covered by an awning. On either side of the walkway were brown beds of earth left empty except for some wilting orchids transplanted from a hothouse somewhere. The flowers were neglected. Unappetizing aromas wafted from the cafeteria into the waiting room. One family was opening stainless steel containers and lacquered boxes. They took out vegetables, griddlecakes, and fried bean curd and loaded them onto aluminum plates. A middle-aged man with a liquor-flushed face uncapped a bottle with his healthy-looking teeth. "The dead are dead but the living must eat," said a woman to an orphaned child with swollen eyes. She looked as if she herself had eaten already; there were traces of greasy red pepper around her lip.

The feathery cloud of smoke issuing from the chimney overhead didn't look at all like the residue from burning human beings, and the cafeteria seemed out of place at a crematorium. Having a cafeteria at such an establishment felt incongruous. People gobbling up food, loud yelps asking for more of this or that, kids pushing and racing around as they played, voices calling out names in search of acquaintances, the odor of kimchi . . . To be sure, it was like a village wedding. From time to time one would spy a young man with an armband around his coat sleeve, smiling a smile as fatigued as if a little more cautious than a groom's grin.

The space in which families waited for their corpses to be burned was like a bus terminal — busy, raucous and astir with the restlessness of waiting. People often paced back and forth between the crematorium with its row of waiting corpses and the other building housing the cafeteria and waiting room. Facial expressions were dexterously altered as the environment changed. From the crematorium came an incessant drone of Buddhist chants interspersed with weeping, and even the people who stayed silent draped sorrow around themselves like a ceremonial stole. Only the occasional sight of a weary mourner dozing off after a night without sleep broke the solemnity and slightly embarrassed onlookers.

Jintae's mother, who still could not steady herself, had been laid on a bench in the waiting room. She looked dignified and peaceful reclining there silently in the no-man's land between the crematorium and the cafeteria. The places of incineration and of feasting were like extremes: it seemed only reasonable to have a buffer zone in between the opposed poles. People who had difficulty adjusting their facial expressions could just lounge about near the devoted daughter-in-law with an ambiguous look, perhaps a smile, perhaps a look of concern, blurring their true feelings. Even strangers from other families in mourning could not pass by her without pausing for a long gaze at the unfortunate woman and expressing their heartfelt concern and sympathy. It was plain to see they were profoundly ashamed that the depths of their grief could never match the intensity of the sorrow felt by Jintae's mother. Anyone could see that her unique blend of silence, distress, and dignity was the very epitome of sorrow in its purest form.

After walking over to the crematorium and back, Jintae's father patted his wife's temple, saying, "Poor thing, how can you be so frail?" With pursed lips, he bent over her as if to straighten her hair, then whispered into her ear in a sharp tone, "We're not even close. Still a whole line of corpses in front of us."

"Spend some cash, then."

Their words were like arrows, each unerringly striking home by anticipating the expectations of the other. Jintae's father stole quietly off in the direction of the crematorium. Before long, the family was duly notified that their turn had come. They told Jintae's mother to remain where she was. In a voice that sounded as if it itself were on the verge of extinction, she protested that the wife of the eldest son could not possibly fail to bid farewell to her father-in-law as he took his leave of this world, and she tottered to her feet. People fought with one another to have the privilege of supporting her. When she came within sight of the corpse, her grief was refreshed and she began emitting loud, unearthly guttural shrieks. Her cries — her tears were used up by now — were more like hysterical yells than wails of mourning, and finally these gave way to manic paroxysms as the corpse was wheeled to the maws of the incinerator. She hopped wildly up and down as if to follow the corpse into the flames. People made a concerted effort to pry her away from the corpse, and the crematorium attendants quickly shoved the body through the grating. The door swung shut and above it a red light came on. At this, Jintae's mother twisted her limbs like a contortionist and swooned. Jintae's father let out a gasp, the two children burst out crying, and a young male relative rushed forward and lifted her onto his shoulder. She opened her eyes only after they had laid her down, back in the waiting room, and had massaged her arms and legs, given her a sip of red wine to revive her, and otherwise made a royal commotion for her benefit.

"Where am I? I really feel like I'm dying," she peeped. Her friends shouted that she should be taken right away to the hospital, given an injection, and be made to rest.

"Certainly, yes, we should've done so before now," said Jintae's father. Seeing that nobody disagreed, he had the car brought around and helped his wife into it. Jintae and Jinsuk followed. Once the family had departed, people's faces at once showed relief. The more genteel contingent of guests slunk away to their own cars, and the rest uncapped bottles of soju* or cola. "Anything to nibble on with our drinks?" someone asked, and one by one the lids came off the lacquered lunchboxes.

Left all alone in the crematorium, Sŏngnamdaek stood there staring at the iron door through which the old sir's corpse had vanished. She told herself it looked exactly like the door of the garbage chute in the apartment where they'd lived. The destiny of man, cast away once his usefulness is at an end, was no better than that of garbage, she thought. Once, she remembered, she had accidentally thrown a fruit knife into the garbage with the peelings. The old sir insisted that she take him down to the basement where the garbage was collected, and spent half the day looking through the trash to find that knife. He stank to high heaven by the time he found it. She'd had a hard time bathing him and

---

*Soju: Clear liquor usually distilled from sweet potatoes, and widely consumed for its combination of relatively high alcoholic content (as high as 25 percent by volume) and relatively inexpensive price ($1–3 for a 375 ml bottle at a market, $3–5 for the same at a restaurant).

cleaning his clothes, but the old sir was very proud of himself, as though he had achieved a tremendous triumph.

At this very moment, Sŏngnamdaek was carrying wrapped around her body the money the old sir had saved up for her from the monthly allowances. The night before, she had made a pouch for it and secured it around her belly, which made her feel full even though her stomach was empty. As she stood there thinking of this and that, the red light over the iron door went out. She didn't know exactly what that meant, but her heart skipped a beat, as it had done when she discovered that the old sir had passed away. From the corridor behind the wall, a voice called out for Jintae's father. Startled, she looked around the room, but nobody from the family was to be seen. She walked over to answer the summons, though she was frightened.

The remains of the deceased had already been brought out. "Remains" wasn't really the proper term; it was only the ashes. All that was left on the rolling steel platform was white ashes with pink embers glowing here and there like a spent campfire. A clerk in a faded blue uniform asked her skeptically whether she would take charge of the ashes. In a moment of bewilderment, Sŏngnamdaek nodded. The clerk was very normal looking. He began sweeping up the ashes with a normal-looking broom and pushed the fading embers into a normal-looking dustpan. Watching the clerk's movements, Sŏngnamdaek thought this seemed not very different from ordinary sweeping; and she thought she had done well to watch. She felt the last remnants of her antagonism toward Jintae's mother being cleanly swept away, along with the petty regrets that made her feel she would have more to do if she stayed around. The clerk disappeared with the ashes he had gathered, and after a long wait he reappeared with a white box tied with a ribbon. Before Sŏngnamdaek could tell him that she was not the right person to receive the box, one of the daughters appeared with her husband and hastened to take it.

Left alone, Sŏngnamdaek did not go to the cafeteria, but instead immediately left the crematorium. She had to ask quite a few people on the street which bus she should take to get to the city without needless transfers, but finally she found out that the right bus stop was quite some distance away. Someone said she could take a taxi there for a base fare of 600 won,* but someone else said the fare would be at least

---

*600 won: Approximately one dollar in 1984.

1,500 won. The difference of 900 won did not matter to her: she had never taken a taxi in her life, and she had no way of estimating the distance, but she was confident that she could walk that far. Her head unburdened by any load, she wondered whether she couldn't walk a hundred *li** in a single day. Her life had been too easy the past couple of years, but gradually her old manner of walking came back to her. Soon she was swinging her hips in high spirits and she felt she could easily bear a load on her head if it came to that. She thought of the depraved insults the gossips at the house had spoken about her the day before. Bitches! She could feel only scorn for those spoiled ladies, whose lives were so frivolous that they interpreted any motion of the hips as what you do in bed. They could never even begin to comprehend what a healthy and tenacious rhythm of life hers was. The sway of her hips came back even without a load on her head, but somehow she was at a loss to think of further insults for the gossips, worse names than "bitches."

"Will they be looking for me at Jintae's house? Even if they do, wouldn't it be something like a search for a mutt that's wandered away from the house in search of its dead master?" Thoughts like this passed through her mind, too. But more than anything, she was savoring the thought of taking off her money pouch and handing it over to her son.

"Good thing I never mentioned the apartment to him. If he'd gotten his hopes up, he would've been greatly disappointed, but he knew nothing of it, so he'll just be thankful for what I give him. I won't give it all to him; I should keep some money for myself to start peddling again. Soon the season for making pickled garlic will be here. Ten kilos of garlic is enough for my head, but, Lord, there I was trying to carry an apartment away on it. When a person forgets her place, she gets punished for her sins. Still, how could she cheat me out of that apartment so brazenly, when it's something she knows, I know, and heaven knows? Damn her to hell, the bitch!"

Sŏngnamdaek felt she needed to let fly with grittier and more pungent curses before she could feel purified, but her swearing was rusty after three years spent in the company of that cultivated household. The oaths she needed didn't come back to her easily. Instead of spewing out curses, she spat once with abandon and picked up her pace.

**Li:* One *li* is approximately one-third of a mile.

There would be plenty of time to unload a string of curses one by one, but the desire to see her son, daughter-in-law, and grandson, a longing she'd long repressed as if enduring psychological torture, pulled her onward and made the innocent gyrations of her hips all the more uproarious.

translated by Chun Kyung-Ja

Butterfly of Illusion

One

That old house had a feel about it.

It was a feel and not the kind of face that for an ordinary house depends on the material it is built from, the size, the quality of upkeep, and so forth. If houses were people, the feel of that house would have been like a premonition evoked by immutable traits hidden deep inside the person, not an impression that shifted with mood, degree of cultivation, or style of dress. This feel was what caused people in the neighborhood either to be drawn to the house or else to take roundabout detours to avoid it. The house stood at some distance from the rest of the neighborhood, but it lay right beside the shortcut to the train station and next to the mouth of the trail leading up to a mountain spring where people went for water.

For administrative purposes, the neighborhood around the house was regarded as falling within the city limits of Y — one of the new satellite cities that had sprung up around Seoul. The residents of Y called the neighborhood by a different name, however. To them, it was the "primitive neighborhood." Despite this label, no huts with thatched roofs or old Chosun-dynasty houses with tiled roofs were still standing. Along the narrow alleyways there were just boxy concrete dwellings, a popular design back in the 1960s when the houses were new, but the structures had become quite run down. These derelict houses lent a condemned air to the neighborhood and made it seem much older than it actually was.

Possibly the kids growing up in the newly erected apartment blocks of Y took the expression "primitive" literally, and imagined the neighborhood's concrete houses as the original abodes of prehistoric men, like the caves or huts still to be found only in Africa or on remote South Pacific islands, places where Stone Age tribes lived on, unchanging over the endless ages that have passed since the dawn of history. But the neighborhood was thirty-some years old at most. When the landowners and the developers first joined forces to establish a new neighborhood on that vacant land, the area had consisted mostly of planted fields and orchards. The local farmers had initially called the new development zone the "village of Western-style houses." At the time, these concrete houses, with square sides like blocks of bean curd, with flat rather than pitched roofs, and with outside walls of glossy ceramic bricks, were objects of wonder and envy. When the farmers gave the new neighborhood its name, they intended it as high praise. Less than thirty years saw the village of Western-style houses degenerate into a "primitive" area.

The old house had been there even before the Western-style houses went up. Like a scrap of refuse left behind from the days when the place was farms, a time loath to evaporate without a trace, the house, despite various renovations and repairs, could not shake off the rustic feel engrained in it to the very bones. The house was shaped like a rectangle with one side gone; there was a spacious wooden floor, and the beams and rafters were made of pine, but the roof was gray slate. The mismatch between the dingy wooden spine of the house and its slate roof was compounded, in a bizarrely harmonious way, with another incongruity, that between the rice-papered windows, some of which were missing wooden panels, and the new sliding glass doors.

Those who had lived in the primitive neighborhood long enough might recall a time when the old house's roof was made of corrugated sheets of galvanized metal. Before that, the roof must have been thatched with straw or possibly tiled in the Western style, but in an area where houses even five years old, let alone thirty, were few, to find an eyewitness of those old days might prove impossible. The label "primitive" stuck to the neighborhood as a whole, not so much to the people or the households, for the turnover in residents was very frequent, much more frequent than in the nearby apartment blocks. According to statistics compiled by the Y city administration, the average duration of residency in the primitive district was a year and half shorter than that in the apartment buildings. Most likely it was just some kind of scam cooked up by real estate brokers, but rumors had

long been circulating in surrounding areas that the neighborhood soon
would be razed and redeveloped. Despite such speculation, once you
bought a place and moved in, you would find it a strange place showing no sign at all of any impending redevelopment. Even after they
figured out that nothing ever gets redeveloped without someone taking
active charge, the property owners had neither the means nor the
know-how to organize a project to upgrade the primitive neighborhood. Many gave up and just put their houses up for sale, and even
those who could not abandon the slim hope of a windfall profit on their
land rented their places out and slipped away. Naturally, it was hard
for the owners to feel any fondness for the place once they realized that
the only merit of the neighborhood had been illusory.

If the primitive neighborhood was like a remote island off the coast
of Y city, the old house was like a still more remote island off the coast
of that remote island.

The children who lived in the apartment blocks and those from
the primitive zone attended the same school. But in the eyes of the
apartment kids, the primitive kids were different, somehow. On his
own, an apartment child might not notice any difference at first
sight, but once it turned out that the other kid was a "native," he was
bound to feel estranged all of a sudden; all the fun chatter about
computer games he had unknowingly shared with the "native" kid
the day before would seem spoiled by a sickening sense of treach-
ery. Had any children lived in that old house, the kids from the
primitive neighborhood might have been similarly aloof toward
them, holding them at bay just as they themselves were kept at
arm's length by the kids from the apartments. But there never had
been any children in that old house. There might have been one or
two way back when it had been a farmhouse, but that was a prehistoric era about which nobody could attest any longer.

Two

At that hour of the day the difficulty in finding a parking spot
should have come as no surprise, yet Yŏngju repeatedly grumbled
disgustedly before jerking her steering wheel in the direction of the
children's playground. The playground was located behind the high-
rise apartment building, and the asphalt ellipse that ran around the
playground and a patch of adjacent greenery initially had been

meant as a no-parking area where children could roller skate or ride bikes. Even when lined parking spaces were extended into this area, it had been like trying to thaw a frostbitten foot by pissing on it. A little breathing space might be opened up, but soon enough everything was back to square one. Luckily, Yŏngju found a beautiful spot from which she would be able to pull out easily even in the early morning when cars were double-parked in the main lot. Another grumbling murmur escaped her lips as she gathered up the heap of things in the passenger seat. It was not much of a heap, really. A jacket she had taken off, a large tote bag, and a few books — a load familiar from days gone by when she worked as a part-time instructor. The only additional items today were two pumpkins. The ripe pumpkins had looked so good piled up in a pyramid alongside a country road that after eying them for a few minutes Yŏngju bought a few. The vegetable seller told her the squash would make a beautiful porridge and without being asked, tried to give her the recipe, but Yŏngju had paid no attention. She knew for certain that her mother would use them to make pumpkin dumplings.

Thinking of her mother, Yŏngju grew wistful and said to herself, "I wish she'd show a little more enthusiasm in cooking. Does she still remember how to make pumpkin dumplings? Better not try to test Mother with pumpkins and such. I ought to be more understanding. What's so strange about losing interest in tasks you've been repeating day-in and day-out for half a century, like trimming vegetables, scaling fish, or tasting soup or stew to see it's properly seasoned? In fact, it'd be stranger if she didn't lose interest. What business do I have looking askance at her just because she's getting tired of doing the very things she's done all these years?" Yŏngju pushed aside the things she had started to pick up, and pressed her forehead against the steering wheel. But by this time her vague anxiety was aimed not at her mother but toward herself.

Her post as a full-time college lecturer was one she had obtained after six years as a part-time instructor, following the three years it took to get her degree. The college where she taught was not on a par with universities in Seoul, but beggars can't be choosers, and she was hardly in a position to choose. It was not as though her survival depended on this job. It was probably her age that made her rush about so madly. The long commute back and forth to Taejon was not impossible, though it certainly was far from easy, and she had been lucky to find a position at all within a commutable distance. Yŏngju's driving was beyond skilled; by this time she was a true expert. Another thing that helped to make the long commute less formidable was that her car, bought new two years before, after she had driven a string of worn-out hand-me-downs, was in good shape and familiar to the point of feeling like an extension of her body. But Yŏngju was pushing forty now. From forty to fifty was as quick as a trip down a slide. That a woman her age had landed a college position at all was a piece of good luck for which to thank the stars. She told herself anyone not totally ignorant of goings-on in the academic world should keep that in mind and be grateful. For the first semester, at least, Yŏngju had been too intoxicated with pride in her accomplishments to feel any fatigue. Lately, however, she had grown more and more ashamed that all the world except her seemed to have been in the know about just how much the going price for a Ph.D. or a professorship had fallen. "Why didn't these things occur to me earlier? If I had known, I would have saved myself a lot of trouble," Yŏngju reproached herself. But then it occurred to her that such ruminations went too far for a woman who once had raised a row in the name of education. She grew disgusted with herself. Her feeling that salaries paid to Ph.D.'s had fallen too far had more to do with her sense of the respect her position should command rather than a strict cost-benefit analysis — the low salary she was being paid versus the time and effort invested in obtaining the job.

"Did you work yourself to death studying like that to teach at some backwater junior college?" Some of her friends had been that brutally blunt.

She might have brushed off such affronts by reciprocating their disdain, saying, "Why, for people of your sort the price of knowledge is measured by an ability to stick like leeches in Seoul for the rest of your life, enjoying your comforts and maintaining your dignity." She couldn't say this, however. That the barbs cut so deeply, leaving her spiteful, probably meant they had pricked her own lack of self-esteem. The work of teaching, of doling out knowledge, was not turning out to be as rewarding as she had expected. The dissatisfaction she felt could be blamed on the poor quality of her students or her own shortcomings as a teacher, but she found herself decrying the pointlessness of knowledge itself, feeling despondent and empty, or else just depressed. In a word, she was plagued by self-doubts, sickened to the very heart.

Yŏngju had chosen to study the poetry of Hŏ Nansŏlhŏn* for her dissertation because she had been deeply touched by the fleetingness of Hŏ Nansŏlhŏn's ephemeral life. To feel moved like that she had not needed to know a great deal about the poet. In actuality, she could not claim to know much more about Hŏ Nansŏlhŏn, her family history, or the era in which she lived than the average person knew from ordinary schooling. Of course, Yŏngju's Chinese was too weak for her to encounter the verse of Hŏ Nansŏlhŏn face to face. What had captivated her was less the sublimity of the poetry itself than her own imagined account of how a women of exceptional genius had been victimized by the social world into which she was born, a world that denied her recognition and in the end destroyed her.

What dissertation research called for, however, was not imagination but concrete information from recognized historical sources, evidence to substantiate arguments. Yŏngju's mentor, who first had encouraged her to give up her post as a middle school teacher to embark on belated graduate studies, was wary of imaginativeness more than anything. The unwelcome advice she received most often was that she must never confuse critical analysis with creative writing. In accumulating the sort of information about Hŏ Nansŏlhŏn deemed appropriate for a doctoral dissertation, Yŏngju lost all the romanticized fascination and empathy she originally had felt for the poet. Instead, she came to feel only weariness. After a while the mere mention of Hŏ Nansŏlhŏn turned her stomach. In place of her pathos what she had gained was a pile of dry leaves, a parade of Hŏ Nansŏlhŏn scarecrows mercilessly slashed and battered, and a doctoral degree.

Yŏngju had been sitting and thinking in her car for some time when the sound of her son's tapping on the window made her raise her head. Choongwoo was dressed in worn sweats and a pair of slippers.

"What's up? *You* are taking a walk?"

"Not out for a walk, I'm out to look for grandma."

---

*Hŏ Nansŏlhŏn (1563–1589): A poet from the Chosŏn period famous for her melancholy poetic contemplations, both in the Korean vernacular and the classical Chinese, on mutuality of love. She was from an illustrious sixteenth-century scholar family — her siblings include Hŏ Kyun, the author of the first Korean novel in the vernacular — but led an unfulfilled personal life which ended in her early death. Her poems were widely admired and helped encourage the writing of women's poetry in mid- and late-Chosŏn.

Yŏngju felt her heart sink, but Choongwoo spoke casually as if nothing was amiss.

"How could you let her go out by herself? How many times have I told you to keep a close eye on her?"

"She's probably around here somewhere. Go on in the house. I'll bring her in."

Saying this, Choongwoo shuffled away. Yŏngju got out of the car after hastily gathering her things, and suddenly full of bile at the seeming indifference of her son's back view, Yŏngju stopped him with a loud call.

"When did she go out? How come you're only going out now to look for her?"

"It hasn't been that long."

Yŏngju couldn't let her son's vague reply stand.

"When, exactly?"

"If I knew exactly when she left, I would've kept her from going out, wouldn't I?" Choongwoo snapped back defiantly, uncowed by her insistent tone.

"So, you didn't even see her go out. What in the world were you doing?"

"She disappeared while I was on the phone."

"With whom? You got distracted talking to a girl, right? Right?"

Yŏngju's son turned around abruptly and walked off without answering. She took a few steps as if to chase him, but changed her mind and turned back toward the house instead. Almost immediately, she regretted treating her son, a good boy who seldom gave her much to worry about, as though he were a habitual troublemaker.

"I don't know why I'm acting this way," Yŏngju murmured to herself. Reflecting on her increasingly tenuous self-control, she felt almost like a crisis was looming. Inside the elevator, she could see reflected in the mirror on one wall a shock of gray hair sprouting wildly from the crown of her head. At that moment, her doctoral diploma struck her as no better than a tattered rag. The looking glass in the elevator was more merciless than the mirror on her dresser or the one in her compact. It was especially pitiless when she was heading back from work. On her way home everything sagged: her shoulders, the skin on her cheeks, her eyelashes, and the hair she puffed up with a blow dryer in the morning. And it was just when everything else was most limp and flaccid that that damned tuft of gray hair raised its head, strand by strand. At every opportunity, Yŏngju's sarcastic sister liked to call that gray shock "the telltale mark of a Ph.D." Going gray as you approached fifty was not uncommon, but still she made cracks at Yŏngju's expense whenever she had a chance, and Yŏngju was insulted by the needling.

The house was empty but the door slid right open. An air of unease filled the house.

"I hope she comes back without raising a big commotion like last time," Yŏngju thought. It had been quite a while since Yŏngju noticed that Mother's amnesia could no longer be ignored. The family had moved into this apartment last year, and Yŏngju's concerns had begun even earlier. Mother would go to the supermarket and drift around on the way back home, unable to remember the number of their building. The family had lived in the previous apartment long enough that the neighbors recognized Mother and led her home or had the security guard alert them to her whereabouts over the intercom. At other times, however, Mother seemed just fine and denied she ever had problems with her memory, growing angry at the suggestion. But soon after they moved, before they could even unpack and settle into the new place, something happened that went way beyond earlier episodes.

One day, Mother went outside at the crack of dawn before anybody else was up. By the time the family finally found her, it was after midnight. After tracking her down, they realized Mother had not simply wandered off and gotten lost. From the outset she had planned to escape. Amazingly, she had taken with her a little bundle and was carrying some wrinkled bills she had been setting aside from her allowance. More amazing yet was the fact that she had made it all the way to Uiwang Tunnel before the police found her. The new apartment was in Tunchondong, halfway across Seoul. It proved impossible for Mother to recall how she had reached Uiwang Tunnel, on foot or by public transportation. She was utterly incoherent. At the news that Mother had been found, everyone in the family was overjoyed as they rushed to collect her. Especially Kyungah, a tender girl by nature, had raced into her grandmother's arms and burst into tears, even though Mother only stood there, staring blankly at the whole family. Choongwoo, too, hugged her from behind and pressed his cheek to hers. Yŏngju's husband took his jacket off and put it around the old woman's shoulders — she was shivering in the chilly autumn night — and bowed repeatedly to the policeman in thanks.

Only Yŏngju had stood there motionless, a bit away from the rest of the family. Her heart froze inside of her; she could not help it. After the children flocked to Mother, her uncomprehending expression slowly gave way to glimmers of recognition until at last she embraced them back and cooed, "My poor babies, where've you been all this time?" In time, Mother's face unfroze and smoothed out. Ever since they were small Yŏngju's two children, Choongwoo and Kyungah, had been physically affectionate with their grandmother. This was not only because Yŏngju worked and was not around much to mother them but also because Choongwoo and Kyungah instinctively knew their grandmother liked to baby them.

Even after they were too big to act like babies, the children still hugged Mother and played with her when she had cooked an especially good dinner or when she waited up to fix them a late-night snack after they had been out. It was their way of paying her back for the favors she did for them. It wasn't at all that the children were cold and calculating by nature. For them as well as for her, it was all just an enjoyable game, and watching them you could not help smiling. Such shared joy, so palpable even strangers could sense it, made Yŏngju jealous at times, but at least she never tactlessly intruded or tried to mimic their games. She had given birth to her children, true, but it was Mother who had raised them almost single-handedly. Having raised the children gave Mother a proud and confident knowledge of her place, a sense of privilege upon which nobody else could encroach, and the natural ease of her bond to the children was almost animal-like — so much so that sometimes Yŏngju, watching the loving interactions among the three, imagined Mother licking the children with a soft, red tongue while all three were nestled in an envelope of warm, fluffy fur.

This time, however, it was different. Yŏngju was sulky; she would not even allow herself to feel her heart growing full at the sight of her children and Mother locked in a loving embrace. Uiwang Tunnel would not let her. The young policeman noticed this disparity in the attitudes of the family members as they collected the old woman, and seemed hastily to have concluded that it was a case of the rancor so common between a mother-in-law and her daughter-in-law.

"With such a son and such grandchildren, why in the world did you leave home? Sure, things may happen that hurt your feelings, but you have to grin and bite the bullet because you are the elder, after all. The world is changed nowadays. You're really lucky to have grandchildren who hang on you like this, you know. You understand, ma'am? The way the world is getting to be, lots of people abandon their parents or throw them out. Would those folks come and pick up their parents even after we notify them? It may seem unbelievable, but there are actually people who slink away to another part of the city just so we won't be able to contact them."

When her eyes met her husband's, Yŏngju hung her head. She felt even worse at being mistaken for a nasty daughter-in-law. The policeman continued to prattle along, pleased that the situation had been resolved so smoothly.

"I knew she was just that kind of an old lady. Just like a stubborn child she was, insisting she had to go to her son's house, but she had no phone number and didn't even know the neighborhood where he lived, just like one of those senior citizens who's been abandoned with nowhere to go but to a nursing home. Finally, she managed to come up with a phone number somehow, and we tried it, but as expected nobody at that number knew her, and they said they had moved into the apartment only recently. But at least that number gave us something to go on, and after much trouble, we were finally able to trace your phone number. It's really wonderful that everything came to such a beautiful end."

So, that was how it was. Mother's destination had been just as Yŏngju had predicted. Yŏngju decided quietly to slip out of the police station and wait for her family in the car, not only because it would be more seemly for a nasty "daughter-in-law" to do so, but also because she wanted to keep the truth from coming out. Yŏngju trusted her husband to understand her on this point and to see the charade through, acting the part of dutiful son to the end. Mother might want this too, Yŏngju thought, a forlorn smile crossing her face.

Yŏngju was Mother's daughter, not her daughter-in-law. That made Yŏngju's husband Mother's son-in-law, not her son. Even Yŏngju couldn't say exactly when Mother had started thinking it degrading to live with her daughter instead of her son. Probably it had been after Yŏngju's brother got married, for that was when Mother's friends and relatives began looking askance at her for not moving into her son's house. The aunts, in particular, began to show signs of wanting to pity Mother. Whenever they clucked, saying things like "At a daughter's house you eat standing up, but at a son's you eat sitting down," Yŏngju felt something inside might boil over and make her spit at her aunts' sense of superiority. These same aunts had nothing on Mother besides the fact that they were determined to live with their sons, come hell or high water. Ever since she was a little girl, Yŏngju had been happiest dreaming of becoming a brilliant success and caring for Mother in a grand fashion. She had not exactly succeeded in doing that, but the thought that even if she had, it would have made little difference for Mother's happiness, made her despondent. Nobody knew Mother better than Yŏngju. She knew Mother's sense of pride was based on the fact that she had spent her whole life on her feet working, not to be provided for in the end, but to provide for her children with her own hands, and that this pride belonged to Mother and to Mother alone. Thoughtlessly to belittle that pride was unforgivable, even for Mother's own sisters.

Yŏngju's brother Yŏngtak was the youngest of the children, born thirteen years after Yŏngju, and shortly after their father had died. After Yŏngju was born, more than ten years passed before Mother became pregnant with Yŏngsook. Then, before Yŏngsook was even a year old, Mother was pregnant again; but before she gave birth she found herself a widow. The only thing their father left behind was the house. At the time, their neighborhood had still been on the city's outskirts, almost in the country, but luckily the house was near a college and they could take in students as boarders. Soon enough, Yŏngju became known as a boarding-house daughter, and she acted the part well, almost as if she were born into it. She ran errands to the grocery store and did chores around the house; soon the work was as natural to her as the tongue to the mouth. She learned how to stoke the charcoal burners for heating the rooms without letting the fires go out. From high school on, she stayed up late into the night with Mother, keeping the books straight, planning the meals for the next day, worrying about the future of her younger brother and sister. When college entrance exams rolled around, it was Yŏngju who consoled her younger siblings, telling them even grasshoppers last only a season, as the family crammed into the attic to sleep curled up like shrimps after renting out every room in the house, even their bedrooms, to students. For Mother, Yŏngju was more of a comrade and confidant than a daughter. They worked together and worried together. Single-mindedly determined to lighten the burden Mother had to bear, Yŏngju was as severe and strict with the younger children as Mother, but never, not even once, did she allow herself to feel any kind of rivalry or jealousy toward them. "Who do you think you are, acting like you're our father?" Yŏngsook and Yŏngtak used to complain.

When Choongwoo returned home he was alone and wore a wilted look. Yŏngju had expected as much and so was not exactly disappointed, but something flared up within her all the same and she jumped up.

"Mom, I'm sorry."

Startled, Choongwoo grabbed Yŏngju's shoulders and apologized.

"It's not you I'm angry at." Yŏngju had a hunch Mother again would be found at Uiwang Tunnel, and it was this that enraged her. Uiwang Tunnel was on the way to Yŏngtak's house. Mother had no occasion to visit Yŏngtak's place more than three or four times a year, but whenever she went Yŏngju always drove her over in her car, and both from their old apartment in Kwachon and from where they now lived in Tunchŏndong they had to pass through Uiwang Tunnel to reach Yŏngtak's house. If Mother remembered only one thing about the way to Yŏngtak's house, the tunnel would be it. Kwachon Tunnel and Uiwang Tunnel were built some years after Yŏngju's family moved to Kwachon. They were starting a new life on their own after living in the big and spacious boarding house, but Mother had adjusted well to life in an apartment. She seemed not to find the small apartment too claustrophobic, maybe because the location on the ground floor allowed her to keep a garden of her own.

Mother's activities gradually covered an ever-widening radius, from the garden to Chŏnggye Mountain, and from there to Kwanak Mountain. She used to bring home gallons of mountain spring water several times a day and soon had a loyal following among the elderly neighbors who had been bred on city water. She was also a wizard at finding wild greens to pick on her outings. Before long, Mother had joined the mountain spring badminton club, the Kwanak aerobics club, and Chŏnggye senior citizens society. It was only natural, then, for her to be greatly displeased when the digging of the two tunnels began on the very slopes where she had been playing. She hated Uiwang Tunnel in particular because it was hard for her to pronounce. Right around this time Yŏngtak's family moved to a new apartment complex on the other side of the tunnel and Yŏngju seized the opportunity to tell Mother the tunnel had been dug for her, to provide her with a shortcut to her son's house. Whenever Yŏngju told her this, Mother's face broke into a broad grin and she was at ease again. While the tunnel was under construction, Mother's lapses of memory became so severe she began to forget the way back home. Yŏngju had to repeat her story about the tunnel time and time again, and every time Mother would respond, "Right, right, they dug the tunnel so I can get to Yŏngtak's house in a jiffy. Who in the world could have read my mind like that?"

The two of them must have repeated this exchange a hundred times over. But there were not many occasions to take Mother to Yŏngtak's, and without having to be told Mother knew nobody any longer went anywhere, even to your own son's house, uninvited.

To the end, Mother never said how she came to be at Uiwang Tunnel that day. Even if she had wanted to, she probably could not have explained how she got there. Aside from the tunnel itself, nothing probably had registered clearly in her brain. Yŏngju believed Mother could not have walked the whole way from Tunchŏndong to Uiwang Tunnel, so she guessed she must have walked part of the way and ridden part of the way. About to bolt the door, Yŏngju came back inside the house and looked for her car keys.

"Where are you planning to go?" Choongwoo asked.

"Uiwang Tunnel," Yŏngju replied.

"She couldn't have gone there again, could she?"

"On the other side of the tunnel is your uncle's house. It was no coincidence that they found her there that day, was it?"

"I know. But maybe she headed for the tunnel because it's the way to Kwachon."

Choongwoo spoke cautiously, trying not to step on Yŏngju's toes, for his mother grew irate whenever Kwachon was mentioned. The old woman's obsessive attachment to Kwachon was incomprehensible to Yŏngju. Perhaps Mother's sudden urge to be in her son's care was inevitable, and something Yŏngju should have foreseen all along. The only thing strange about this wish was that it had not surfaced sooner; after all, it was the everlasting desire of every mother in the land. But Mother's peculiar attachment to Kwachon — just an apartment complex, when all was said, even if the family had lived there for ten years — seemed senseless, and what Yŏngju could make no sense of, she was inclined to dismiss.

"If your grandma likes Kwachon, it's only because Kwachon's closer to your uncle's than here," Yŏngju interjected in an unnecessarily curt manner.

"If you're so convinced she's set on uncle, why did you bring grandma back from his house in the first place?"

"Listen to you. You sound like grandma belongs to somebody else's family."

"Mom, calm down. You're the one thinking like that, not me. Really, why are you acting like this? It's not like you at all."

"Maybe it was a mistake to bring her here. Now, it'd have been better if I hadn't. If she's at Uiwang Tunnel again, just watch me this time, I'm not going to bat an eye."

"Anyway, she hasn't even been gone an hour. No way she could have gotten that far."

"You don't think she got there on foot last time, do you?"

"Don't you remember what her feet looked like that day?" Choongwoo frowned a bit as he spoke.

Yŏngju remembered breaking into tears after making Mother soak her badly blistered feet in warm water. How vexed and angry she had been! And how far off Yŏngtak's house must have seemed to Mother! The distance as well as Mother's determination to get there at all costs were plainly spelled out in the ravaged skin on those toes. Yŏngju could not sleep that night because of those blisters, the worry and the loathing they aroused in her. She stayed up wide-eyed all night, and called Yŏngtak the next day to discuss the possibility of his taking Mother in. Actually, it was more pleading than discussion. Before he got married, Yŏngtak used to proclaim loudly that he would take Mother into his house and care for her once he got married. Yŏngju had not said outright that he did not have to do that, but in her heart of hearts, she was secretly proud. It was not that she hoped he would take Mother off her hands one day; she was just grateful that Mother would not become some chattel tossed about from one child to the next. Yŏngju did not like the tone of her own entreaties as she asked Yŏngtak to take Mother — after all, Mother deserved no less — but it was hard for her to change her tone. Perhaps it was Yŏngtak's reaction, which was not at all what she had expected. He just listened to her talk without revealing his own feelings, and remained reluctant to make any definite commitment. What he finally managed to say, in a jeering tone, was: "So you're no different, after all." Yŏngju could not understand what he meant by this. She was deeply offended, all the same, yet she could say nothing in reply.

Perhaps she was at a loss to generate any indignation or anger because she despised herself for silently accepting a social order in which bearing a son who fails to care for you in your old age is the most miserable fate possible. Yŏngju thought to herself that she deserved any unpleasantness that came her way.

"I'll let you know after I talk it over with my wife."

When her brother Yŏngtak had responded like that, Yŏngju couldn't help but retort, "Tell me what *you* think. That's what I want to hear."

"Isn't it the woman who ends up taking care of old folks? I could order my wife to take care of Mother if I wanted to, but I really don't want to issue commands."

Yŏngtak was living happily together with a woman he had dated for several years before marrying, and the two of them had a son and daughter. Plainly, Mother's presence would be an intrusion. As Yŏngju knew, time was always needed to prepare oneself, emotionally as well as practically, to assume an extra burden in one's life. She told herself she should be more understanding, but still she was perturbed by how annoyed she felt at her brother's silence. She thought: "He's the eldest son, the head of the family at least in name, so how can he act like this?" But her unforgiving attitude toward her brother's was blended with a sense of guilt as she asked herself, "How can I be this way?" She was at a loss to decide exactly whom she was trying to blame. But more unbearable still was the change in Mother.

The root of the evil was Yŏngtak's promise, whether or not he really meant to keep it, that he soon would be back to take Mother home with him. Mother had her bags packed and each day waited anxiously for him. Often, she muttered to herself, "My son told me he'll be here. I wonder why he's so late," looking out the window anxiously, like someone stranded in a waiting room. Worse yet, Mother had started distancing herself from Yŏngju's family with looks clearly meant to push them away. Unable to bear this any longer, Yŏngju had gone directly to her sister-in-law and pressed her to accept Mother into their home.

But Mother lasted not even three months at Yŏngtak's before coming back to Yŏngju's apartment in Tunchŏndong. Actually, to speak of her as "lasting" there was misleading. With each day that went by, Mother had lost more and more of her self-reliance. The one who couldn't last had been not Mother, but Yŏngju herself.

After pushing Mother into her brother's hands, Yŏngju couldn't help calling daily to see how she was getting along. Whenever Yŏngju called, Mother simply repeated over and over again, "Dear, I want to go to Kwachon. Please, take me to Kwachon." For Yŏngju, these words had a pathetic ring. Kwachon was where Yŏngju's family had lived before moving to Tunchŏndong, so Yŏngtak and his wife interpreted Mother's plea as a wish to go back to live with her eldest daughter. Still, the couple acted faultlessly, as though they would die first before asking Yŏngju to take Mother back. Yŏngju grew more and more uneasy about Mother staying at her brother's to the point of feeling her brother and his wife were being cruel in refusing to ask her to take Mother back.

From the day Mother moved to her brother's house, Yŏngju had not had peace of mind for a single day, for she also interpreted Mother's pleas to go to Kwachon as a wish to come back to the daughter's house. How could she possibly ignore her Mother's words without repressing all recollection of the many long years she had spent with her mother, not only as her eldest daughter, but as a friend. Still, Yŏngju endured this predicament as if being tortured with leg screws. Spitefulness made her tell herself that she would never be the first to offer to take Mother back from her brother's family — they would have to beg her first. At the same time, Yŏngtak's own obstinacy made him vow that his older sister would have to beseech him before he would deliver Mother into her hands again. These feelings, though seemingly in direct opposition, in reality were the same thing. What both of them valued was not Mother, but the dated notion that for a parent to live and die at a daughter's house while there is a son alive is a shame beyond all shame.

Whether or not she realized that this invisible tug-of-war was under way between her daughter and son, Mother's queer syndrome of constantly wishing she was elsewhere was getting worse day by day. The choice between her son and daughter was no longer important to Mother. What she wanted was to be in Kwachon; Kwachon was neither here nor there. From the outside, Mother looked like her mental faculties were deteriorating, but it could have been that they actually were improving. She had set up a no-man's land of sorts called Kwachon, away from her daughter's house, away from her son's house, and away from having to be shuffled between the two as if she were a chattel. All she was asking was to be taken to this buffer zone. Finally, Mother started running away from her son's house, too. Yŏngtak's wife had taken such thorough precautions, however, that the old lady never managed to get much farther away than the edge of the apartment complex.

Not only was Yŏngtak's wife the head of her building's tenants association; she was rational in the extreme. On the pretext of keeping Mother from getting lost and into trouble, she dressed her only in such clothes as would make it hard for her to get far if she left the house. If Mother went out in her pajamas or nightgown, the children playing around the apartment complex quickly would notice her. Once noticed, she was to be reported to the security guard. Dressed as she was, Mother probably never managed to stray much beyond their own building, let alone to escape from the apartment complex.

When her attempts to run away persisted, however, an additional lock appeared on Yŏngtak's front door. Though the apartment doors ordinarily opened from the inside even when locked from the outside; the new lock prevented someone inside from opening the door once it had been locked from without. When Yŏngju questioned the need for this new lock, Yŏngtak's wife stared at her with marble eyes, asking what else they could do when the rest of the family was out? Such devices seemed unavoidable for a household with an elderly member unless one wanted to hire somebody to keep a constant watch. The way Yŏngju saw it, everything Yŏngtak's wife did was perfectly proper. This very thoroughness, this perfection of Yŏngtak's wife struck Yŏngju as alarming, and it chilled her to the bone when she imagined Mother screaming with fear as she shrivelled and wasted away. Yŏngju had been willing to overlook that first lock, but a few days later another lock appeared, this time inside on the door to Mother's room. After resigning herself to the fact that she was unable to leave the house, Mother apparently had taken to roaming all around the house, opening and shutting doors while muttering to herself. She would open and close the same doors again and again, even peering into the closets and the bathroom; to Mother the place seemed to have an unending series of rooms.

"My, here's another room. And one more here? What sort of house has this many rooms? A pity they are left empty! Damned fool of a woman, why doesn't she rent these rooms out?"

All day Mother wandered about muttering such things. Yŏngtak's wife, unable to stand it any longer, had locked her up in her room.

"I wouldn't have done it if I hadn't had to. As it was, I just couldn't live like that, on edge all the time."

Just by looking at her sister-in-law's haggard face, Yŏngju could tell things indeed must have been unbearable for her. But Yŏngju herself was getting tired of having this desperate struggle to deny each other's human dignity trivialized by her sister-in-law as something that set her nerves on edge. By this time, Yŏngju was through hoping the relationship between Mother and Yŏngtak's family would get better. She simply hoped they would throw up their hands in despair and admit to her that they couldn't manage caring for Mother any longer. But even that seemed far from a simple matter.

That day, Yŏngju had gone over to Yŏngtak's to visit Mother. As always, Yŏngtak's wife greeted her with a cold, sterile expression that betrayed nothing about her inner feelings. Yŏngju's face, however, had apology written all over it, an apology for coming over too often. Yŏngtak's wife was civil enough to bring in some tea for Yŏngju, but she would not open the door to Mother's room.

"Is Mother taking a nap?"

"If you're so curious, why not go out on the veranda and look in through the window?"

"What? What in the world are you talking about? Is it so much trouble for you to open her door? You've gone too far this time."

"I learned it from Mother."

For the first time Yŏngtak's wife was complaining, tears in her eyes. She said Mother's symptoms had worsened lately; she had started climbing out through the window onto the veranda and from there stared into her son's room night and day.

"And when our eyes meet, she asks who I am. Do you know how that makes me feel?"

She did not explain further about her feelings. But Yŏngju could feel how mortally sick and tired Yŏngtak's wife was of the whole thing. Anger and contempt made Yŏngju feel as if her heart would burst. After a while, she went out on the veranda and took a peek into Mother's room. Mother was glaring at the old woman in the mirror, shouting at her, "Who are you? Huh? Out of my way! I'm telling you, get lost!" She was stamping her feet in vexation and rage. Just as Mother could not recognize the old woman in the mirror, Yŏngju found it hard to accept that the old woman confined in that room was Mother.

It wasn't that she had grown emaciated or anything physical like that. She was dressed in a comfortable outfit, one well-suited for an old lady, and looked much neater than she was in her baggy drawers. But Yŏngju had never before seen such cowering defensiveness in Mother's eyes. She had always been a person who seemed at ease, like a house with all its doors open. The change in her eyes wasn't all. Her small frame was tense down to every last muscle and her hair seemed to stand on end. Yŏngju could feel that extreme tension as if it were in her own body. She knew that if anyone so much as touched her, Mother would pounce and start biting. What a horrible world this had become for Mother to stand against all alone.

Without again asking her sister-in-law to open the door, Yŏngju opened the window and crept into Mother's room from the veranda. Mother did not ask who Yŏngju was, and she made no move to attack her. She just stayed there in the corner, crouched against the wall. Mother was terrified, as if facing a giant with no means of defense — not even her hostility and anger could save her. Yŏngju embraced her. She smelt of soap; the scent was not unpleasant. The room itself was simple but immaculate. There were even a couple of landscapes hanging on the walls. It had a bathroom attached, and in this apartment would be considered the master bedroom. From the beginning, Yŏngju had been deeply appreciative that her brother and his wife had given up this room to Mother. She told herself she had to keep that in mind now. Yŏngju patted her mother's back — so small it fit entirely within Yŏngju's embrace — and began stroking it gently. Perhaps what Yŏngju was seeking to calm with her strokes was not Mother but her own wrath rising within her. She knew she had to take Mother home with her, but thought she ought to tell this to her sister-in-law calmly and rationally, using civil words and without getting red in the face.

Her brother was not at home, but she had no hard feelings against him. She could well understand what he had suffered stuck in the middle between Mother and his wife. Her feelings for her brother were closer to motherly love than to affection between sister and brother, not just because of the age difference but because of the many years she and Mother had shared the grave task of raising a poor little boy fatherless from birth, trying to make him feel the same as any other boy. It was so hard for Yŏngju to overcome her own distracted state of mind that she went on stroking Mother for a long while until she seemed to start feeling uncomfortable.

After Yŏngju took Mother back to her place in Tunchŏndong, Mother reverted to her old self incredibly quickly. Even in the car on the way, Mother's look of distrustful panic soon dissipated. Yŏngju's family greeted her as if she were just returning from a short trip, and to them her condition did not seem to have worsened in any serious way.

Even Yŏngju began to wonder whether she had blown things out of proportion — perhaps her sister-in-law mindset had made her too quick to think ill of her brother's wife and had distorted her perception. She was almost ready to reproach herself.

The danger of Mother's running away was still real, and Yŏngju had to be most wary, so she made certain Mother never was left home alone. In a household with no full-time housewife, that was the hardest thing of all. Kyungah, a junior in high school who was busy studying for the college entrance examination, was excused. When they didn't have classes, Yŏngju and Choongwoo took turns staying home, but the two of them could not always do the job. In between, they hired a maid, and aunts occasionally came by to keep an eye on Mother.

Once Mother began helping out with this and that around the house, the family's tight watch over her relaxed, a bit at a time. The chores she did were nothing much. Maybe she trimmed the tips off bean sprouts, shredded bellflower roots into strips, or inspected mushrooms or fern brakes, telling Yŏngju whether they were Korean or not, that was about all. When Yŏngju didn't let her do even small chores like these, Mother grew disheartened, saying there was no point for a body to waste time in idleness when death would rot the flesh soon enough. Yŏngju was greatly relieved to hear such things from Mother again. They were the sorts of things Mother used to say back when they ran the boarding house together. Hearing her talk this way, Yŏngju felt like a child again, a little girl who waited for her mother to return from an outing and then rushed to meet her in the dim light of dusk, to be sheltered by the folds of Mother's skirt with a peaceful and contented heart.

Better yet was the return of Mother's amazing skill at folding laundry. She would take clothes down from the clothesline still slightly damp and fold them with such precision that even long johns looked as if they had been ironed. It was a skill nobody else could even begin to match. Mother's hands were still graceful and dependable. Ah, those hands that folded clothes as if they had been pressed — when Yŏngju caressed Mother's hands, she was seized by a warm urge to kiss those adored hands.

Mother's memory, however, had not returned to normal. "Mother's memory was still fading in and out without warning," Yŏngju thought now, "so maybe I relaxed too much." At times, when it was hard to find someone to look after her, she had left Mother alone in the house. She was reluctant to impose on the aunts every time, but more than that, she feared they would program Mother to believe that, come what may, one had to die in one's son's house to meet one's proper fate. The aunts were forever repeating such things. Yŏngju doubted that this notion, long engraved indelibly on Mother's brain, could have been completely erased, but at the very least she could try to keep the aunts from freshly bringing to the surface an idea better left repressed in the depths.

Three

Lotus-shaped paper lanterns hung from all the eaves.

It was a few months after a Buddhist symbol and a signboard reading "Ch'ŏngae Temple Mission" had first appeared on the old house. There were lanterns to spare even after the eaves all around the house, back as well as front, were decorated, and the extras had been hung from cords strung over the front yard. It was April 1, the first Buddha's Birthday celebration since the house had been consecrated. Seen from the primitive neighborhood, the lotus lanterns looked like a big cluster of pink balloons, making one imagine that at any second the house might take off and soar into the sky, suspended from heaven-bound balloons. This expectation was preposterous, of course, but it nonetheless reflected a certain ebullience in the air, a festive mood that had swept over the neighborhood as if borne in on a warm gust of wind.

Even before the lanterns went up, people in the neighborhood were happy just to see the temple signboard on the house. But not one of the Buddhist believers in the neighborhood belonged to that temple. More than half of the residents probably counted themselves as Buddhists, whether their participation in the faith meant attending prayer services at temples or only occasional visits to Buddhist oracles for insights into the future, but none of them belonged to this temple. Even so, it gladdened them to see so many lanterns hung on the temple, for so many lanterns seemed to them to mean a good-sized congregation. This reaction was unlike the residents, who were not in the habit of feeling selflessly uplifted at the good fortune of strangers.

Their sentiments may have stemmed from the fact that before its conversion into a Buddhist temple the house had been occupied by a fortune-teller. Most people considered a Buddhist temple to be higher class than a fortune-teller's house, and more seemly for the education of children. Not that they had been particularly antagonistic or aloof toward the house when the fortune-teller lived there. The location of the house was such that it was more or less automatically separated from everything else. Whenever strangers came around asking for directions to the house of the lady fortune-teller, people just pointed over beyond the vacant lots, saying it most likely would be that old house yonder.

The fortune-teller's house had no signboard or flag to announce itself, but nobody in the neighborhood was unaware that a fortune-teller lived there. At the same time, nobody knew anything about the lady fortune-teller who lived in the house, whether she was pretty or ugly, a gifted seer or just a quack; they just knew a lady fortune-teller must live there because of all the strangers who popped up at random asking about her. Most of the inhabitants of the primitive district, not so successful at what they were doing, were the sort who went to fortune-tellers to try to improve their luck. Among them were some who went to shaman's rites so often it was like their sole hobby, but not a single person in the neighborhood claimed to have visited that fortune-teller's house. Jesus was not the only one who got no recognition at home, it seems.

Even now that Buddha's Birthday was being celebrated in the house, the children were the only neighbors who went near the house. They huddled in groups, peeping inside from time to time. Just as a breeze carries aloft the lightest objects first, it was the children who were swept up in the festive mood; the adults in the neighborhood didn't even nod. The neighbors for whom April 1 was a religious holiday had already left to catch their busses and trains, bound for the various temples to which they belonged. The house was wide open, and inside the sliding doors a dainty little gilt Buddha was perched on a velvet cushion, smiling a graceful smile. Many congregation members were busy looking for the lanterns with tags inscribed with the names of their relatives. The colorful traditional silk dresses worn by many temple-goers were a treat for the eyes.

This temple housed a priestess. In truth, the lady fortune-teller and this priestess were one and the same person. Even the little statue of the Buddha was the same one she had used in her days as a fortune-teller. The only change was that the gold of the Buddha had brightened a little about the same time the temple signboard was hung out front. The statue had been freshly regilded. Today's believers were mostly yesterday's regular visitors to the fortune-teller, and the few new members of the temple congregation were just people who had heard from the regulars that the Buddha of this house was particularly efficacious.

The old regulars found nothing strange or unseemly about the fact that the fortune-teller had become a priestess. Even when she was simply a fortune-teller, she had been a follower of Buddhism. All along they had believed her powers of prophecy or clairvoyance had their source in the Buddha, and nothing about this had changed. The ritual of bowing before and after having your fortune told was unchanged with the conversion of the house into a temple. Then as now, believers visited the place out of a burning desire to decipher some insight into their husband's coming prosperity or their child's future success from a phrase or two casually spat out by the lady. And because they took her powers to be a manifestation of the power of the Buddha, they had taken to calling the lady "Boddhisattva" even before she took her vows as a priestess. Now that she had been officially ordained as a Buddhist cleric, they felt no discomfort at all in calling her a "natural-born priestess."

If anything had changed, it was that one day each month was set aside for reading of the sutras. The texts were read by an old monk who came down from Ch'ŏngaesa, the main temple of which this was an annex. On Buddha's Birthday, the Lunar New Year, July Seventh, and other days of observance, as well as for funerals and occasional devotions commissioned by believers, the monk came down from Ch'ŏngaesa. But the believers of the annex congregation had not the slightest idea where Ch'ŏngaesa was. That their natural-born priestess deferred to the old monk, using an honorific term for "coming down" when he visited from Ch'ŏngaesa, made them vaguely imagine a handsome temple well hidden up in the mountains somewhere. But they were not very impressed by the Ch'ŏngaesa monk. He had the imposing appearance suitable to his age, but almost never did he show any sign of prophetic gifts. The general opinion was that he was extraordinarily gifted only in recognizing a certain category of members — high-society wives who wished to hide their status. This capacity only damaged the harmony of the congregation and did nothing to further his own authority. In short, the believers put up with the Ch'ŏngaesa monk simply as a necessary side-effect of the evolution of the oracle's house into a Buddhist temple. They hoped the priestess would soon learn to do the invocations and prayer chants on her own. Their natural-born priestess had never said so herself, but among the believers she was known to be studying to enter a Buddhist academy.

On this Buddha's Birthday the monk from Ch'ŏngaesa had not yet arrived, but the cooking was in full swing in the kitchen, where a huge iron kettle hung from the wall. An abundance of all sorts of fruits, sweet pastries, and fancy rice cakes were spread out on the patio next to the kitchen. Because it was the Buddha's Birthday, the temple was providing both lunch and an evening meal to the congregation. Plenty of hands were already at work steaming and seasoning vegetables and making soup. The voice of Makŭm's old mother, who was supervising everything, was so vigorously fluid it was hard to believe she was approaching seventy. The priestess's secular name, as well as the legal name on her birth certificate, was "Makŭm."

Makŭm's mother probably felt more triumphant on this day than on any day since Makŭm was born. The old lady was only ordering people around; all the actual work was being done by her daughters-in-law. She also had a son-in-law who, if she only jotted down a list, would drive all the way to a wholesale market in Seoul to buy whatever she wanted. If the business went on prospering like this, within two or three years they would have to raze the house and build a bigger temple, or else develop a new temple site somewhere else. The mere thought of it made Makŭm's mother arch her shoulders with pride. As she looked the house over, the old lady's eyes shone with greed as well as deep pride. Not that there weren't a few things that made her uneasy. She felt a little apprehensive about renovating the house, especially now that this once ill-starred place was so full of life and flourishing with good fortune, like dying embers rekindled to burn high once more. She worried that putting hands on the house to change it might chase away the good luck.

As a rule, however, greed overwhelms caution. A plan had already been under discussion among the elders of the congregation and the Ch'ŏngaesa monk to commemorate this beautiful day by agreeing to build a bigger temple at this site; the plan was well on its way to fruition. It could not really be said to be very long ago that Makŭm's mother had opened her eyes to the business of giving hope and comfort to the human heart, but if there was one thing she unquestionably had mastered, it was the knowledge that few businesses promised such a reliable way to make money as easily as swimming on dry land, or that the proverb "Well begun is half done" fit so well.

Makŭm's mother sat outside on the patio watching the preparations and nagging, but at the same time she was busy drawing up a rough estimate of how much money had come in so far that day as offerings and how much more would be laid on the Buddha's altar. Her expression would change capriciously from the broadest of smiles to a frown of dissatisfaction. This business was finally taking off so well that it seemed like a dream. At one minute she would be proud of it, but at the next she remembered hearing about the vast sums rushing into bigger temples, filling iron pots with bills, so many they had to crush the money down to make room for more, and this made her boil with envy because the money coming into her temple seemed a mere pittance in comparison.

Another thing that left her dissatisfied was the befogged expression on the face of the priestess, as if her mind were elsewhere. She could scarcely stifle the disgust she felt toward her daughter, who tried to avoid eye contact, let alone any form of touch. She wondered whether her daughter realized that for a business like this to succeed, mother and daughter had to be in complete synch, from hand to feet. "How dares she look down on her mother," Makŭm's mother thought, "now that the poor wretch has become a big dragon, after all she owes me for getting her this far?" But the old lady knew that Makŭm had her reasons for acting this way. The old lady's eyes shot daggers in Makŭm's direction whenever her daughter wasn't looking, but when their eyes met, she was all smiles. It was not something she found pleasant to do, but the daughter may have been trying to avoid her for the same reasons. There was a kind of silent agreement between mother and daughter to avoid making eye contact, and Makŭm's mother came to the house only on days when there was a prayer service or a meeting. On regular days, she left her daughter alone in the house.

The daughter had long been the sole source of income for the family, starting back when she was a fortune-teller and continuing now that she was a Buddhist priestess. The daughter tried to steer clear of her mother, avoiding not only eye contact but conversation, too. But she left the finances to her mother's discretion and didn't bother herself with such things. She did not even know how much money she herself made in a day. To find that out, she would have had to start talking with members of her family. Perhaps she had adopted her habits just so she could avoid having to deal with them. Makŭm was the means of livelihood for her family, Makŭm's money was her mother's, and Makŭm's mother's money was her mother's as well.

Makŭm's mother was a genuine native of the area. She knew the prehistory of the house. But she no longer lived in the primitive neighborhood. She lived in a high-rise building in a spacious apartment that looked down from its high floor on the primitive zone as if it were an eyesore marring the landscape. Makŭm's mother had been born in the area when it was a cluster of farms, before the apartment buildings went up and even before the primitive neighborhood houses had been built. She had been married off into another family in the area, and had lived a harsh and difficult life as a young wife. Even that far back, the old house had stood there in the middle of an empty field. Makŭm's mother had been born into a house much worse than that old house, and her husband's family's house was much worse even than the one she had been born into. She had nothing to do with the old house at all. When the chaos of the Korean War broke out, she fled the neighborhood for the first time. When she came back, the neighborhood was much changed. Many neighbors had moved away and many houses were empty.

The old house was still standing, despite some deterioration, but it was unoccupied. People said the landlord who owned the house had been cruel to the tenants and laborers who worked under him, and that the whole family had been massacred during the war. Those who knew about the incident called the house ill-starred or cursed, because of the vengeful massacre of the family who had lived there. Many people refused even to walk by it, and would take the long way around, instead. From time to time, the abandoned house became a den for beggars and vagabonds. More and more it took on the appearance of a haunted house. Even after many years had passed and the neighborhood population had changed so much that those who knew what happened there during the war were few and far between, an atmosphere of evil clung to the ill-starred house. People's aversion to it was deepened by outlandish and frightening tales that continued to circulate.

Makŭm's mother and her husband, a day laborer in an orchard, had five children. Busy raising them, the mother never escaped the neighborhood, and never even had a house of her own. But not once had she looked at that house and wished it hers, not for all the thought of a good night's sleep in a spacious house of her own. It was simply a condemned property, not a house.

One day a thin wisp of smoke was seen rising from the house. Almost nobody paid it any mind, even to wonder whether a new beggar had taken up residence inside the house. This was even before the primitive district was constructed. Amid the fields and the orchards a handful of farmhouses still spotted the land here and there, but the signs were clear that the farms would vanish before long. Even so, nobody had foretold that the prices of land in the area would soar sky-high. Only Makŭm's mother first noticed when the house began to show signs of life. Nobody else could have recognized the man who had come back to live in the house as the brother of the dead owner, the sole survivor of the massacre. After witnessing the slaughter of his brother's whole family as a young man, the brother was traumatized. Having no relatives left to turn to, he had entered a Buddhist monastery and had only just returned to the lay world after almost two decades as a monk. Makŭm's mother had not been scheming to do him in from the outset, but somehow the mere knowledge of who he was made her itch just thinking about it. She vaguely thought that one day she might be in a position to make good use of that information. She kept watch over the house from afar, and her heart grew more and more tense as land prices around the house began to climb. It seemed unlikely to her that a man who had spent so many years as a monk would voluntarily turn his back on that life one day just because a means of living awaited him in the secular world.

One day a "Zen Temple" emblem appeared on the house. The connections the erstwhile monk had forged at the temple must have been all right; men who fit the profile of "intellectual" frequented the house. It was never a busy place, but a few people constantly came and went. Makŭm's mother and father began to work in the house as domestic help. They learned that the visitors to the house were men who came to study Chinese language or Buddhist sutras. Monthly meetings of fairly large groups were held. Partly to reduce the number of mouths to feed at home, young Makŭm, who had barely finished primary school, was sent by her mother to the house to be a live-in maid and errand girl.

Times were hard, but Makŭm's mother told herself it was her duty to teach her children a skill if she couldn't send them even to middle school. From the time she was very small, Makŭm had a sad and ominous aura, and she displayed an uncanny power to predict what would befall others. These traits made her mother think something useful might come from having her daughter learn some Buddhist sutras, even if only from eavesdropping as she worked.

In those days the primitive district was still called the village of Western-style houses. The neighbors kept a respectful distance from the rundown house with the Zen emblem. The strange man living there, who was neither a monk nor a layman, was referred to as a "spiritual master." Of course, because of the reputation of the house, none of the residents of the district of Western-style houses went there to be instructed in the Tao or to study Buddhist sutras.

Not long after Makŭm was sent to live in the house as an errand girl, when she was just fourteen years old, the spiritual teacher violated her. Makŭm told her mother what had happened: she was terribly upset and did not want the same thing ever to happen again. The mother jumped up and down with rage and threatened the spiritual teacher. Planning to extort even more money from him, she then helped him to acquire clear legal title to the house and to claim ownership of the surrounding fields. In time, due to Makŭm's mother's machinations, the house became Makŭm's property and the spiritual teacher retained the empty fields. It was a good deal for both sides.

Makŭm's ordeal led her to hate men, but it also made her even more sensitive at reading people's thoughts from their faces or their manner of speaking. Her mother exploited these talents to promote her daughter her as a fortune-teller, but Makŭm was unreliable and had no lust for money, so the business failed to prosper as well as the mother had hoped. Even so, Makŭm brought in so much money that not only her mother but her siblings as well got used to sponging off their sister's career as a shaman. The fortune-teller's oracle metamorphosed into a Buddhist temple not only through the cooperation of the spiritual teacher who sold his surrounding land to buy a temple in the mountains, but also because Makŭm readily agreed.

Makŭm also expressed a desire to study, but she was too old to start studying again. Just as she showed no interest in making money, it was not in her nature to be a scholar. She trusted nothing other than her intuition. Still, she wanted some excuse to go somewhere other than where she was, it didn't matter where. What she wished to escape was perhaps less the place where she found herself than the people to whom she had been bound up to then. Everyone she knew, her family included, seemed absorbed solely in taking things from others, whether money or status. No means which worked to this end were too unprincipled for these people. Makŭm's ability to see this truth at an early age was an important asset in her fortune-telling. Nevertheless, she told herself that not everyone on earth could be like that. She had never had a child of her own, but when she looked at her mother, she felt not all mothers would be like her. This tortured her the most. The belief that not all mothers would be that way was the truest truth she treasured in her heart of hearts, a truth confirmed by the quiet smile of serenity she saw on the Buddha's face whenever she awoke suddenly from slumber in the depths of night.

How much money had come in? After Buddha's Birthday passed, the temple again was like a temple should be, quiet through and through. Makŭm thought of moving the lotus lanterns from the yard to the ceiling overhanging the patio, but when they swayed in the breeze she felt like a pond was floating overhead, and the priestess looked up at the sky and smiled. Then she walked over to the backyard to pick some greens from her garden. Much food had been prepared, but all the rice cakes had been given away to the believers and all the leftover dishes had been taken home by her family. Nothing was left for her to eat. That mother of hers, who had never seen her daughter relish a meal, told herself that any food left behind for her daughter would just spoil and be wasted. So rather than giving any thought to getting Makŭm to eat, she just tried to take everything with her.

What's more, as though Makŭm were enjoying a feast every day, her mother never forgot to bully her by warning that as a priestess she had to abstain from meat and fish even if she really liked them, else the believers would desert and move to a different temple. Makŭm had a hardened habit of making just enough food to keep from starving, for she had no interest in cooking and no talent for it. When she was a child, her mother had never taught her the proper ways to prepare food. It had not been she who had sown the seeds in the backyard garden, either. She had no idea how to prepare the greens properly, but she grabbed a handful of plants at random from the garden. She was about to start cleaning the vegetables when an old lady quietly came into the house. At first glance, Makŭm could see the lady had not come to have her fortune told. Her unseasonable clothes and bright face dazzled Makŭm's eyes for no apparent reason. The old woman smiled and chided the priestess.

"Don't even know how to trim vegetables? Tut, tut, what have you done with your years?"

The old woman sat down innocently across from Makŭm and began trimming the greens. Makŭm realized for the first time that you should skin the stems when you trim green shoots.

"I guess you wouldn't begin to know how to wash them, since you don't even know how to trim them. You clean, ah-uh, like this." The old woman took the vegetables to the hose in the yard and scrubbed them until the water turned green.

"I guess you wouldn't have any leftover water from washing rice, huh?" she said and told Makŭm to bring out some rice. The rice, too, she scrubbed a few times against the inside of the pot and then set aside the milky-white water. Looking around the old-style kitchen, she kept exclaiming her admiration, and then put the rice on to cook, after which she ladled out some bean paste from a large clay pot and began preparing the soup. All this the old lady did as easily and naturally as if she were working in her own old kitchen. The priestess racked her brain, trying to figure who this old woman could be, but she drew a blank. From experience, she knew that anything she came up with after straining to remember was seldom correct. The right answer ought to come right away. But she was not a bit frustrated; rather, she was greatly pleased. Joy was crawling slowly up her spine. Never before in her whole life had she felt like this.

The two lovingly shared the meal the old woman had fixed. The vegetable soup was so good that the priestess doused her rice in it and finished a big bowlful, but the old woman kept on insisting she should eat more, since she looked so frail and weak. It was enough to confuse any onlooker as to who was the host and who the guest. But then, from the moment she walked in, the old woman had acted as if she were coming home. Watching as the old woman immediately started worrying about the next meal, saying she should cook something really tasty for dinner, the priestess felt an impulse to act like a baby in front of her. This was a quite new feeling for her as well. She had never before been spoiled by another and the experience enraptured her, as if she were absorbed in a pleasant dream far from any feeling of reality at all.

She bought several things from the grocery for the grandma to prepare for dinner. She got bean curd, bean sprouts, and dried anchovies from the mini-supermarket in the primitive district. Stepping into the kitchen, she helped the grandma prepare dinner in a give-and-take fashion. She was chided about pouring the costly sesame oil carelessly. The grandma scolded Makŭm a great deal, but the fortune-teller felt not at all intimidated. It was a revelation to her that a person, to be precise an old person, could be so untroubled, so free and easy.

When night came, Makŭm spread out her bedding and lay down next to the grandma. "Easy come, easy go" — Makŭm thought. She feared the grandma might leave as suddenly as she had come. Cautiously, she took the grandma's hand in hers. Small and wrinkled, it was still soft.

"Want me to tell you an old tale?" the grandma asked, taking Makŭm's other hand in hers. "Once upon a time, long, long ago, there was a widow who lived alone with her young child. The widow started having an affair. She took to going to bed with all her clothes on in order to slip out to meet her lover once her child fell asleep. When the young boy found out mommy was slipping away at night, he went to sleep with mommy's shirt string tied fast to his wrist. When he set his mind at ease and fell asleep, mommy snipped the string in two and raced out like a gale."

"That's so sad, grandma." Murmuring this, Makŭm fell fast asleep. When she awoke from the kind of deep sleep that renews you, body and soul, it was morning.

Grandma was no longer beside her, but Makŭm could hear sounds from outside. Grandma was folding laundry on the wooden porch. "When you are old like this, you should just die. How could I have forgotten to do this laundry before going to sleep?" She took the clothes, damp with the morning dew, smoothed them flat and folded them with sharp creases. "They need to see the sun again. Then, they'll be fluffy." Listening to her chatter on like this, Makŭm marveled. Where had such a rare treasure rolled in from? The more she thought about it, the more amazed she became. Her underwear and her temple robe, which had been as wrinkled as dried pollack because they were left unshaken after they were wrung out, were now as smooth and tidy as if just ironed.

Thus began her dreamy life with the grandma, a sweet and comfort-filled life. Makŭm vowed to give up wondering where the grandma had come from and when she would go. She had no idea who the grandma might be, apart from the fact that she seemed more at home in Makŭm's house than the priestess. All grandma's rambling about her past amounted to nothing. It didn't seem she was being vague on purpose. When she was pressed, she made no sense. If Makŭm fastened upon a comment and followed it up with questions, the grandma struggled to remember with a perplexed look on her face, but soon she grew tired and started saying something totally beside the point. Once, as she gazed absent-mindedly at the statue of the Buddha, she said Jesus freaks were good people too. She told Makŭm she once fell sick on the street and almost died, but when she woke up Jesus freaks were praying for her. But when Makŭm asked to hear more about it the following day, grandma talked of an entirely different matter altogether. Staring at a far-off greenhouse, she said her back was giving her trouble lately because she had spent the winter there. This made no real sense to Makŭm, yet it didn't seem completely incoherent. What Makŭm intuitively realized was that the grandma kept losing the thread of memories that came floating back to her now and then. But it was clear to her that grandma was fully satisfied with her current situation.

"Fish like the water in which they used to play, and people, too, are fond of places where they've once lived." The old lady said this cheerfully and stretched her arms to relax herself. This gave Makŭm the idea that the grandma had lived in this house long ago, and had come back after so long. When such notions occurred to her, she was not at all displeased. She considered it a matter of karma. She had been grandma's granddaughter once upon a time in a past life and now was her granddaughter again; that was all.

But then grandma would stare vacantly at distant hills and murmur, "My son said he'd come to pick me up. Why isn't he coming?" Makŭm would feel her heart plummet and her mood would be spoiled. It wasn't that she feared the son would indeed come to retrieve the old woman. Rather, she felt bad because the grandma seemed to be an elderly parent purposely abandoned by her children.

Four

Yŏngju's guess that Mother had again headed toward Uiwang Tunnel was way off. She stayed up all night, and the next day checked out all the places Mother possibly could have gone. Finally, she reported Mother's disappearance to the police, the local ward office, and the family welfare bureau of the district office. She discovered to her surprise that there was a national hotline for reporting missing persons. She made hundreds of inquiries in all directions, but days passed with no progress. She took out an ad in a newspaper. She asked, as a favor, that a friend of her husband's, who was in the broadcasting business, announce a plea over the radio in between popular shows. These efforts did yield a few leads, but when she looked into them, they came to nothing. It wasn't just once or twice, but several times, that she ran crying all the way to Suwon after someone called in to say an old woman had been seen panhandling at Suwon terminal.

There were even cruel prank callers who, after saying they were with Mother right then and asking Yŏngju to come with enough money to pay the caller back for a bowl of noodles bought for her, hung up without saying where they were. She went to the prosecutor's office to check on the list of deaths of unidentified persons. In the process, a few times she experienced the ordeal of having to view the corpses of old people who turned out to be total strangers. Her husband and her brother more often handled those steps. Even after she had done everything she possibly could, she could hardly just sit at home and wait. Rather than sit still at home even for a minute, Yŏngju drove her car every place she could imagine that an old lady might want to go. The state of her house was unspeakable. But thanks to these efforts, Yŏngju confirmed that Mother had been seen a few times in Kwachon.

The family had lived in the Kwachon apartment for so long that many neighbors could still recognize Mother. One man claimed to have seen her, but he said he had just greeted her, thinking she was heading home after a visit. He said she had been neatly dressed and cheerful in demeanor as always, so he never in a million years could have imagined that she was lost. If he had known she was being sought, he would have kept her with him and contacted Yŏngju. Yŏngju felt exasperated and wanted to stamp her feet in frustration. Even though it seemed too late to do such a thing, she decided to print up flyers to distribute as newspaper inserts. For several days, Yŏngju went to every newspaper distribution center from Kwachon all the way to Pyungchon, Sanbon, and Anyang. Afraid people were in the habit of tossing out such inserts without even looking at them, she then decided to print up posters and stick them up on street corners. Even if putting the posters up only within a limited radius of where Mother had been seen was a big job, far beyond the capacity of Yŏngju's family by themselves. But just having something she could work on to try to get Mother back was a salvation. Still, everything took time and work, and Yŏngju and her immediate family could do only so much.

To share the work and confer about whether there might be better ways to try to track down Mother, Yŏngju often met with her brother and her sister. Naturally there was a lot of talk when they got together, and criticism usually centered on Yŏngju. Yŏngtak often began with the words, "What does a sinner like me have to say?" but he and his wife seemed most self-righteous. Yŏngtak's wife didn't interfere by offering small suggestions to do this or that. She merely looked on with a cold demeanor, but Yŏngju often sensed that the icy smile on her face was asking what more need be said now that the necessity to keep Mother under lock and key had been so irrefutably proved. The younger sister, Yŏngsook, seemed to sense this, too.

"You should have borne with it a bit longer. You acted so sanctimonious and brought her back home, but now all you've managed to do is let them off the hook. I don't have to see her to know Yŏngtak's wife must secretly be thinking it serves you right."

"Is now the time to argue who deserves the blame? We don't even know whether Mother is alive or dead. Then too, what I tried to do was to think about Mother first, about what she would want. I didn't know things would turn out this way, but I still think that I wasn't wrong."

"My, my, who can top the superiority of a sister with a Ph.D.? The police said not to worry about that, no? Didn't they say they'd contact you right away if she were found dead? Through the fingerprints or something."

"What does my having a doctorate have to do with anything?"

"No child ever got such full mileage out of a mother as you did, no? Wasn't it enough to have kept mother working so long, no, you had to get greedy for a doctor's degree? It's your greed that kept Mother here at her daughter's house until she was so old, and finally this happened."

How could Mother and her younger sister be so different? Didn't her sister know who was responsible for providing her own college education, and Yŏngtak's too? Mother was always proud of her children's college educations, but she always gave half the credit to her eldest daughter, and she felt sorry about the debt. If Yŏngju had not been trapped into the work of helping her mother run the boardinghouse, she could have earned her Ph.D. years earlier. These regrets she had heard from Mother many times, and had she not been determined to put Mother's conscience at rest once and for all, she never would have had the guts to tackle graduate studies so late in the game.

Like a true boardinghouse daughter, Yŏngju had met her husband among the students who lived with them. He knew her family predicament inside and out before marrying her, and didn't object in the least to living with his in-laws even after his wife had become a middle school teacher. There was an old saying that even a humble man who had only three sacks of barley to his name would never move in with wife's folks, but Yŏngju's husband behaved in such a way that nobody felt awkward or sorry on his behalf. When asked about his family situation, he said he lived with his wife's mother with as much pride and satisfaction as any woman could muster when answering that she lived with her mother-in-law. Her husband never looked so wonderful and Yŏngju was never as proud of him as at those moments. Mother too was grateful to have such a son-in-law. Even now, Yŏngju's husband was the one who thought about Mother most at odd moments, at unnoticed times. Yet Yŏngsook wanted to pick on her brother-in-law, even such a paragon as he was.

The spring weather had been warm for several days. On a certain mild day, Yŏngju was thinking about the possibility that Mother was sleeping outdoors, having no home to go to in her befuddled state. Yŏngju felt less horrified by these thoughts than she had been weeks before, on account of the warm weather. Her husband wore a sad face and remarked that he missed the bean paste stew Mother used to make out of pickled radish. He happened to mention this when Yŏngsook was around. The whole family knew that nobody prepared that dish better than Mother. Even though Yŏngju's husband had made this comment in a forlorn manner, Yŏngsook got into a rage and threw a tantrum.

"If even a maid had left the house," she shouted, "you would find better things to say about her than that!"

Yŏngju wondered how her sister thought of Mother if she insisted on taking such a harmless comment to be a supreme insult that belittled her. Yŏngju herself missed Mother most intensely when she thought of the way she used to fold clothes, and she could more than understand the true feelings in her husband's heart.

Nearly six months had passed since Mother left the house. It was almost summer. Yŏngju had reprinted thousand-sheet stacks of posters many times over, but they were still a long way from having covered Seoul and its suburbs. Phone calls with possible leads had ceased coming in a long time ago. It had become almost a daily routine of Yŏngju's to make the rounds of various institutions for the elderly to put up the posters and check whether Mother could be there. There were many nursing homes and similar places not registered with the family welfare bureau. She could find such places only by word of mouth.

One day she was on her way home from a futile trip to an unregistered home for the elderly. She found herself at a nondescript spot on the outskirts of Seoul, but for some reason she felt like stopping there for a rest. She got out of her car and took a deep breath of air. It didn't seem particularly fresh. She was near the entrance to a squalid-looking neighborhood. As she was thinking she might want to put a poster up there, her eyes chanced to come to rest on an isolated house some distance away. It was incredible that an old farmhouse like that was still standing so close to Seoul. It was not a traditional house in a cultural sense or anything; it was just an old, troublesome-looking house, but Yŏngju slowly approached it, drawn there by some inexplicable force. Even as she walked up, Yŏngju paused to wonder what was drawing her to the house. Out of the blue, she thought about the house in Chongamdong where Mother had kept boarders. It was just a random association; there was not really anything similar between the houses.

Taking in a sharp gulp of air, Yŏngju looked past the signboard announcing the house to be Ch'ŏngae Temple Mission. She saw Mother's sweater hanging from the clothesline, fluttering in the wind. It was as if Yŏngju were sucked into the house. She was gasping for breath. Lotus lanterns hung overhead, and the golden figure of the Buddha bespoke the house's conversion into a temple. Apart from these things, it was no different from any other country house.

On the wide floor in front of the Buddha, two women in gray monk's robes were sitting under the lotus lanterns, chatting idly as they peeled some tubers. The shimmery haze of a mirage, an air of boundless ease, amity, and peace enveloped the two women. Perhaps because the robe she wore was much too large for her small frame, Mother looked to Yŏngju like a butterfly that had temporarily folded its wings to rest. No, no, it wasn't only because of the loose robe. It was because of the lightness of being, the freedom of having completely shaken off the weight of life, the wastes of living. Before this, who had ever made Mother so free and so happy? Who would have thought that a woman past seventy could be such a bundle of innocence, unsullied by life?

"No, this couldn't possibly be real. It is an illusion I am seeing," thought Yŏngju. She could not approach one step closer to Mother, even though she was only a touch away. For where Yŏngju stood was reality. Reality and illusion, no matter how close they were, and no matter how transparent, were two distinct worlds, the haze between them absolutely impassable.

translated by Ryu Youngju

Farewell at Kimpo Airport

The old woman found her young granddaughter's kindness out of character and so awkward that it secretly annoyed her. "Ha!" she thought, "Now that I'm off to America, even you are kissing up to me. Don't think I can't see through you . . . " The old lady's narrow mind never deviated from its cramped orbit, so accustomed had she grown to ill treatment at the hands of her family.

Like the girl's mother, her eldest son's wife, this granddaughter of hers was standoffish, not loving in the least. The old lady had already begun to grow suspicious when the young girl had volunteered to escort her around Seoul. When they entered the museum, the young girl put her arm around the old woman and diligently explained, in a loud, clear voice, that this was a copy of Palsang Hall at the Bŏpjusa temple complex, and that was a reproduction of an altar at Bulguksa, a Buddhist temple over a thousand years old. But the old woman understood not a word of it. She was unused to kindness of any sort. As she looked over toward where her granddaughter was pointing, her first thought was what a magnificent place it was. But she soon got a grip on herself. "Phew," she thought, snorting disdainfully, "this is nothing. In America there are lots of buildings over a hundred stories tall, and I'm about to become an American grandmother. Ha! You thought I'd be impressed by this?"

The old woman's hair, figure, and face had nothing in them to suggest the slightest generosity. She looked totally cramped and unfeeling. Only when she was belittling others did she feel a sudden triumph and pride that brightened her face and gave it a semblance of attractiveness, as if a little lamp had been lit inside her. Lately this little lamp was on far oftener than it was off.

The old woman would leave for America shortly — all procedures had been completed, thanks to her daughter. To be sure, this "thanks to her daughter" was as unsatisfying as ending a feast with a drink of ditch water, but when she reminded herself that three of her four sons, all but the eldest, were in America, she lifted up her head and felt high and mighty. To the old woman "America" called to mind first and foremost a country of riches, a place where everybody had more to eat and to wear than they could ever need. In her mind it was no larger in scale than metropolitan Seoul — the area could be traversed with a flap of her ragged skirt and a few brisk steps. And if she could not get along with her daughter, she told herself, she could go live with her son; and if she didn't hit it off with that son she could move on to the next. Actually, however, the old woman's daughter was the only one of her children in America. Her second son was in Germany, the third in Brazil, and the fourth on the island of Guam. These three younger sons of hers all somehow had been sidetracked and were now scattered in these non-American locales. But all their original destinations had been America, and from the moment they began their frantic quest for connections allowing them to emigrate, her sons' mindless laments of "America, America, if I can only get to America!" had been driven like spikes into her ears. America's popular image among Koreans of the time — a promised land, difficult to reach but, once attained, a place where everyone grew rich overnight — had taken deep root in her mind. So, her sons simply had to be in America. In her mind, Germany, Brazil, and Guam were local districts in America, just as Nusang-dong, Ahyŏn-dong, and Ch'ŏngjin-dong were districts in Seoul.

Even worse, when the old woman thought of Brazil or Guam she lacked the wherewithal to map them as far apart as, say, Seoul and Pusan in Korea. This is not so surprising, considering that she grew up in Kup'abal as the daughter of a dirt-poor farmer, and first came to Seoul to marry a rootless day laborer who had finally settled in Hyŏnjŏ-dong, just over the hill of Muakjae. In that same neighborhood she had given birth to her children, endured the war, become a widow, and painfully raised the children on her own, never taking even a day to see the sights around Seoul, let alone the world beyond. The closest she ever came to seeing the sights may have been when she was a naive young bride: Word of a grand shamanistic ceremony at the Hyŏngjebaui swept through Hyŏnjŏ-dong, the neighborhood just beneath the Sŏnbaui. In no time the shrill whistle of pipes and the beat of drums filled the air. She truly loved a spectacle. Telling herself the household chores could wait, she slipped away and joined kids from the neighborhood to dance, hips gyrating, all the way up to the Sŏnbaui. All day long she watched the festivities. Having already written off the day, she then headed up to the ruins of the fortress on Mt. Inwang and gazed out over Seoul. While she was daydreaming about getting all dressed up and visiting the zoo, Hwashin Department Store, and the Tongyang Theater like other people did, she suddenly grew flustered and thought of home. Looking north toward Kup'abal, her home was only a few kilometers away, but it seemed so far off over distant mountains that in the end all she could do was weep. That was the entirety of the universe this old woman had ever seen, so it was only natural for her to shrink the strange world of America to fit a tunnel-vision formed so many years before.

What's more, had she had a chance to escape Seoul with the flood of refugees in June 1950, the old woman's constricted universe might have been expanded a bit, but flight had been impossible for her. The first house she had called her own, a hovel at the end of a dead-end street in Hyŏnjŏ-dong, was leveled by a bomb and her husband was killed. When Seoul was finally retaken, her eldest son, the pillar upon whom she had relied, went off to fight. She was left all alone with a cluster of young mouths to feed. And that was not all: At the end of her terrible suffering came disgrace. Though she was four years past forty, well beyond childbearing age for most women, she found herself pregnant with a posthumous child. Horrible as the Chinese Red Army might have been, she was in no shape to go anywhere. She prayed the baby would die, a miscarriage or stillbirth. As much as she wished for the thing inside her to perish, it was not to be. A daughter was born, her youngest and only daughter, who was now in America.

That daughter was bringing her mother to America! As the saying goes, "A dragon may rise from even a trickle, and the child you scorn treats you better than the one you spoil."

As she reflected on the halo of filial piety bestowed by her devoted daughter, the old woman grew even haughtier and her gait took on a swagger. As she entered the museum with her granddaughter, she noticed people lining up and slowly filing past glass cases, peering into them intently, from which she gathered the cases must contain something of great interest. The young girl's touch grew still more affectionate. Maybe she was just afraid of losing her grandma — the crowd was larger than she had expected — but she wrapped one arm tightly around the old woman's waist and skillfully cut a swath through the crowd and up to the glass display case. The granddaughter was tall for her still tender age, a full head taller than the old woman. Her white collar looked crisp against the navy blue wool of her smartly cut school uniform.

Inside the display case, which the old woman was certain must house some dazzling golden treasures, there were only chipped clay pots and broken shards of earthen bowls. She was struck dumb, but her granddaughter's eyes shone. "These are patternless celadon and those pots over there have a comb's-tooth glaze," she said, trying to explain the exhibits but using terms beyond her grandmother's grasp.

The old woman tut-tutted, telling herself it was disgraceful, absolutely disgraceful, to call these things treasures and house them in such a magnificent place! A clay pot should be called a clay pot, a broken bowl a broken bowl; seeing such high-flown names on all that junk made her sick.

The old woman's face was no longer lit with that nice little lamp of self-assuredness, but rather it bespoke something closer to condescending pity. Noticing this change, the young girl was overwhelmed by frustration and despair. She knew that look. She knew it well, because she had seen it too many times. It was exactly the same sterile look of condescending pity that had surfaced as soon as her uncles and her aunt had bought their plane tickets and had stayed frozen on their faces till the day they left. Her uncles had all worn that expression and so had her aunt. Lately, when the girl thought of her uncles in Germany and Guam, or of her aunt in America, their features blurred in her memory. But with each passing day she recalled more vividly how desperate they had been to leave Korea behind at all costs. As they scurried about seeking connections and fulfilling procedures, their frenzy had been utterly desperate, like the writhing agony of a beast in a trap or the panic of rats on a sinking ship.

From the start they all had wanted nothing but to get to America. After losing their father in the war they began to haunt American army bases from a tender age. They cut their teeth as shoeshine boys or houseboys and matured into handymen or waiters in the officers' canteen. As time passed they grew fairly confident in English conversation and even mastered that peculiar Yankee gesture of shrugging the shoulders and raising a corner of the mouth when stymied by something. Over the years, however, most of the American forces were gradually withdrawn. Thus the boys' base jobs did not last. When they tried to find work with Korean organizations, their lack of schooling proved a constant cause of rejection. Perhaps the curious combination of a lack of educational credentials coupled with the ability to speak some English predestined them to yearn for America. When they were penniless children, the mysteries that first captivated their young minds were "made in America" and "the dollar." It was only natural that they longed to make a pilgrimage to the origin of these wonders.

Each of the boys, after he had been let go by the American base, had become frustrated working at a series of lowly jobs in Korean companies, would continually grouse: "This filthy pit of a place makes me puke, and I can't take it any more." Hence their determination to desert to America. Their niece was still very young at the time, but the ensuing bloodshot-eyed panic, the chaos and pandemonium it created in her home, haunted her like a nightmare.

In trying to forge with strangers the connections needed to emigrate to America, the three young men were repeatedly duped by con men. And their "entertainment expenses" snowballed, too. The young girl's father, as the head of the household, had been pleased when his younger siblings earned money to defray some expenses. But he was no selfless Buddha — and when they began to use up his money, not a day passed without squabbles. Inevitably, whenever the brothers fought, the mother and her daughter-in-law also had words. The old woman sided with her younger sons and the daughter-in-law with her husband.

Whenever the two sides roared and brawled the words most often heard, unremarkably, were "America," "America," and "America." America this, and America that.

"Idiot, so you think America's the be-all and end-all? Even if our family's pillars crumble and our roots wither, you imagine that if you can just reach America somebody there will feed you? If you can make money in America, why can't you make it here? I've had it up to here! You're America's problem now! I'd like nothing better than to send you to America, but I've got children of my own to look after."

"Ha," said the second son. "Did you put me through school? What have you ever done to earn my respect as the older brother? All I'm asking is for you to send me to America. If I can just get there, what's a little money? Whatever you loan me I'll pay you back tenfold. Your acting like this only makes me more determined to go to America. Only in America can I live like a human being."

"Honey, let him be," chimed in the wife of the elder brother. "Let him go to America or paradise or wherever he can make it to on his own. We'll just wait and see how it turns out. Unless you want to make beggars of your children, it's high time you got hold of yourself and stopped listening to his foolishness. Ha! You think just anyone can go to America? Like they say, a bad calf's horns grow out of its rump. Now that we're in hard times, he gets wild ideas about running off to America."

Once things had gone this far, the old woman was not one to sit quietly and listen.

"Why, I've never seen such a shameless bitch. I've been listening, and you don't know when to hold your tongue. When your brother-in-law was working and bringing his wages to you, you grinned so much your fat kisser looked like a washtub. Back then you saved him the best food and the warmest spot; you spoiled him then, but now look at you. Bitch, I want back every cent my son earned and gave to you, and I want it back this instant! You took it here, you took it there, you took it saying you had to save money for him to get married, you took it saying you were putting it into a savings account so we'd have more money later, but what happened to all that money? Hand it over right now. Then I'll send him to America myself. Woe is me! When a daughter-in-law lines her own pockets, how can a family avoid ruin? Woe is me! Doomed, I'm doomed!"

At this, the young girl's father would slap her mother, telling her to shut her trap and mind her own business. Then her mother would let out deafening wails as the grandmother pounded on the floor, screaming, "Hit me, hit me! You're beating your wife, but I'm the one you want to hit!" The second brother, as if delivering a soliloquy on stage, would join in, "I'm so lonely," "I'm so pitiful," and "Not a soul cares how I feel." Even now when the young girl thought back on those battles, she had no idea why the combatants had taken the sides they did.

Things kept going awry until her uncle finally gave up on America, but that did not mean forsaking the quest to go abroad. No longer was reaching America the goal, now it was just getting out of Korea. Once he had made up his mind to leave, in spirit he was already gone. His flesh, regrettably, was marooned at home; it seemed a hardship for him to reacquaint himself with the house and with Korea.

Inexplicably, he started flying into rages, scowling at people, and using foul language. Often he was beside himself, writhing as if bound fast and immobilized. His was the thrashing of a trapped and powerless beast. When he got drunk all these excesses combined to culminate in rampages that brought misery upon the whole household. When he had finally exhausted himself, he would lie down to sleep, whining like a little girl that he wished he'd studied more or learned a decent trade. Each of the three younger brothers went through this same process of torturing himself and the family. Despite everything , in the end every last one of them found a way — dubious or not — to get away to Germany or Brazil or Guam, and each found some sort of job.

As the younger brothers got ready to emigrate, their madness did not subside. If anything, it worsened. As happens in the course of such procedures, they ran into minor snags that they automatically assumed would go badly wrong and block their departure, like the setbacks they had suffered earlier in trying to go to America. All this unnecessary hysteria made them dread every step in advance.

They were constantly restless. Even when they were home, sitting still was too difficult for them. Regular as a pendulum they paced back and forth from one end of the room to the other, hands thrust in their pockets, shoulders hunched, faces grave. Each of them mumbled the same spiteful monologue: "Fuck, everything these goddamned Koreans do is screwed up! Shit, I can be stubborn too, stubborn as hell. And if I ever do get out I'm never coming back to this godforsaken place. No, but when I take a piss I'll be sure to aim it in this direction."

All of this and more the young girl recalled like it was just yesterday.

The girl's mother stood by and mocked her brothers-in-law, saying that the half-wits needed to pace faster to wear out their socks. The girl shuddered to remember how her uncles had looked back then, always as if they were dragging leg-irons; she even seemed to recall the clank of chains.

That the girl's memories of those days had stayed so vivid was partly because her uncles' despair over emigration had been so glaring, painted in primary colors, without the slightest pretense of camouflage to salvage their dignity. Besides, those scenes were forever linked in her mind to troubling memories of the conflicts and deprivations their departure had occasioned. It was impossible, she knew, that she had ever really heard any clank of chains. In fact, that sound had not been in her memories at first. It was something she had unconsciously added after she matured a bit and began embellishing the hazy images of her childhood.

The girl had grown more and more perplexed from wondering why her uncles had fled from their fatherland, wild and desperate as convicts cutting their chains or beasts gnawing their traps, as unconcerned with proper ways and means as rats abandoning a sinking ship

Letters came from her uncles every once in a while. At first, hoping for a bit of money, her family had waited impatiently for such letters, but in time their expectations eroded. The letters mentioned nothing of earnings or of sending any money home. There was only talk of how busy they were. So busy, in fact, there was no time for writing letters, no time for being homesick, they said. It seemed at once a boast and an excuse for not writing more often.

The girl wrote most of the replies. Her father was totally dissatisfied because his brothers sent no money and felt they could get by with a few lines scrawled as a matter of duty. "Ha! They're the only busy ones! As if we're not busy?"

The correspondence had degenerated into a duel over who was busier. One could say the eldest brother and his wife won this duel: The girl's uncles were too busy to write often, but her father was too busy to write at all.

It goes without saying that the old woman wanted to send letters, but she did not know how to write. In the end the young girl had to write for her. The old woman dictated every last detail of her letters. She began by saying how she was worried sick wondering how they were and how much she missed them. A concoction of despair and exaggeration followed as she announced she probably would die without ever seeing them again. She ended by begging for money, saying her life was hell, she had not a cent to her name, and she was mistreated by her eldest son and his wife. But the young girl always left out the pleas for money. Deceit on the scribe's part, you might say, but the girl found it impossible to record that voice of a mother begging her son for money.

Writing such lines as "Dear Makbong, Time flows like a rushing river and all too soon spring has flown . . . ," the granddaughter could get completely into character as an aged mother longing to see her son. But when it came to the pleas for money she felt she personified the Republic of Korea and was begging for aid from Brazil or Guam. It was just too demeaning, and the girl could not bring herself to do it.

The old woman had no way of knowing any of this, of course. If her dreams were the least bit portentous, she would begin a vigil in expectation of a letter. If by sheer coincidence a letter did arrive, to her it was a confirmation of her prophetic dream. Even when she saw that the letter was nothing more than a routine greeting, she pestered her granddaughter to read it to her over and over again, thinking she might have overlooked some subtle clue as to when the money would be coming. The girl had reasons of her own for being interested in the letters from her uncles. Now that their wish had been granted and they had left Korea behind, now that they were, to some degree, free of their birthplace, she wanted to know what Korea, their fatherland, meant to them. But time and time again the girl's attempts to figure this out, like the dreams of her grandmother, came to naught.

Some of the letters complained of a nearly maddening hunger for *kimchi*. The young girl found this pleasing and a bit gratifying. But this sweetness did not last. All they had to do was marry and their wives would furnish *kimchi*. And, after all, wasn't it a mere cry of the palate and not of the soul? It was nothing as lofty as patriotism or love of one's people, but the young girl was mystified to the point of vexation over how the human spirit and one's fatherland were bound. By exploring the nature of these feelings, she perhaps hoped to free herself from the confusion she had felt at her uncles' ranting and raving before they left. Still, nothing was any clearer and in a few days her grandmother would be gone as well.

The young girl dreaded sending off yet another relative. Her emotions, however, differed from regret. She really had no tender feelings for her grandmother. As any daughter would, the young girl sided with her mother. It was a relief that her mother at long last would be freed from the hardship of serving a mother-in-law. In addition, her grandmother's circumstances were not like those under which her uncles had emigrated. Her daughter, doing well in America as a nurse, had formally invited her and paid all the expenses for her departure. Unlike when the girl's uncles left, there had been no deceptions by swindlers, no problems with procedures, and no fights over finances.

What the young girl found hard to swallow was the drawn out period between the decision to leave and the actual exodus. It had been exactly the same with her uncles. Once their departure date had been set, even though they still ate their rice from the same old pot, sitting at the same table with the same *kimchi* and *doenjang*,* for some reason they glowed with the satisfaction of a hearty American meal replete with steak and butter. They affected a certain languishing attitude as if to underscore the disparity in their situations, and they never passed up a chance to express their pity for the rest of the family. This the young girl found intolerable. At the same time her uncles could no longer simply pass by the gangs of children playing in the alley. No, like those big-nosed strangers whose hobby is to display their charity by calling on orphanages with donations of supplies in hand, they clicked their tongues and wore concerned looks in an effort to broadcast their pity. "Oh, dear! What were these poor wretches thinking, churning out so many children. The door to suffering is wide open, wide open . . . " Even when they looked up at the sky: "The sky is goddamned blue. It's hopeless, simply hopeless." They talked about everything in this tone.

Once she sensed the old woman was acting this same way, the young girl's arm, until then offering gentle support, went limp. It was not that the young girl had taken the old woman to the museum in hopes of cultivating in her an appreciation of Koryo celadon. The girl herself possessed no such appreciation, and, in fact, it was her first visit there, too. Quite arbitrarily she had settled on the museum as a place to spend the money given her to take her grandmother to a movie and lunch as a last gesture of devotion before she left.

To find a theater showing not an American but a Korean movie had been hard enough. When they finally did find one, above the entrance hung a painting — as big as it was disgusting — of a woman with disheveled hair and contorted face, who had blood trickling from the corner of her mouth. A purposely ambiguous caption read "The Aesthetic Apex of Korean Rancor."

The old lady had been docile all the way to the theater, but the garish movie signboard seemed to rub her the wrong way. She grimaced and suggested they eat lunch first, saying even the Diamond Mountains looked better on a full stomach. They went to a *komtang*** restaurant where the old woman displayed an excellent appetite, polishing off an extra-large bowl of *komtang* and two plates of *kimchi*.

---

*Doenjang: Fermented soybean paste famous for its pungent odor and taste, *doenjang* is one of the key staple condiments found in Korean kitchens. It is also used widely as a stock for various soups and stews.

**Komtang: A hearty soup with an opaque broth made from boiled cow bones.

The girl thought once more of her uncles' letters. And she thought of her uncles, her aunt, and her grandmother. Just as a kite soaring through the sky, however unfettered it seems, is tethered to earth by its string, they too, wherever they fled in this world, would never forget the taste of *kimchi* and so would never escape their Koreanness. Then, as young girls will, she fell into a silly reverie, wondering whether the secret bond between the nation and all those who had left it came down to nothing more than the flavor of *kimchi*.

Still more foolish had been the decision to pass up the movie and take the old woman to a museum instead. The two of them emerged from the restaurant still intending to see that movie, but the old woman shuddered, saying it might give her nightmares. Most likely this too was due to the lurid poster. The young girl felt the same but could think of nothing else to see in Seoul. The girl all at once felt she had been standing in the noonday sun for ages. She was overcome by a stifling sense that there was absolutely nowhere to go. She lent the old woman her arm and they walked back down the alley past the restaurant and out onto a main street lined with shops selling cheap shoes. The young girl was still very frustrated, unsure where to go, but she kept up a calm front for her grandmother's sake. Even so, the old lady, pleased at having eaten her fill of *komtang*, appeared positively delighted and, as if to say "I know what you're thinking," spoke to the young girl in a charitable tone.

"Don't trouble yourself. What's all this fuss about sightseeing? As if there's anything worth seeing in this place anyway. No need to throw money away. As for me, when I get to America I'll do plenty of sightseeing. Hold on to that money and use it when you really need it."

Abruptly, the young girl decided to go to a museum. This made her feel proud and dignified.

Thus they had ended up at the museum. But even after happening on exhibits more striking than the broken pottery, the old lady was no less dissatisfied and no less bored. In each new gallery they entered, she gravitated to the cushioned chairs and wanted only to sit and rest. She kept demanding to know how much farther they had to go and was openly mortified that they had paid good money to enter such a place. In the end the girl was compelled to leave her grandmother behind and tour the museum by herself. Bringing the old woman to the museum had been an impromptu gesture; the girl had entertained no illusions about the prospects of changing her outlook.

The old lady followed behind her granddaughter, wondering when the tedious outing would end so she could go home and lie down in peace. As they entered one gallery — she didn't know which it was — the air grew cool. The fluorescent lights overhead were dim, making the room a bit dark. Here and there, rays of daylight streamed in, exposing even the dust on the floor, which led her to think this might be the last gallery. Through the exit door in the blinding autumn sun she could see a ginkgo tree, its foliage turned a beautiful shade, swaying gently. The sight almost made her hear the music of golden chimes.

The old woman's face flinched with joyous surprise and then immediately froze into a solemn expression of awe. This was not because the exit was at hand. On display in that last gallery was a grand array of statues of the Buddha. There were so many that the old lady was briefly at a loss before settling on the largest of the figures, a stone Buddha, and bowing to it reverently. She bowed again and again. Nobody had told her about this, but somehow she just knew that in America, that country of the rich where they had everything under the sun and wanted for nothing, the one thing they did not have was the Buddha. Upon realizing this, she felt cast alone into a boundless void, gripped by desolation and terror. Even the pride and delight she felt at joining her devoted and prosperous children in America could not begin to relieve the sense of isolation and fear that overwhelmed her at that moment.

The old woman believed in miracles and she liked to pray. Not only to the Buddha but also to the animistic deities whose images adorned the walls of the shrine she visited — Sinjangnim, Yongwangnim, Ch'ilsŏngnim, and Sambuljesŏk.* She had seen and prayed to these spirits so often since her marriage that they felt like family. Other times, her wishes were made at rock shrines like the Sŏnbaui or the Hyŏngjebaui* at the foot of Mt. Inwang.

She had never had a chance, unlike some women she knew, to bang the gongs at one of the grand shamanistic rituals at the shrine. Neither had she ever offered a big donation or made a pilgrimage to one of the ancient temples in the remote mountains. Nevertheless, possibly because she had had no chance to do those things, she loved to share her

---

*"Animism and rock shrines": It is common for Buddhism in Korea to fuse with the native elements of shamanism and animism. Worship can take place either at a temple proper or at certain propitious natural sites.

fondest hopes with the Buddha, the mountain spirits, and the stone shrines. When anything troubled her it was to them that she turned.

Whether the wishes she expressed came true was not the crucial thing. What the old woman loved was the intoxicating shiver she felt in praying: the feeling that all would turn out for the best, that she was not alone and had nothing to fear, that she had a link to the powerful and had forged a spiritual nexus with all the gods.

This unexpected encounter with the Buddha was inspiring, and her apprehension lest this be her last such chance sent a feverish flood of wishes gushing forth all at once. She could scarcely settle on any single desire. The first thing that came to her was long life for Kilnam, her only grandson, who was still a toddler but someday would carry on the family line and honor the ancestors. Then it occurred to her that the safety of her eldest son was more urgent — he had been very anxious lately, for the astrologers had proclaimed it a perilous period for him. Next, she felt it was more important to pray for his economic affairs to improve, but almost immediately she worried even more about the fate of her younger sons who were overseas. This brought her to fret over her daughter, the nurse, and this in turn led to doubts about whether she herself could get on an airplane and fly to America without some mishap, and so she yearned to pray for herself. All these pressing worries spilt through her mind, but she did not forget to worry about the distant future; she needed to pray for her fate in the next world. The old lady was utterly confused, so inundated was she with matters calling for prayer.

"Lord Buddha, Śakyamuni Buddha, only, hear my prayers. Only, only . . . Lord Buddha, you know my heart, don't you? You know my heart."

Overwhelmed, the old woman never before had found it so hard to express herself. But after a moment, her heart calmed apace, the rush of worries subsided, and her attitude was perfectly pious. She had faith that the Buddha would understand everything and grant her every wish. She was thankful. So grateful was she in fact that she called the young girl over, took the rest of the money, and set it humbly in the Buddha's lap. She then repeated, "Lord Buddha, you know my heart," bowed once more and gazed respectfully up at the statue. The Buddha's stone visage was smiling beneficently as if to say: "Indeed, I know your heart through and through." The old woman's heart glowed with a joy bordering on ecstasy.

Dusk was not far off, yet outside things still radiated with the brightness of midday. They had surveyed a full five millennia of history and a single fall afternoon had not yet faded.

"Let's find somewhere to rest a little before we go."

The sunlight made the old lady dizzy. She was so tired her whole body seemed to droop. Still, she felt relieved, too. She wanted to rest and to savor that sense of contentedness for a while longer.

The museum stood on the grounds of an old palace, and a group of elegant young ladies dressed in colorful silk skirts and striped jackets were strolling along the edge of a pond. The exquisite hues of their clothes were mirrored in the water, composing a beautiful painting that fractured into bits as the skirts rippled in the breeze. Young men in suits trailed behind them, eagerly squeezing off rounds with their cameras. The old woman's eyes, perhaps because of her fatigue, looked distant and unfocused like the eyes of one oblivious to the world. Her skin, riddled with age spots and deeply wrinkled, resembled the bark of some ancient tree. The young girl gently touched her grandmother's hand.

"Tenderness," thought the young girl.

"What did you say your aunt is doing in America?" the old woman mumbled quietly, as if to herself.

Supposing her grandmother had been thinking about her aunt all this time, the young girl was taken aback and feared the conversation might take an ugly turn.

"She's a nurse."

"How much did you say she makes in a month? I mean in Korean money."

"About 250,000 won . . . "

As the old woman's eyes came whirling back to life, the lamp of her arrogance was relit.

"Your mom went too far with your auntie. People just don't do things like that."

She was talking about what had happened before her aunt left for America. The young girl agreed about her mother's excesses. Unlike her uncles, her aunt had left without making a fuss or using any family money. She had done all the emigration procedures on her own. The girl's mother seemed to think this praiseworthy for, as a token of thanks, she promised to buy a fancy outfit for her sister-in-law to wear on the trip. But the day before her aunt was due to leave, her mother came home with only one piece of clothing, a top that remotely resembled a short coat. It reeked of cheapness and shabbiness. Even the old woman saw this at a glance and immediately flew at her daughter-in-law, saying it was not just anywhere but to America her sister-in-law was going, and asking if she thought it proper to send her off dressed like a charwoman. The daughter-in-law, ever eager to do battle, shot back in a contemptuous tone,

"Mother, you keep harping on America, America, America. You think if someone just gets there, then they're a big success, but they're not. You think auntie is going to America on a state visit? If you must know, she's going to wipe up shit. Shit. Mother, you've got to get a hold on yourself."

The daughter-in-law indulged in blatant overstatement, using "going to wipe up shit" to describe the job of a nurse's aide, just to mortify her mother-in-law. If this were not enough, she went on at length to say assistant nurses were hired to do jobs nurses didn't want to do, and what could nurses hate more than cleaning up after patients who had shit on themselves? She capped her diatribe with her own theory that such work was so foul they couldn't find Americans to do it for any amount of money and so had to import foreigners.

That evening the aunt came home in a shiny new pair of boots that came clear up to her knees. The old woman, who had been livid and wild-eyed all day, immediately demanded to know how much the boots cost.

As soon as she heard the reply, that they had cost 7,000 won, the old woman began, "You bitch, you hopeless bitch, you're off to America to wipe up shit and you need 7,000-won shoes? You look great, just great. A 1,000-won coat with 7,000-won shoes, just great."

This tirade continued through the night. Wringing the blameless boots, the old woman grumbled, "Bitch, going to wipe up shit in America! Hopeless bitch you are." It was the last night the old woman and her daughter spent together in Korea. Such was her whisper of motherly love as she sent her only daughter away.

At last the old woman's own departure was only one day away. But not even her final night in Korea was a satisfying one.

She wanted to spend her last night with her grandson, Kilnam. This she truly wanted. He was still young and an only son, so his mother spoiled him, which was probably why he minded only her and never listened to his grandmother. Still, she told herself, if only they could sleep together for one night they would get along just fine.

She wanted to cuddle with him, to admire that precious little treassure of his that one day would carry on the family line, to be kicked by him as he slept, to cover him with a blanket, and to kiss his chubby little cheeks. More than anything else, she wanted to hold him close in her arms all night.

As luck would have it, however, the day the old woman was to leave was the sixtieth birthday of her daughter-in-law's mother, so the daughter-in-law went to her parents' house the day before. Apparently, she planned to spend the night there and come directly to the airport the following day, for as she left she perfunctorily played the dutiful daughter-in-law, telling her own daughters not to forget to cook *bulgogi** for their grandmother that evening and again for breakfast the next morning.

The old lady really had hoped Kilnam would stay behind, but he doggedly refused to let go of his mother's skirt. His mother might have made him stay home. After all, he was no longer nursing. There was no real reason she couldn't have. But instead, as if doing a big favor for her mother-in-law, she took him along, saying, "Okay, okay. Let's go together. Grandma needs to get her rest tonight."

So hurt was the old woman that she secretly wept the whole night. Even after she finally got a little sleep early in the morning, the missed chance remained a dull pang of resentment constricting her breast.

The next day her daughter-in-law barely made it to the airport on time, then immediately began scurrying about urging her husband and daughters to see grandma off quickly because they had to get back to her parents' house to pay their respects at the birthday ceremony. With all of them in a rush, the old woman felt she had no choice but to hurry off, and this only worsened the bitterness she was feeling. Suddenly she flung her arms around Kilnam. He said it hurt and started crying. She let him go but tightly squeezed his little hand. Again he complained, tears welling up.

The young granddaughter scrutinized her grandmother. The spend old lady was dressed in a loud shiny skirt and a jacket of synthetic brocade. She had a silver hairpin askew in her small, unkempt bun of gray hair. A red bag on which the word "BONANZA" was embossed in white hung awkwardly around her neck and over her chest. As she realized that her grandmother's incongruous attire made her look ridiculous beside the other travelers, and that to the end she persisted in doting on Kilnam, the young girl's heart throbbed with an almost physical ache.

**Bulgogi:* A popular dish of thinly sliced beef, marinated in soy sauce and garlic.

To her, both sides — the sending and the departing alike — seemed way out of line. She had felt more comfortable seeing her uncles go. They had strutted triumphantly away, ranting, "See if I ever come back," and "Whenever I take a piss I'll aim it this goddamn way." In her own vague manner, she thought she had deciphered the hypocrisy of her uncles' generation.

The old lady's daughter-in-law, saying there was no time to spare, pressed her to board immediately. Never knowing whether she meant there was little time to reach the birthday party or before the plane took off, and with that same knot still burning in her chest, the old woman waded into the crowd, finished the emigration procedures, and proceeded to the tarmac from which the plane was visible. A bus stood waiting to carry passengers to the airplane. She followed the others and boarded the bus. Most of the passengers were young.

One youngster kindly asked her where she was going.

"Oh, what's it called? Where in America did they say it was? Oh, yeah, I think it's called Ssang Poriko."

"Oh, you mean San Francisco. I'm going there, too."

The youngster clowned around, giving the old woman a hug. She was glad for the attention, held his hand tightly and then let it go saying, "My, what am I doing? I shouldn't, but before the bus leaves I have to tell my family I've found a trustworthy traveling companion. Sending an old woman like me off all alone they're probably too worried to leave."

She hurried off the bus. Actually, she just wanted to see her family, especially Kilnam, one last time. The old woman ran to the escalator, looked up to the lounge and yelled, "Hey, you guys! I found someone to go with me to Ssang Poriko. A very nice young man. Don't worry about me."

But there was no reply. She saw only strangers, who snickered at her. She stared a while longer, but among the crowd in the lounge there was not a single familiar face. Her family must already have left for the party.

She wanted to check once more but could not, for her vision kept blurring. She grew embarrassed under the gaze of strangers and, as if to hide from them, got back on the bus. From the time she got off the bus until she boarded the airplane, the old woman felt as if she were traveling through chaos itself. She hovered on the brink of unconsciousness, her vision so hazy she could not even make out her most immediate surroundings. The young man she had met before tried to help her, but soon he grew distracted and went back to joking and laughing with the other youngsters.

Finally, and with a grave shock, the old woman became conscious of the plane's taking off. The jarring was not physical, such as anyone might feel, but a tremendous shock felt by the old woman alone and unfathomable to any other.

If an ancient tree standing anchored for centuries were to be suddenly and totally uprooted by some titanic force, the shock to that tree at that moment might come closest to describing how she felt. Not until the old woman's senses had emerged from confusion did she become aware of herself as this uprooted ancient tree.

The young people on the airplane, like the old woman's sons, felt not the slightest tinge of sorrow at leaving Korea. All had happy, beaming faces. That was why she could feel no sort of bond with them. She felt entirely isolated.

"Why, Grandma is crying, eh? Crying like a baby. See? We're not crying. Don't cry, we're all in this together." The young man was back, acting up and making faces, trying to cheer up the old woman.

"Well, I guess they have been uprooted, too, you could say," thought the old woman, "but they are saplings, and young trees can put down roots wherever they go. But not me, no. I'm a dead tree."

The old woman now realized how much she loved this land even down to its shabbiest parts, this land against which her sons had gnashed their teeth in loathing, and from which they had so desperately struggled to escape. As if peering at her own corpse, she imagined again the awful scene in which the giant tree was uprooted and toppled to the ground in a paralyzing terror, its thousands of roots exposed, dry, and withering. She wept in heart-rending grief.

Could any other soul in this world ever have wept as pitifully as this, I wonder? Could anyone else have had the horrid misfortune of seeing her own corpse while alive? The old woman's crying, that wail mourning her own death, was heart-rending.

The young people found it intolerable. So disagreeable was it that had they not been aloft they gladly would have fled, thinking nothing of the fare. In all their lives they had never heard so disturbing a timbre.

translated by John M. Frankl

Mr. Hong's Medals

On that particular street there were a surprising number of key-chain vendors. Plenty of other vendors, too, all crowded on top of one another — selling nail clippers, bottle openers, Swiss Army-style utility knives — but for some reason my glance kept returning to the key-chain vendors.

"How much?" I asked, squatting in front of a vendor who had a bigger selection on display than most of the others.

The youth looked up from the newspaper he was reading, barked that some were 300 won and some were 500, then went back to his paper. His gaze was strangely grave, almost fierce. What the young man was reading so absorbedly was a long op-ed column by some college professor calling for Korea to outperform Japan.

The notion occurred to me that he might be a descendant of an independence fighter from the Japanese occupation.

Just then I had no coins on me, it happened. Fortunately, the youth was preoccupied with reading the paper, and my rummaging in my pockets did not distract him. For some reason I didn't even have any 1,000- or 5,000-won bills, only 10,000-won notes.

I was inclined to buy something from him, but I felt uneasy about asking him to change a large bill — 10,000 won would purchase everything on he had display — more uneasy than I felt about not buying anything. I smiled sheepishly and stood up.

The youth glanced over at me once more.

"No padlock vendors here, eh? Why's that?"

Feeling awkward and at a loss for anything to say, I ended up blurting out this ridiculous question. He didn't bother to reply.

It wasn't that I needed a padlock. Both at home and at the office, all my doors were lockable whenever necessary. The porch door, bedroom door, bathroom door, dresser drawers, desk, chests, and even the refrigerator all had locks built into them. I had not a single door in need of a padlock, in fact.

The Paris Bakery stood about halfway down that same bustling yet slowly deteriorating block. I took out my directions and looked again. The place I was headed for was down the alley between the bakery and the shooting gallery. Turn left at the Y junction where an inn stood, then it was the third building on the right. The mouth of the alley was so narrow that from a distance the bakery and the shooting gallery seemed to abut. I had no doubt I was headed the right way, but even after I found the alley right where it should be, I felt downcast and defeated as though I'd taken a wrong turn.

I had been telling myself I ought to buy something for the old man, but thinking it would be easy to buy him a cake at the Paris Bakery, I was still empty-handed. My mistake had been in imagining from the name "Paris Bakery" that it would be a clean, upscale establishment. Such misleading names were becoming more and more common. Even in the countryside little shops put on airs by calling themselves "San Francisco," "Venice," or "Monaco." Anyone unaware of the practice deserved to be mistaken for a North Korean spy. Perhaps I made such a foolish false assumption because I'd just recently passed through Paris while on a business trip overseas. A brief stop it had been. Maybe the brevity of my visit was partly responsible for the mixture of envy and admiration I'd felt, realizing "People live like this, too!" The bruise on my heart lingers.

At the sight — through the film of dirt on the front window — of a gaudy red and yellow cake on display, I was overcome by disgust. The inside of the bakery was dimly lit and the concrete floor was uneven. Then and there I changed my mind, thinking, "I'll give him money instead, money will be better."

It had been through Sŏngpyo that I'd learned that old Mr. Hong from Nŏwu village had long been laid up sick. Lately, his condition had worsened so much he couldn't even recognize people.

A few days before, while visiting a client's office, I'd chanced to run into Sŏngpyo. It had been over ten years since we'd lost contact. He looked fat and prosperous.

"Hey man, how about a little exercise once in a while?"

Lacking anything to say after the customary greetings, I needled him about being overweight.

"You know, me and the old lady, taken together we go over two hundred kilos. And my little girl, the fifth grader, she's over fifty kilos already. No wonder our old car couldn't handle it. The rear springs kept sagging, so this time I went for broke and bought a big six-cylinder model. Not cheap, I can tell you. Don't know if it'll hold up, though."

I was repelled by Sŏngpyo's habit of steering any conversation toward boasting, especially about his wealth — he certainly hadn't changed. Still, reckoning I wasn't likely ever to see him again, I lingered talking to him a bit longer, then rose to depart, politely saying I'd call on him sometime. Even as I tried to leave, he kept on bragging about how he'd recently moved into a nice apartment, offering unrequested details about how big the place was, how much he had paid for it, what a great investment he had made, and so forth.

"Oh, yeah, your uncle, Mr. Hong, he's still doing all right?"

Fed up by this time with his boorish harangue, I interrupted him by asking after old Mr. Hong from Nŏwu.

"Huh? Well, the old man . . . "

Sŏngpyo stammered as if his conscience was not at ease, but after initial evasions it gradually emerged not only that the old man was ill, but that he wasn't expected to live much longer.

"You wait till now to tell me? If I hadn't asked, I'd have missed my last chance to see him before he passes away. I'll stop by and see him in a few days."

I took out my address book and started to write down the address Sŏngpyo had mentioned for his new apartment. Only then did he say that Mr. Hong wasn't living with him anymore.

"It's been some time already since I got him a place of his own. What are you so surprised about, anyway? Nowadays it's tough even to live with your own parents under the same roof. I let him live in my house long enough. He got his own place, but did he have any savings, or any capacity to support himself? I'm taking care of all his living expenses — everything. Not many nephews are so good to their uncles these days."

Sŏngpyo at first had seemed defensive about the matter, but gradually his tone grew self-congratulatory and by now he was in high spirits.

"Did your uncle take a new wife, then?"

"Take a new wife?"

Sŏngpyo snorted loudly and then laughed with unnatural abandon. His huge gut heaved to and fro like a hill rocked by an earthquake.

"Not just anybody can marry, you know. You need to have money or, at least, you should be able to, uh, discharge your manly duties. . . ."

Before finishing the sentence, he was howling with laughter again. Was it right to talk about his uncle that way? In front of me, no less? Neither Sŏngpyo nor Mr. Hong was a relative of mine, but being from Nŏwu myself, I knew their roots better than anybody else.

Sŏngpyo's cruelty at Mr. Hong's expense made me squirm. It was hard to tell whether he was insulting me as well.

"You mean to say the old man is dying all alone? Is that it?" I asked sullenly. Sŏngpyo wasn't troubled in the least by my tone and went right on as before.

"My old lady's life has been hell, you know. When Uncle got so ill he couldn't even control his bowels, we had to hire someone to clean up his shit. Hiring that woman was an education, I tell you. Seems cleaning up shit is a specialized profession these days. The witch absolutely refused to do any other work beyond cleaning up his shit and washing his laundry. Fearing people would say she neglected him on his deathbed, my wife has to look in on him at least every few days. She thought she'd have it easy when she married into a household without in-laws, but she definitely has her hands full these days. And how do you think she vents her frustration? Day in, day out, she nags at me, 'yap, yap.' I have to watch out for her moods and humor her. It's nearly as much work as clearing away his shit."

He went on and on about the shit with so much animation that I felt like pinching my nose and fleeing as hastily as possible. Mr. Hong's current residence, which I'd barely managed to get from Sŏngpyo as I excused myself, was the house in P District for which I was presently headed, down the alley between the Paris Bakery and the shooting gallery, left at the Y junction, and then the third on the right. As I sketched a map to record the directions, the outrage and hatred I felt toward Sŏngpyo as he railed about shit turned gradually into relief as I came to believe old Mr. Hong from Nŏwu was receiving humane treatment after all. Sŏngpyo's attitude, his shamelessness, had just rubbed me the wrong way. P District was known as an elegant residential district near the heart of the city. The sound of the place, just around the corner from the Paris Bakery, called to mind a bright and comfortable home. It had to be that way, I told myself.

Now, embarrassed by my mistake, I cast a contemptuous look at the hapless Paris Bakery, then loitered for a bit outside the shooting gallery. The interior was so dark you couldn't tell whether anybody was inside. Several pistols lay strewn along a wooden platform that jutted almost into the street. Sunlight reflected eerily off the weapons with a metallic shimmer. I had the unmanly habit of flying off the handle at the mere sight of a gun's muzzle. Once when my small son was playing, he aimed his toy gun at my chest and shouted "Bang! Bang! Bang!" I didn't play along by falling down and feigning death. Instead, I snatched the gun, threw it in the trash, and gave the boy a slap as I demanded to know where he'd learned such a nasty game. My wife never let me forget that incident. Over and over, every time we had a fight, she reminded me of that episode and used it to illustrate my failures as a father.

Heedful of the muzzle, I went ahead and picked up one of the pistols laying outside the shooting gallery. Despite its metallic appearance, it was plastic. The lightweight barrel was capped at the muzzle by a cork. Even though I'd certainly happened on such playthings before, the discovery that the gun wasn't real still made me uneasy — it was as if I'd been duped. For an instant, I considered returning home without going to see the invalid. I wondered what surreptitious motives might be leading me there, beyond the wish simply to see the old man.

How sick was he, old Mr. Hong from Nŏwu? If he couldn't even control his bowels, probably he wouldn't recognize people anymore. What's the point of visiting a man who's barely alive, who's already lost his lucidity? Besides, we hadn't been so close that I'd be condemned for failing to visit him. Our connection was such that it mattered very little how I learned of his illness. I easily could have found out after the fact by reading the obituary notices in the newspaper. Whether I paid my condolences or not was of no consequence.

Nevertheless, I didn't turn back. I wanted a clear picture of Mr. Hong's current plight. It wasn't clear whether I was looking for a peaceful or a wretched end for him. If he turned out to be miserable, I wouldn't be able to forgive Sŏngpyo. Sŏngpyo's gluttonous appearance alone had made me gnash my teeth with rage. On the other hand, if the old man was blessed to be living out his last days in clean and comfortable conditions, that might also leave me uneasy somehow.

"What do I want, then?" I interrogated myself, unsure whether I wasn't entangling myself in some outlandish conspiracy. The only thing I knew for sure was that I wanted to see how Mr. Hong was dying.

P District no longer showed any trace of the elegance I had recalled.

The once magnificent tiled-roof residences looked so dilapidated that they seemed about to sink into the ground. Streets that used to be swept smooth and spotless each morning were slovenly and the pavement was cracked and uneven. Cheaply rebuilt walls expanded to the very edge of the eaves made the houses look ugly and made the narrow alleys still narrower. As I felt my way down that sunless filthy alley to the Y junction, I already looked down on the people of the neighborhood — stigmatizing the lot of them as inferior beings.

The third house on the right was a very old place, too. Pillars askew and a partly collapsed threshold at the front gate made it resemble an unseaworthy ship on the verge of capsizing. There was no nameplate or number on the gate. I stood back from the front entrance and looked at the moss growing between the tiles on either side of the roof's sinking ridge. Then I surveyed the scene visible through the cracks in the door. The house was about to fall down, but it appeared spacious. Judging from the number of trash cans teeming with refuse in the courtyard, several families seemed to be living there.

I pushed open the gate and coughed loudly. A woman squatting in front of a fireplace just inside the house shot a glance my way. She was swirling laundry in boiling water with a stick. A good-sized inner yard could be made out through the inner door. Probably several families rented rooms in there, but I told myself that Mr. Hong would be lying in the room where the woman was. A fetid odor issued from that space, bringing to mind Sŏngpyo's rants on shit.

The woman boiling the laundry was fixated on her work, and did not look my way again. She seemed accustomed to people coming and going, with so many other people living in the house.

"Hello. Can I ask you something?" Confidently, I went ahead with my question.

"Go inside and ask. I don't live here so I don't know anything."

"I heard an old man from Nŏwu is living here."

"Well, I only work here so I don't know anything about this place. Go on in and ask, why don't you? Six families live here — if there's no man from Nŏwu there might be a man from Yŏwu."

Even as she joked, the woman kept her eyes averted from me. I disregarded this and questioned her further.

"He's an old man. A Mr. Hong. I came to see him after hearing he's critically ill."

At this, the woman slowly rose.

"I don't know his name, but the only old man waiting to die in this house is here in this room."

"So your job is to attend to him?"

"Yes. But who are you, coming to see a bag of bones whose children ignore him?"

"He's from my hometown. I'd have come sooner, but I had no way of knowing. Does the daughter-in-law stop by often?"

"What's the use? She comes when the food runs out so she won't be accused of starving him. But she doesn't even go in to see him."

"Would it be all right for me to see him?"

"It's already been ages since he stopped being able to recognize people. Still, it would be proper for you to visit him. Yes, that would be proper."

The woman quickly wrestled the laundry tub over by the spigot in the courtyard, then slid open the door to the room. A very disagreeable odor emanated from within. It almost made me vomit. As she stepped in ahead of me, the woman said,

"I clean up after him every time he goes. The stink is from the bedsores. Rotting flesh is much nastier than excrement."

Thanks to the woman's presence, I barely managed to suppress my urge to flee. Her eyes implored me to go through with the visit. I did my best to breath naturally, then took off my shoes to go into the room. I had to stoop to go through the low door. Inside it was dark. The woman's face shone with a gentle yet forceful motherliness. She coaxed me, murmuring, "Come on, now, come on," as if I were a child given a bitter pill to swallow. I made it into the room, but then stood there stiffly, my head pressed against the low ceiling.

"Well, you came to see him, so you might as well see him up close. I know I said he's unable to recognize people, but even if he can't express himself, he probably knows what's going on. One day his daughter-in-law left without going in — she only made a fuss outside — and the old man's unhappiness was plain to see in his face. It's likely he hears everything, even if he can't talk, so if you have something you want to say, go ahead, speak up!"

She nudged me in the back and I plopped down in a heap on the floor. "Could this actually be Mr. Hong of Nŏwu, the father of Eunpyo?" I wondered to myself, as I gazed at the old man in front of me, lying there with his eyes staring into space. Maybe I wanted to scream out loud that this wasn't the Mr. Hong I was looking for, and then just run away. His figure, once short but sturdy, now was as small as a child's, just skin and bones papered with a hint of flesh. He was so tiny his body barely made a wrinkle in the blanket spread over the vinyl-clad mattress. I've never seen anything so pathetic — his scrawny bare shoulders were visible inside flannel pajamas that were too big in the neck. Instead of saying anything, I started to pull the blanket over his unspeakably gaunt shoulders, but my heart sank at the sight of a deep hollow between his neck and shoulder blade. Then, as if cornered with no exit, I had to conclude that this man was Eunpyo's father for sure.

I knew that everybody's skeleton must look like that beneath their flesh, but when I saw that pitiful hollow, all at once I thought back to the days when Mr. Hong used to go around with gleaming padlocks dangling front and back. His first job after coming south from North Korea was as a padlock peddler. Back then, there weren't any factories left intact to manufacture padlocks, so all his merchandise was used, not new. American-made padlocks that leaked out through military channels were the costliest and most profitable. Mr. Hong used to shine up those brass padlocks with a special solvent, then set out to hawk them. He hung them from a kind of poncho that he wore bunched together front and back.

To my childish eyes, Mr. Hong looked as grand as a general, his chest full of medals, headed out to inspect a million-man army. It wasn't only the shining gold color of the polished brass padlocks he wore front and back; it was because his bearing and his gestures embodied a lofty spirit, a certain pride.

"Who am I toiling like this for? It's all to see my nephew, Sŏngpyo, the eldest grandson of the Hong clan, the boy I brought south with me in place of my own son, it's to see that boy do well in school, make a success of himself, and become a powerful man. Nothing's more important. Young people these days don't understand me, but my departed ancestors down below all understand."

He was so cocksure of himself, I found myself feeling guilty when I wondered how it could be such a noble deed to abandon his own son to bring his nephew to the South.

What allowed him, a lowly padlock peddler, to live as proudly as some celebrated general, was nothing else than his moral self-satisfaction, or perhaps it'd be better described as moral intoxication. At times he may have eluded the human conflict and the suffering that stem from such pure moral commitment; probably not once had he questioned or reconsidered the validity of that morality itself. Never had I seen his conviction waver.

Eunpyo, the son he'd abandoned back home to rescue his nephew, the oldest male of his generation and future head of the Hong clan under Confucian precepts, was my age. Eunpyo grew up in Nŏwu — a small hamlet all of whose inhabitants were members of the Hong clan — and my family lived in Pŏmbaui, a village slightly larger and more open to the world than Nŏwu. Nŏwu was only one valley over from our village, so we often crossed the ridge to play or fight with each other. Eunpyo was a bit stronger than me, but then I had an elder brother who made my life easier by carving wooden tops and making kites for me. I used to pick fights with Eunpyo, relying on my brother's backing; and Eunpyo sometimes repaid my kindness with his own superior strength.

By the time we entered primary school together, we had stopped fighting and begun constantly to hang around together. Often, Eunpyo came to my house to get me, or we did our homework together after school at my house, and he would stay for dinner when we worked late. I think Eunpyo was less drawn to me than to my older brother, who was nice to him. Sometimes I threw temper tantrums because I didn't like my brother being equally nice to the two of us; and it made me jealous when Eunpyo paid more attention to my brother than I did myself.

"You have an older brother, too! Ask your own brother, and stop pestering mine!"

When I challenged him and snatched away a top or a game my brother had made for him, Eunpyo used to frown and protest, "Sŏngpyo's not my real brother, he's only a cousin."

In those days Sŏngpyo lived with his mother — she'd been widowed shortly after he was born — in the house of his devoted uncle, his father's younger brother. People often said the custom of caring for the widow and children of one's older brother as if they were your own is a beautiful aspect of Korea's Confucian traditions. But Eunpyo's father took the custom to extremes. He raised the two boys so that the difference between the favored and the neglected was always clear for all to see, whether it was food, clothing, or something else at issue. In times when rice was scarce, he would heap white rice in Sŏngpyo's bowl while making Eunpyo eat cheaper dark barley or yellow millet, depending on the season. At the New Year, he gave new clothes only to

Sŏngpyo, not to his own boy. When he bought shoes, he got costly sneakers for Sŏngpyo and black rubber ones for Eunpyo.

Maybe the women of the Hong clan could be evenhanded in some matters if they wished, not in buying clothes or shoes, but in scooping rice in the kitchen. But Mr. Hong's reign over his household seemed very strict and the family members dared not oppose him on most things, even behind his back. No matter how well the wives of the two Hong brothers got along, Eunpyo's mother couldn't but be uneasy. Sŏngpyo's mother, widowed at such an early age and forced to rely on her brother-in-law for her livelihood, must have felt uncomfortable, too. Seeing how Eunpyo often bought extra sweets when we went on school trips, boasting how his aunt had secretly given him money, I could guess even then that her mind was uneasy.

For some reason, however, all the Hongs of Nŏwu went out of their way to praise the favoritism shown Sŏngpyo. To me, those villagers were bizarre people. Backed by the unending praise of his own kinsmen, Mr. Hong from that time kept growing bolder and bolder. Even before fleeing South and becoming a padlock vendor, he went around swaggering as if he had a chest full of medals. Even the vagrants of the village had to listen to Mr. Hong's sermons if they had the misfortune of running into him. By neglecting his own child and pampering his adopted heir, Mr. Hong felt he had attained a moral perfection that not a soul could impugn.

Because our village was close to the 38th parallel, it was among the first to be invaded by the Northern Army when the Korean War erupted. It was also one of the last the army left, in defeat. From my child's perspective, the soldiers' killing of people was as if they were playing a game with toy guns. Eunpyo and I, holding each other's sweaty hands, watched Northern soldiers lash people to a poplar tree by a stream just outside the village and savagely shoot them. The executed villagers couldn't lie down even in death; they could only hang their heads. The bright sunshine that day, the bark of the poplar trees glistening in the light as if coated with silver, and the gun barrel that sprayed death — for a long time these nightmares haunted my memory.

Thankfully, on that occasion my father had gotten away to my mother's hometown in time. After the Northern soldiers left, a head count was done and it was no exaggeration to say that no adult males survived except a few who were taken away for forced labor. Mr. Hong managed to stay on in the village, protected from harm, without fleeing or being taken away to work, purely due to his perceived virtue. It was not a reputation gained by generosity to others or accumulation of good deeds. I could not understand or accept this so-called virtue based solely on his preferring his nephew to his natural son. Even back then, I suppose I was troubled at seeing how Mr. Hong's flight to safety sealed Eunpyo's unjust fate.

That winter I wasn't allowed to play with Eunpyo or even to see him. My family watched me like hawks so I wouldn't go anywhere near Nŏwu. They whispered that typhoid fever was going around in Nŏwu. I had heard women's curses — things like "Bitch, I hope you catch the typhoid" and "When the typhoid gets you, you won't even sweat." But never had I imagined anybody really would fall ill with typhoid. Typhoid was a fantastic peril, like goblins or ghosts. And now it was not just any family that had fallen sick, either, but Eunpyo's. It was said that Eunpyo had become ill first, that Sŏngpyo came down with it next, and that even their grandmother had caught the disease.

The reason the disease hadn't spread, we were told, was that a unit of American GIs had come from the town and done a thorough disinfecting of the Hong house. My mother comforted me, saying my friends wouldn't die because the Americans were giving them medicine in addition to using a disinfectant to kill the germs. Still, I could tell the disease was serious from my mother's lament that the old grandmother might not make it, even with the medicine.

Then, too, the grown-ups worried about whether they ought to go to Nŏwu to pay their respects to the dead, in case a funeral invitation arrived. They talked about how, in the old days, families infected with typhoid were massacred. These were grotesque tales: nobody was willing to shroud or bury the corpses, so neighbors burned them up along with the whole house once the stench from inside grew unbearable.

"What nonsense! That was then, this is now. I'm told even foreign soldiers are fearlessly going there to disinfect and dispense medicine. As neighbors, how can you even talk about such things? "

My father was annoyed but still I didn't see him muster the courage to go to Nŏwu himself.

"It hasn't spread to any other houses and that household is recovering without relapses, so the American disinfectants and medicine must be working after all."

Some people were willing to go this far in changing their minds, but still nobody willingly went to Eunpyo's house. A rumor circulated that all three victims of the disease had survived, but they were just like ghosts — their hair had all fallen out and their legs had shriveled up so they could only crawl around. The closer Hong relatives seemed to be going to the house before long, but even then those of us in Pŏmbaui dreaded to go anywhere in the vicinity of Nŏwu.

The American unit that had contained the typhoid outbreak quietly left their quarters in the school in town and headed off somewhere else. As if the North Korean Army weren't terrifying enough, rumors went around that the Chinese were joining forces with it, to come back south again. This was a rumor far more ominous than the ones about typhoid.

On a freezing nasty day that winter, we had no choice but to leave our village and flee south. Not a single ox had survived the summer fighting, so we had to carry all our things on our heads and our backs. If one of the old and weak held out — saying he'd rather die at home than on the road — the man of the house often left his wife behind to look after the old. Since most babies in arms also had to stay behind, in reality most of the refugees on the road were adult male survivors and boys who could handle the trip.

As my family passed by Nŏwu, I tugged at my father's pants and whined for him to stop by Eunpyo's house. My father said nothing and just walked on, staring straight ahead. Just then, Mr. Hong was leaving his house, too, a wooden A-frame on his back. But it wasn't a bundle of his belongings he was carrying on the frame. It was Sŏngpyo. I couldn't tell whether his hair had fallen out, for he was wrapped in a cotton cape and had a quilt pulled around him, leaving only his eyes showing. Seeing a good-sized teenage boy like him being carried that way, I imagined the debilitating effects of typhoid must be truly terrible.

"Are you only bringing Sŏngpyo?" people asked.

"If I can take only one, I should save my nephew. Don't you agree?"

"Couldn't agree more."

Neighbors who knew him well chimed in halfheartedly. Mr. Hong wasn't the type to abandon his elderly mother, either. He'd left his wife and his brother's wife behind, and this left him with a choice between the two immobilized boys. I felt a violent antagonism toward this man who, seemingly so self-assured and complacent, looked as though the decision had caused him no agony at all.

Our group, including Mr. Hong, was about to depart from Nŏwu when we heard a woman wailing loudly. Given that cries of "Eunpyo's father,

Eunpyo's father!" were heard amid the howls, it had to be Eunpyo's mother.

The earsplitting shrieks stopped us in our tracks. All except Mr. Hong, that is. He kept trudging along quite unperturbed, his frame bobbing on his back. For the longest time after that, I couldn't forget that deafening wail.

Even after reaching the south, we continued to be neighbors of Mr. Hong. His authority was awe-inspiring; arrays of polished padlocks dangling both front and back, he looked like a smug general as he went about doing business at all hours. Was it so great to desert one's own child in the very clutches of death to save a nephew, raising and educating him as your son? Overwhelmed by the man's blind self-assurance, I prayed that his absurd grandiosity would be unmasked as a fraud.

A truce was concluded in time, but even then we could not return to our village. We had believed that we surely would be able to return, for our home was below the 38th parallel. We felt embittered and victimized by the demarcation line when we discovered that the demilitarized zone had jagged south and devoured our village.

I told myself that even Mr. Hong would not have chosen to carry Sŏngpyo instead of Eunpyo south on his back if he had known the separation would be permanent. Immersed in the sorrow of losing our hometown, my brother and I tried to excuse Mr. Hong's conduct in this humane way.

We were wrong about that, however. Mr. Hong went one step farther and bragged that he had rescued his nephew because he had foreseen that things would end like this. Around the time his business, animated by his grand mission to educate his precious nephew, sprouted into a small shop, my family moved to a better neighborhood. Our financial situation had improved a bit, too. Still, we kept in constant touch and had frequent opportunities to see Mr. Hong.

Biannual gatherings for refugees from the same hometowns up North were happy events. Everyone in all our families took part, and Mr. Hong also attended — always with his nephew in tow. Moreover, the solidarity among us exiles was so strong that we kept in close touch even with people we had never known very well back home.

I met Mr. Hong occasionally at weddings and similar events. Sometimes he was with Sŏngpyo and sometimes alone. Naturally, by now he showed no sign of having once been a padlock vendor who traipsed around dangling padlocks front and back. To me, however, he always seemed to be wearing those padlocks like they were medals of honor.

I could not forgive him for the way he boasted of having cold-bloodedly deserted his own son and of having endured hardships of all kinds to assure his nephew's success. It seemed to me that even now he was spending each night polishing his personal history, just as, when he was a peddler, he once had polished his padlocks until they glistened with a golden patina. Wherever he went he shone, thanks to his unique personal achievements. Certain people from back home, especially older men, tried to conceal their own moral failings by patiently listening to Mr. Hong's bragging and by according him exaggerated praise and respect.

Nevertheless, because the earsplitting wail of Eunpyo's mother still echoed in my ears, I remained determined to live to see that pomposity punctured and Mr. Hong become the butt of jokes.

Weddings of people from our home village were still frequent, but funerals were growing frequent, too. At such gatherings, a generational shift was under way: there were fewer and fewer old people as time went by. Those who admired and listened to Mr. Hong were fewer and fewer, too. As it dawned on him that his personal sacrifice was no longer making him shine, Mr. Hong's dejection became noticeable. Fearful of losing this opening, I let the younger people know about his past. Their reaction was quite contrary to that of the older generation. My generation had already freed itself from Mr. Hong's antiquated moral code. His great virtues were hardly more than bad jokes. If his morality was a laughingstock, then Mr. Hong himself was even more of a laughingstock. The more intelligent among us were extremely indignant at Mr. Hong's cruelty toward his own wife and son. To us, he had no more dignity than a loathsome beast.

From that point forward, Sŏngpyo and his uncle very seldom showed up anywhere together. The uncle's appearance became shabbier and shabbier. Rumor had it that Sŏngpyo was raking in lots of money, so the old man's threadbare appearance became even more conspicuous. Rude youngsters teased him maliciously.

"Why did you walk all the way here, Mr. Hong, when you could have asked your rich nephew for a car?"

"For an uncle with such a rich nephew, you look far too ragged. Your rich nephew couldn't have gotten you a cheap suit, so it must be the bachelor life that makes you look that way. Why not ask your rich nephew to hook you a new wife!"

After my father passed away, I stopped going to the hometown reunions. I had showed up at those assemblies only because I couldn't bear my father's nagging. By this time, I regarded Seoul as my hometown. My children had been born in Seoul and I was entering middle age. Under the circumstances, it seemed natural for our family to identify itself through the children's birthplace instead of through my father's.

"Mr. Hong, do you know who I am?" Sitting by Mr. Hong's bed, I nearly yelled as I tried to attract his vacant gaze.

"He doesn't see anybody," the woman said from the side where she stood.

"Can he talk?"

"He recognizes people when they talk."

She repeated what she had said before, that even if he couldn't express himself in words, the old man probably understood what was said to him.

"How long has he been like this?"

"It's been three months since I began taking care of him. He was like this even before that, I think. I heard they'd hired a parade of people like me."

"Be quiet for a second. He's trying to say something."

I cut her off, thinking I saw the old man's lips moving.

"Well, I'm telling you he can't comprehend or speak. He's doing that because he senses people around and thinks that he'll be given food. I don't know what it really means to live, but even in his condition, he's still so eager about food. It's pitiful and yet disgusting to see him pant for food like that every time anybody comes near him."

"If that's the case, why don't you make him something to eat?" All of a sudden, I was feeling indignant.

"How can you get mad at me like that? Don't worry, I feed him enough so his intestines don't dry up and kill him. As it is, he can barely get out of the puddle of his own waste. If I gave him all the food he wanted, you'd find me drowned in a pool of crap. Is that what you want?"

Defending herself thus, the woman headed out the door and clanged some pots around.

"Mr. Hong, do you recognize me? Mr. Hong?"

I yelled again, thinking he was pursing his lips because he wanted to say something. It wasn't just his lips. His glazed eyes seemed to gain focus and shine. But it seemed even that effort at expression was too much for him; the gaunt hand jutting out from under his blanket shook convulsively.

The woman brought in a pan of thin gruel and tried to shovel some in between his pursed lips. But to her surprise he clenched his teeth and rocked his head back and forth like a baby.

"Oh, no. Seems the end is near now. When they refuse to eat, they'll soon die, that's what they say . . . "

The woman was flippant as she took the spoon away. But it seemed to me more likely he was refusing food because he wanted to speak. Anxiously, I shouted at him again as I pressed his trembling hand.

"Mr. Hong! Mr. Hong! Do you recognize me? Mr. Hong! Say something!"

After a moment, he seemed to be clenching his fist. Then the movements of his lips became more distinct. His formerly expressionless eyes now glistened with a subtle joy, and I clearly discerned what he was saying:

"Eunpyo. Eunpyo."

That was what Mr. Hong was saying. Not once since he came south had I heard him utter his son's name, not once since he had abandoned his son for his nephew's sake. It seemed possible that seeing me — Eunpyo's best friend — could have released long dormant sorrow within him. He might be thinking, "If Eunpyo is still alive somewhere, he must be about the same age." But he had never said anything like that. To me it had always seemed that not only had he ceased speaking of his son from the day he left him behind, he had erased the boy entirely from his memory. Even when he boasted about fleeing south with his nephew in place of his son, he used the word "son" as a generic noun without a real thought for Eunpyo himself.

The "Eunpyo" uttered by the old man was so faint only I could make it out. To me, however, it was deafening. Mr. Hong had gathered all his remaining strength to voice that deafening sound. The earsplitting wail Eunpyo's mother had emitted over thirty years before was returning at last to echo with a vengeance.

Deep down, I had been anticipating this moment for a long while, but when it came I was startled to feel totally empty instead of fulfilled.

As I walked back out into the street lined with key-chain vendors, the sun was sinking in the sky. I recalled the sight of Mr. Hong, his padlocks dangling from his chest as he came back home around dusk, packets of salted fish and rice in hand. No longer did I entertain any illusion that the padlocks were medals of honor — perhaps it was the fish and rice. He was nothing more than a shabby, lonely padlock peddler.

It had taken thirty-two years for me to see him for who he was.

translated by Chun Kyung-Ja

Thus Ended My Days of Watching Over the House

I left the tea for a moment to nudge open the living room door and peek inside. Facing me was my husband, Professor Min, looking as dignified and nonchalant as ever. I could see only the back of the visitor I had just let in. I hadn't noticed it when I viewed him straight on, but from behind, his old-fashioned crewcut definitely made him look like someone from the authorities. My heart began to pound all over again.

I was sorry I hadn't turned him away at the front gate. My husband had occasional visitors, but it had never occurred to me to ask whether he liked being called on at home. Most of his guests were current or former students dropping in for a friendly chat rather than on vital and pressing business. For this reason we had long held a tacit understanding: when he was busy or looked as though he didn't want to be disturbed, I could pretend he was out. Although I have to admit to a minor satisfaction in wielding this power, I never abused it to suit my own moods. Nor was I so arbitrary as to turn anyone away just because I didn't like the impression he made.

School was currently in the middle of the long winter break, and I knew my husband had finished up the previous semester's grading a few days earlier. With no manuscript or article in urgent need of completion, he seemed blessed with some rare free time. I had no real excuse to refuse a guest.

But the moment I confronted this visitor at the gate, my pulse began to race. I thought I should tell him my husband was away on a trip. There wasn't anything particular in his manner to criticize; on the contrary, he seemed unusually friendly and polite. His ordinary looks gave me the illusion that I had met him somewhere several times before. Still, like an infant troubled by an unfamiliar face, I somehow sensed that his business was entirely different from that of other visitors. That's what frightened me. I was about to send him away, but then he looked over my shoulder into the house and a flash of recognition crossed his face.

Ours was a small house. Between the front gate and the porch was but a narrow space — no wider than an alleyway, really — that served as our yard. The living room, which doubled as my husband's study, was right beside the porch. It was morning and I could picture, as easily as if I had eyes in the back of my head, my husband drawing the curtains to let sun in for his bonsai trees. To refuse the visitor now had become impossible.

"Should I make the two of you breakfast? Or should I just bring some tea?" I asked.

I felt a little relieved that my husband looked so unperturbed, but, to be honest, this was a silly question on my part. I did not as a rule go to the trouble of cooking except for specially invited guests. Besides, it was already quite late; my husband was the only one in the family who hadn't eaten. But I had an instinctive dread of this stranger, a fear that I couldn't get over. What I said was a pretext, plausible enough to excuse my having snuck into the living room.

"Oh, no, thank you. We have to go right away."

The visitor, turning my way, answered instead of my husband. His use of the word "we" rubbed me very much the wrong way.

"I still haven't eaten. I usually skip breakfast during the semester. Maybe that's why I wind up eating brunch instead of breakfast and lunch during vacations." My husband smiled at the visitor.

"'Brunch.' Quite an interesting word, indeed. I make do with brunch too, and I don't have a day off all year, much less a vacation. In fact, I haven't had breakfast myself."

"Well, in that case, why don't we go after we've eaten?"

"Oh, no. Please let me treat you to a meal elsewhere."

"I usually don't like to eat out in the morning."

"I'm terribly sorry to upset your daily routine with such a trivial matter, professor . . . "

I had no clue to what the two of them were getting at or how well they knew each other. My sense of fear began to deepen.

"Dear, please get my things ready for a trip." These were the first words my husband had spoken to me. "A change of underwear, too."

"Underwear, too?" I asked, wondering if this mention of clothing held a special meaning.

Without answering, my husband turned to the visitor, "I should pack long underwear, too, don't you think?"

"Oh, no. You needn't worry about anything like that. This shouldn't take more than a few days, and I'll do my utmost to ensure that you're quite comfortable. Ah — ma'am, please let the professor change his clothes here."

"Here?" My voice was quaking with fear in spite of myself.

"Yes, right here in this room . . . My, quite a few books you have. I'll just do a little browsing while you change. Don't mind me." His voice was gentle but charged with a strange force that preempted the slightest objection. I could feel the strength slowly seep from me, like air from a balloon.

This feeling of helplessness persisted as I packed my husband's clothes in the bedroom. Though terrified, I lacked the energy to figure out what was frightening me. My hands shook continuously, making it very difficult to do the packing. It was like being forced into heavy labor after illness has sapped your strength so much you can't lift a feather. But fear, tension, and a sense of compulsion drove me on.

When I returned to the living room with clothing for my husband to change into, he looked calm and indifferent, as before. The stranger's back was turned. Had I been worrying for no reason at all? I felt annoyed.

But just as I was about to help my husband change his clothes, the visitor spoke.

"Pardon me, ma'am, but would you be so kind as to bring me a cup of tea?"

I turned toward him to protest because this seemed to be nothing more than a request for me to leave. "Now I really should find out who he is and why he's being so pushy," I told myself.

He had been flipping through a family album and at that moment happened to be looking at a color photograph taken last spring, showing the five of us gathered by the cherry tree that was blossoming in front of the house, smiles on our faces. I had no idea why this man had suddenly appeared here and was bossing us around, but it certainly seemed his primary goal was to take our happiness hostage.

I slunk off to the kitchen and returned with the tea. My husband had finished changing except for his necktie.

"Could you help me with this?" My husband was as matter of fact as he normally was when going out. I looked over at the visitor first. He was pretending not to have heard, so I hurried to my husband. I suddenly found myself hoping he would caress me in front of the stranger. No chance of that, though; with his straight-laced upbringing, my husband never touched his wife outside the bedroom. Still, I thought he really should. There was no other way for us as a couple to make a concerted show of resistance against such tyranny.

But my husband stood up stiffly and did nothing more than raise his chin a bit for me. It was all I could do to take the two drooping halves of the tie and match their lengths. "It's nothing," my husband said in a measured tone. "Don't worry." He stole a glance at the visitor for some sign of support.

The man was still looking at the photo album, but chimed in as soon as he saw an opportunity to speak up. "Of course, ma'am. Nothing is going to happen to the professor. Just look at it as though we're traveling for a few days."

"Really, that would be best. Please tell Mother I'm on a trip. The same goes for the children. You know how sensitive Mother is. Take special care that she suspects nothing. See that she gets her meals at the right time, of course, and do all you can to seem unconcerned. You, too, should just think of this as though I've gone on a trip. Oh — and please keep an eye on the bonsai for me. Make sure they get sun and don't forget to water them. Watering them can be tricky, you know. Remember not to fill the pot until you've dampened the soil on top with the spritzer . . . "

As I struggled feebly to help him with the tie, I felt a sudden urge to choke him with it until he cried out like a wounded beast. The impulse passed in a moment, but it was very intense while it lasted.

As I finished knotting the tie for him, my husband patted his collar and looked at me. I gazed right back at him. Here I was, hoping for a caress so much I could barely stand it, and he was lecturing me on how to take proper care of his mother and his plants. The thought of all the time he and I had lived together turned my stomach.

"May I say goodbye to my mother before we leave?"

In asking the visitor's understanding, my husband's expression took on a servile cast for the first time. The visitor again acted as though he hadn't heard. I hoped that he would continue the pretense for a while so I could see how far my husband was willing to degrade himself for his mother.

"She isn't feeling well these days. She's always had high blood pressure and a few months ago when she heard I needed an operation to have a gallstone removed, she fainted in shock. She's been in bed ever since. I'm concerned that this might deal her another severe blow. Please let me say goodbye to her as if I'm going on a trip."

The visitor lifted his head and smiled with extreme modesty, a modesty more effectively humiliating than arrogance, I thought; I waited to hear what he would have to say. Uncertainty briefly played upon his face, but then he said, "Fine. I have elderly parents out in the country myself."

"Thank you."

Naturally, I followed after my husband as he went to say farewell to his mother.

"Please stay here, ma'am," the visitor said softly.

"Do as he says."

My husband gestured for me to stay, making no pretense of hiding his fear that he might be prevented from seeing his mother if I followed. I stayed behind in the living room with the stranger, who went on looking through the album as he tried to make small talk with me.

"Your family truly looks happy. I envy you."

"Why are you taking him into custody?"

"Custody? Oh, nothing of the sort."

"Well, then?"

"Just a polite request for the professor to come with me. I'm his escort."

"So he could have turned you down?"

"Fortunately it was easy to convince the professor that we require his cooperation and he didn't refuse."

"He's been a straight arrow all his life. Those dwarf trees are the only vice of his I know about. I can't think of anyplace outside the campus where his cooperation could be needed."

"I realize all that. That's why he has so many devoted students. But, as you know, among them are some troublemakers who have been disrupting the social order."

"Can that be a crime on his part!?" I flared up.

"Please calm down, ma'am. I never said anything about anyone committing a crime."

"Who in the world are you? What right do you have to come over to someone's house first thing in the morning and . . . " My lips were trembling.

"I've already explained that to the professor. And it's not first thing in the morning; it's already eleven o'clock. Time for brunch." His tone was gentle but frosty.

My husband returned.

"I told Mother I'd be gone a week or two."

"That long?"

"Better to err on the safe side. Same goes for you, too, so go on like you always do. Maybe this will turn out to be a more valuable experience for me than any trip could be."

All of a sudden my husband was making awkward attempts at talking tough, like a frightened boy putting up a brave front. The merest shadow of compassion passed over the visitor's face. I averted my eyes so I wouldn't have to look at the contrast between their expressions. Choking sorrow welled up within me. I felt a desperate urge to cling to the stranger and beg him not to take my husband away. Oh, if only I were younger and prettier, I thought.

"Well, let's go." My husband took the initiative. With a shrug of his shoulders, the visitor followed.

I had intended to see the two of them off down the alley to the thoroughfare, but at the front gate the visitor stopped short. In a businesslike voice that seemed to belong to someone else, he said, "Why don't you stay in here, ma'am?"

"But when my husband sets off on a trip I always see him to the end of the alley."

"Your husband is not going on a trip."

His voice was low but clear; his expression, stiff and icy. I might as well have been shoved violently aside.

"Please come back soon. Dear." I barely got the words out.

"I will. Just be sure to stay calm. Remember, act naturally, everything is normal."

The two strode off and disappeared out the alleyway. I waited until I was so frozen that I couldn't stand outside any longer.

Calmly, I cleared away the visitor's teacup, straightened the scattered books, and washed the underwear my husband had changed out of.

I wanted to flop down wearily, but recalling my husband's parting remark about behaving normally, I set to work at a busy pace, like a student overwhelmed with homework.

"Hey you, bring me some food! I'm starving to death. My tummy's burning up. What are you so busy with that you haven't even thought about bringing lunch? Do you know what time it is?"

It was my mother-in-law, calling from her room in the back.

I had been walking a tightrope in a precarious attempt to maintain my sense of day-to-day calm, and her sudden outburst — an iron mallet beating on a metal drum — was so tremendously raw and horrible I shuddered.

Today was hardly the first such outburst I had heard. Plagued by diabetes and high blood pressure, my mother-in-law was always famished. Not only that, she was now quite old and senility had taken her into a second childhood. When we learned that my husband, her only son, was to have a gallstone removed, we had not kept anything from her; after all, it was not a particularly dangerous procedure. But as soon as she heard the word "surgery," she fainted dead away. She had been in bed ever since, and as her senility grew progressively worse, the only thing she was making clear was her voracious appetite. She'd start demanding breakfast at dawn and lunch well before noon: "I feel like there's lye in my tummy," she'd say, or "My innards are shriveling up and sticking together." She still had a way with words.

Her ears remained quite sharp, and so, in addition to her three regular meals, she would pipe up whenever the sound of eating was anywhere to be heard. And then she would shriek like a baby ejected from the womb: "Now don't be sneaking food, children. Give me some! Eating in secret when there's an old woman around!? You'll get yours!" Still, her shrieks never struck me as being out of synch with the daily rhythm of our respectable, peaceful household. They had never even seemed an intrusion.

Just as everyone in the family took after my husband in his love for the dwarf trees, we all followed his lead in caring for my senile old mother-in-law. We worked together with as much devotion as we could muster and felt a certain moral superiority about this in our hearts. If her cries about lye in her stomach came even slightly later than usual, my heart would beat faster and I would peek into her room to check on whether something was wrong. When she slept, I would prick up my ears in concern. Not until I heard the sound of peaceful breathing could I relax. That's how deeply all of us in the family felt.

On this day I felt guilty because my mother-in-law's voice had irritated me and because I had prepared her lunch in a hurry. As for me, I had been planning to eat brunch with my husband. I hadn't eaten a thing all day, but now I had absolutely no desire to eat — and when you're not hungry, nothing is more unpleasant than someone else's appetite. My mother-in-law kept yelling about the pains in her stomach. By the time I had prepared her lunch tray, her complaints had aggravated me almost to the point of snapping at her.

Her special diet for diabetes and high blood pressure meant I must spend extra time preparing her food. My husband was more concerned about his mother's abnormal appetite than anything else. Although she enjoyed meat, I generally served her fish. To get her to be satisfied with vegetables instead of rice I had to coax, trick, and threaten her. Today I was in no mood for any of that, however. I just set the tray down and waited in silence for her to finish.

I watched as she grabbed the fish with her fingers and chewed it down to the bone with her pearly-white dentures. As she spit chewed-up bones onto the corner of the tray, then licked bits of fish off her fingers, I couldn't help but be aware of a loathing toward her that was lodged deep within me. This emotion occupied but a small part of my feelings toward her, which for the most part were appropriately high-minded and moral; nonetheless, that hatred was like a pocket of compressed air. Firm. Dangerous.

The children returned in the evening. Our daughter was in her final year of high school and her brother was in the ninth grade. Even though they were on vacation, they came home late. Both were taking supplementary classes at school in the morning and had tutors in the afternoon. I told them their father had gone on a trip. Worn out with their own work, they didn't look particularly interested in what we grown-ups were doing. Once more I felt proud because they were already taller than I was.

I didn't want to lie to them, and I found myself hoping to tell them what was going on so that they could share my concern. My children were no longer so young. And precisely because they weren't toddlers, they wouldn't be satisfied with merely hearing what had happened to their father. They would want to understand it as well. It would be important for them to know *why* their father had been taken into custody, not just the simple fact of it.

I was not, however, in a position to tell them why — I didn't know myself. If I couldn't make them understand this, then learning that their father had been taken away would be as traumatic as hearing that he was a shameless criminal. Best not to share my anxieties with them, I decided.

My husband and I had a good relationship, but there was a line between us that was not to be crossed. He didn't care what I did for the house once he turned over his salary to me. Likewise, I pretended not to know anything about his field of sociology or what he was thinking. We had grown quite used to this system and were comfortable with it in several ways. None of this had ever caused me any doubt or dissatisfaction.

After the children went to bed and I was alone, for the first time I thought about the invisible wall between my husband and me. Which of us had first erected it? I went over our relationship in detail. He often had spoken disparagingly about men who wanted to know every last detail about what their wives did at home. Had this been an indirect way of telling me not to get too curious about his work? If so, I concluded, then he was the one who first established the boundaries.

I'm not sure why I was picking on him. Maybe it was because my inability to help my now almost grown children to understand what had happened to their father made me feel inferior. He had urged me to go about life normally, but without knowing where he was or what ordeals he might be enduring, I couldn't bring myself to prepare elaborate meals, so I just cooked whatever was easiest.

"Tell me, is this how you're going to treat me when my son is gone? Where's my fish?! Not even a fish tail on this tray! How dare you! It's not right. Not right at all. Just wait till he comes home. Don't think I won't tell him everything." Such were my mother-in-law's protests every time I set down her food. She'd pull the tray toward her, push it away again, hurl her silverware down, and make every sort of racket.

One day the visitor appeared and relayed the news that my husband was healthy, was satisfied with his surroundings, and would be home soon. The real reason he had come, however, was to search the study.

Given all this, I found it pure torture to put up with my mother-in-law's unbelievably raucous shrieks. I had no will to whip up meals to suit both her finicky diet and her insatiable appetite. Oh, grumble she did, but her enormous appetite didn't diminish in the least. She would lap up every last bit of food on her meal tray and then right away begin cursing and clamoring that she was still starving. It was only with great difficulty that I put up with her bawling. This, I thought, is in no way compatible with day-to-day peace in our family. Well, what was the everyday peace we were blessed with, anyway? That her fits previously hadn't clashed — and had even seemed in harmony — with the family's sense of calm was truly miraculous.

Gradually I began to consider her an outsider. If, as they say, it's a family duty to bear up together when one member is going through hard times, then neglecting this responsibility was equivalent to renouncing one's qualifications to be in the family. In my mind, I already had ostracized my mother-in-law from the family and marked her as an enemy of the rest of us. What was hard to put up with now was not so much her outbursts, as the idea of harboring an alien in our midst. Waiting on a parasite day in and day out — that was true hardship.

In spite of all this, every morning I opened the curtains in the living room to make sure my husband's beloved bonsai trees were getting their ration of warm sunlight. I watered them the way he showed me. I even got up in the middle of the night to make sure the charcoal stove was still burning and keeping the living room warm. I felt no love for those plants, however. My husband was enthralled with the bonsai, as though Mother Nature's essence had been distilled into them, but I had no interest in those forcibly stunted trees beyond a touch of pity.

One day, though, I received a strange jolt as I examined the pot containing my husband's most prized pine. The tree's branches spread above as gracefully as those of a lone pine standing on a cliff, but the trunk had coiled around itself like a snake. These agonized twists and turns were almost certainly the result of the tree's being constrained to grow artificially. Had my husband also been grooming his family into a showpiece of calm and respectability as nothing more than a hobby?

Why couldn't my husband hurry up and return? Please let him come back before I get to the point of mistreating his plants too, I prayed; I had to come up with my excuse beforehand, because I knew I would end up ignoring them before long.

The more I neglected my mother-in-law's meals, the more frantic she got. She hadn't shown this much energy since being confined to her sickbed. Oh, she still had to use a bedpan, but she would stride into the kitchen and rummage through the cupboards, flinging open the doors and slamming them shut.

Whenever I came in, holding her meager dinner tray, she would kick up an enormous fuss. She was a one-woman riot. "Oh, what a wretched lot I have. See how horribly my daughter-in-law treats me the minute my precious son is out of sight! If there's a kind soul in this neighborhood, come, come quick and see how I suffer through this miserable life of mine. Ohhhh, I can't stand it, I can't stand it. I know you're starving me to death, but I won't die. Never. I refuse to die. Not until I see my son. I'll stick it out to the end, no matter what." Such were the recriminations she shouted aloud for the neighbors to hear.

After showering me with a round of this abuse, she would wolf down every last bit of food on her tray. The longer her tirade, the more difficult it was to put up with — it wasn't so much her words as that horrid voice. Honestly, it was as bad as having to put up with someone banging on tin cans.

Finally, I lost control. Something inside me snapped. My feelings — passionate, human emotions — had been suppressed too long within me, coiled and hardened. If I hadn't allowed them to explode at last, I'd have gone crazy. Well, I thought, it's about time to let my mother-in-law see what is really going on. Time to apply the coup de grâce and show her just what I think of her appetite.

"Mother, you shouldn't be grumbling about your food. Our circumstances don't allow it. Do you have any idea where your precious only son is at this very moment? He has been arrested."

"Arrested?"

"Yes, arrested — like this."

I imitated someone being handcuffed and shoved my two hands right in front of her face. Of course, my husband hadn't left like that at all.

"Like this?" She made the same gesture with her own hands, her face growing pale with terror. It was the same look she wore upon hearing about my husband's surgery. Then she collapsed.

I waited. My mouth was dry. I swallowed hard and waited some more. It was obvious enough what I anticipated when I disclosed to her what was really going on and made that horrible gesture: I was waiting for her to faint again.

The first time had been very hard, for I'd had to help my husband recuperate from the operation and care for her at the same time. I had accepted her condition then as an appropriate response — after all, she believed her only son to be in a life-and-death situation — and didn't allow the trouble it caused me to affect our relationship. It was a miserable thing to have happen, but because we all loved each other, it was something that could reasonably occur.

But to have to put up with her collapsing a second time . . . I had no confidence that I could endure a situation that would be much worse. And yet to me it seemed nothing in comparison with the emotional agony of having to embrace an outsider who had intruded into our family.

But she didn't faint. Instead she began to screech and wail at the top of her lungs. "Oh no, oh no! Am I dreaming?! Is this real?! My poor son, honest to a fault. Who could believe such a malicious story? Oh god, oh god! He must be so cold in this brutal weather! He must be so hungry!"

Thanks to her cries, my children also learned what was going on with their father, and we became like a house in mourning. It must have been an extra burden for them, I told myself, what with their entrance exams coming up.

When my mother-in-law's wailing petered out, she immediately set upon her food. She practically licked her plate clean, just like before. By the next meal she had begun complaining about her food again. "Since when did you become such a skinflint? Your husband comes first and you think nothing of your mother-in-law, eh? The older you get, the more you need meat to keep your strength up. I'm going to eat to keep up my strength so I can see my son. I'm not going to die, not before I see him. Go ahead, pray to the gods for my death, and see if it works. I refuse to die."

Laying particular stress on the words "I refuse to die," she glared at me. I glared right back at her without flinching. "Sure, sure, you should live a long, long life! Live long, eat to your heart's content, get back all your strength and then some, and raise hell, yelling all you want! Outlive your own son and your daughter-in-law! Do that!"

My mother-in-law hurled an empty bowl and shoved the table aside. My children came running to console me and scowled at their grandmother. Nothing of the sort could ever happen in a respectable household, but how could I scold my children? We were no longer a respectable family.

I felt I had gotten a weight off my chest, but at the same time feelings of pity for my mother-in-law crept up on me. I began to prepare the foods I had previously denied her — thick beef broths and grilled meat. At each meal I brought her a heaping bowl of white rice without mixing in other grains. I even bought her cakes as sweet as honey for snacks. These foods were all equally catastrophic for her diabetes and high blood pressure. Never once had I dreamed of giving her such things when my husband was around and we were still a respectable, peaceful household. One reason we had moved her to a back room and fed her there was to keep her far away from such temptations.

Eating rich foods again after so long sent her into a state of ecstasy. Every meal I brought her these delicacies, and in her delight, she forgot all about her concern for her only son. At first I may have brought her these tasty morsels out of pity, but it dawned on me that my real motivation might have been to estrange her from the family. Then I could hate her to my heart's content.

I now felt full of energy for the first time since my husband had left. But what was stimulating my vitality was hate. As I watched my mother-in-law devour her rich foods, my true feelings toward her came to the fore: stunted, horribly twisted feelings. The old hatred I had felt ever since marrying the only son of a widow was now allowed to strut and swagger; I trembled with this energizing sense of joy. Hate was indeed the surest reward of life. My days, which ought to have been empty without my husband, now were burgeoning with fulfillment.

I even wanted to instill some of my hatred in my children. And so I would nonchalantly say to my daughter, "Do you realize how poorly your grandmother treated you and me when you were born? She was upset that our first child was a girl. For three weeks, the seaweed soup she gave me stuck like thorns in my throat."

My daughter responded by opening up to me as she never had before. She had been in agony because the field my husband wanted her to study in college was not really what she herself wanted. She asked for my help in talking to him about it. She even revealed to me that she had long thought how wonderful it would be if she could get married three different times during the course of her life. She asked for my opinion. "Would that really be so immoral that I wouldn't be forgiven?"

I also drew my son aside and exchanged idle remarks with him. "Don't even ask about how your grandmother treated me when we got married! It was as though I were a concubine instead of a daughter-in-law. If your father and I were getting along well, she became furious. She wouldn't feel better until she saw us arguing. Was she ever unfair to me! I've been so worried I might wind up like her that I've decided to send you off to live on your own the moment you get married. So if you meet a woman you like, don't let her give you a hard time about marrying an only son, okay?"

Since I was so casual in talking to him about things usually left unsaid, he too confided in me. In fact, he confessed he was planning to live as a bachelor because he had no faith that he could be as devoted and filial as we were if he got married. "Oh, my poor baby," I said, stroking his back tenderly.

Our home truly was no longer peaceful or respectable. Every day I was peeling off another layer of the wrapping that enveloped our former peace and respectability. I was so absorbed in all this that I wound up forgetting to look after the dwarf trees for several days. They hadn't died yet, but they had become unrecognizably withered.

I refused to water them or give them sun again. With no feelings of love aimed at them, it seemed the trees would shrivel up and die as a matter of course. One frigid day I tossed several bonsai trees that were vulnerable to the cold out into the yard, pots and all.

Finally my husband returned. As if really back from a trip, he even brought gifts for his mother and the children. He looked weary, just as though he actually had been on the road. None of us believed this, but he kept up the pretense.

Perhaps he could even repackage the family peace and respectability that had been torn to shreds in his absence without too much difficulty. They might even look as good as new. I have no intention of stopping him. I might even end up helping. After all, the wrapping is of no great importance; the important thing was that I had seen what actually lay beneath it all.

Maybe I won't be able to bear it if I don't get to see my husband's true face. He wants to wrap; I want to tear away. For the first time in our marriage we will experience conflict. Nothing else will make our lives worth living. Already I was relishing the days ahead.

My husband gathered up the pots I had tossed outside, while I heated water for his bath. In spite of the wrongs I had committed in his absence, I was elated. Why? Because we now would meet each other wearing our true faces; because from now on what we would have to do was to get to know one another; because I had figured this out by myself while he was gone; and because I expected that this would be more worth living for than anything we have experienced till now.

Thus ended my days of watching over the house.

translated by Stephen J. Epstein

A Certain Barbarity

Instantly I felt an affinity to a poet who, in a poem I happened across in a magazine, said he lived in a neighborhood where shit trucks come to haul away shit. I don't know much about poetry, nor do I personally know a single poet. I had always vaguely thought of poets as beings so pure and immaculate that they'd never tread on filthy ground; as beings who lived aloft in airy realms; in short, as a special breed of noble superhumans, a species entirely different from common creatures like us.

And now this poet says he lives in a neighborhood where shit trucks routinely make their rounds, which means he probably lives in a neighborhood just like ours. And every morning he takes a shit not in a fancy bathroom but in an outhouse, wiping his ass with a page ripped from a weekly magazine. No shit! Right away I felt I could befriend this poet as if he were one of my own neighbors, tapping him on the shoulder and what not.

In our alley, when neighbors run into each other in the morning on the way to work, we trade greetings with a little nod, say a few words about the weather or about hangovers making our heads throb, even though we've never been properly introduced and don't know each other's names or jobs.

Now whenever I exchange such casual greetings, I can't help wondering if it could be the poet I've encountered, and, if so, how I would appear to the eyes of a poet. Just in case, I make a lame attempt to smile and end up wearing an obscure grin quite out of keeping with my station in life. For, you see, I've heard it said that what poets most detest is a snob.

Not that I mean to say I was actively searching for that poet who'd made a poem out of a neighborhood frequented by shit trucks. The mere thought that there might be a poet's abode right out there among the houses in our alley made my heart full. Not that I love poetry or poets so much. I was just intrigued to see the face of a man who's taken up such an utterly useless vocation.

In this alley, where we managed to buy a house of our own, most families are headed by men more or less my age, conscientious salary-men like myself who go to work early in the morning and return home by seven or eight. The women are housewives, pretty much like my wife. They bear no more than two children, wear long housecoats, take pleasure in shopping for household goods, and form a savings pool to buy electric rice cookers or faux mink blankets.

The spirit of cooperation among us is so strong that we have the shit truck come to empty all our cesspools at once, and the households all take turns sending someone outside to keep an eye on the men dipping out the shit, lest anyone be cheated on the number of the barrels hauled away. There are even fights with the workers on occasion. Not a single housewife in our neighborhood is so high and mighty as to frown or show any sign of disgust at the smell of shit.

I had grown to love the hard-working folks in our alley and to appreciate the harmony they showed, but every now and then I enter-tained myself with thoughts like: "Wouldn't it be exciting if one day Mr. Kim across the alley, who we've always assumed is an upstanding salaryman, were taken away in handcuffs for being a pickpocket?!" Or, "Wouldn't it be a kick if Young-ae's mother, the head of the neighbor-hood savings pool, found herself a lover and the sound of her being thrashed by her husband echoed all the way to our house?!"

My wish to discover a poet living in our neighborhood was not so different from these idle daydreams of mine. In short, secretly I was longing for a new face, a free spirit, anyone other than the standard issue of our alley.

My hopes were fulfilled in a quite inconceivable manner. One Sun-day we woke up to find that the pavement in front of the house right next to ours had been torn up. I thought our neighbors must have had some problems with their water pipes, but then was told that they were changing their outhouse into a modern bathroom with a flush toilet. The neighbor couple, Chŏl's parents, seemed busy overseeing the workmen, but they were needlessly arrogant, totally ignoring the other neighbors who had come outside to see what was going on.

"Honey, what's the point of remodeling ours alone? The other houses still have their old-fashioned barbaric outhouses, so the shit truck will go on showing up every other week, leaving that god-awful stench behind, you know. It's just so upsetting."

Frowning daintily, Chŏl's mother complained to her husband in a loud voice, as though she wanted to be sure all the onlookers would hear.

Good gracious, how on earth could that woman be so . . . ? Chŏl's mother had long been the most belligerent woman in the neighborhood when it came to fighting with the crews of the shit trucks. When the workers claimed they had emptied five barrels, she shrieked back at them at the top of her lungs, saying they were full of shit to try to lie when she, with her very own eyes, had seen that only four barrels had been taken. Then she gave them hell for filling the shit barrels only half full instead of all the way to the brim. On and on she'd go with all sorts of complaints, staying out there in the street long after her own cesspool had been drained. She was the kind of woman who couldn't rest until she was through minding the business of everyone else in the neighborhood. She would peep into her neighbor's outhouse, then snap at the workers not to fill up the barrels too full, saying that if they filled them to the brim the sewage was bound to spill all over the street, and then who would be responsible for cleaning it up?

Such being the state of things, Chŏl's mother always parked herself in the alley with her jaws flapping constantly from the moment the shit truck arrived until it left, deeply inhaling the stench with each breath, and I almost thought she had a perverted fondness for the smell of shit.

Needless to say, my impression of her was far from positive. I was repelled by her mean, garrulous, and stingy nature. In fact, such meanness and stinginess were common characteristics among the women living in that alley of ours where the shit truck regularly called to deliver us from the rising tide of shit. The only differences were in degree, not in kind. In Chŏl's mother's case, these shared traits were just stronger and more naked. So, maybe I was just venting my loathing for everything base and squalid in that alley of ours by faulting Chŏl's mother, whose bright colors made her a convenient flagbearer for all the alley's ills.

That very woman now had become a totally different person, acting so prim and proper. With her forehead furrowed into a frown and a trace of a pout on her lips, she almost resembled a lady of some sort. Not the kind of woman ever to be involved in the business of ladling shit, and certainly not the kind to run her mouth endlessly as she squawked with neighbors.

The change from squatting in an outhouse to doing one's business seated on a white ceramic throne in a modern bathroom, could this indeed bring such a total metamorphosis overnight? Chŏl's family asked us to share our outhouse with them for a few days until their toilet was completely finished.

"Sure, sure. What are good neighbors for? Feel free to use ours anytime, please."

My wife readily, even ingratiatingly, assented, for no apparent reason.

Every morning the members of Chŏl's family paid a visit to our outhouse before we did. Not only did they show no appreciation, but the way they held their noses and grimaced as they left was a truly sickening sight to behold.

My wife cleaned our outhouse with the utmost zeal, and even bought a roll of toilet paper and hung it inside. For three days I had to sacrifice a little pleasure of mine, the pleasure of reading old magazines in the outhouse. The full flavor of a weekly magazine is best captured when it is read in an outhouse, not a current issue but an old one, not intact pages but pieces put together as if solving a puzzle. For several years I've been plagued with constipation, and so it usually took me a good half hour once I entered the outhouse. The enjoyment I got from close reading of the magazine pages provided as makeshift toilet paper had been a welcome distraction from the agonies of constipation.

In the course of reading outdated magazines I am continually surprised both at how very easily people get excited and then at how they no less easily forget. People have long since forgotten about the case of Pak Dong-Myŏng. "Was he an armed robber? Or was he a hit-and-run driver? No, wait, he was a pop singer caught smoking marijuana!" — that about sums it up. Then one fine day I would not only discover who he was but also learn about the many women who had loved him. Where else but in an outhouse can one savor this guilty pleasure of being refreshed by a survey of long-forgotten scandals? As long as these magazines are published in this land, there should be outhouses. For three days, however, my wife had been scouring our outhouse until it was as spotless as any flush-toilet-equipped lavatory, depriving me of my usual pastime.

Fortunately, the use of our outhouse by Chŏl's family ended after three days. At last they had become the first household in our neighborhood with a flush toilet. In spite of myself I could hardly deny that human dignity is greatly affected by the place and the posture one assumes when shitting. Chŏl's mother was now full of grace.

It was not just our family, either. All the neighbors must have felt the same. The next time the shit truck came, we had no choice but to have our shit ladled out and hauled away, but we all felt sorry that the stink of shit would go on invading Chŏl's house. We ended up, of course, doing everything as usual, but somehow we couldn't help but feel frightfully nervous.

One day my wife gave me an update on all the rumors about Chŏl's family that had been circulating up and down the alley.

"Honey, guess why Chŏl's family installed that toilet all of a sudden? I bet you have no idea why the whole family suddenly is acting so aloof. You see, soon the family will be rolling in money. Chŏl's father's distant cousin, I hear, lives in Japan and he's going to come soon for a visit. He struck it rich in Japan and is looking to invest in Korea, so he's coming over on some sort of market survey visit, planning to set up a suitable business here. And he sure sounds like a decent fellow. You see, even though he's a rich man and all, he would rather stay with his Korean relatives than at a hotel, to taste the atmosphere of Korean family, he says. But then, all his immediate relatives are in North Korea, and his closest kin in the south are Chŏl's family. So, just think of it, a real windfall for Chŏl's family, don't you see? A man's lot can change in hours, they say. That saying fits Chŏl's family like a glove. I guess they'll get out of this filthy alley soon enough, too. They haven't just fixed the toilet. They also put up new wallpaper, repainted the house, and even put carpet on the floor. It's a brand-new house now. And they go on buying things, god knows what, day after day. Honey, isn't there anybody among your relations who's gone abroad and made a success? Nobody, not even a long-lost cousin? Phew, how boring!"

A few days later, my wife approached me with a new report.

"Honey, he's come, he's here. What do you mean, 'Who'? Who else? The Chŏl's rich relative has finally arrived. I must say, the rich are different from us. You see, he's brought his pet dog, too. Chŏl had it outside in his arms, and I tell you, I've never seen such a cute and pretty dog in my life. It's hardly bigger than your fist, but so ferocious that if you so much as touch it, it'll bark your ear off, its fur all bristled up, and the fur, my, it's a solid red, just like flames."

Later, I myself had a look at the dog Chŏl was lugging about, but the part about the fur being a fiery red was a gross exaggeration. It was brown, a bright brown with a reddish tint, and the dog was also bigger than a fist, as big as those toy poodles that are becoming common in Korea. A pretty dog it was, though, with intelligent-looking eyes.

A few days later, my wife again took up the topic of Chŏl's family.

"Well, hard to say how much money that Korean-Japanese brought with him, but they say he brought no gifts at all. How could somebody do that? Money is money, but gifts are gifts, you know. All he brought was a few changes of clothes for himself, and a big cardboard box full of cans. At first, the family thought the cans were treats for Chŏl, at least, but, no, they were nothing but food for Botchang."

"Botchang? Who's Botchang?"

"The little dog. You see, that fist-size Japanese dog's name is Botchang."

"Shit, why not call him 'Kudŭl chang'?"*

One day, I came home from the work and was changing when I overheard my five-year-old daughter talking as she played with her little brother, but I couldn't make heads nor tails of what she was saying. The little one, barely past his first birthday, was busily toddling about. After staggering around the room, he usually ended up plopping down in the arms of his mom or his sister. My wife and daughter each liked to hold the baby, so they competed with each other, both holding their arms out, saying, "Come here, dear, come this way. Be a good boy and come to mommy," or "Come to me, baby. Come to your sister and I'll give you some sweets, look at this, look at this, yummy." Such was the "Home, sweet home" scene in my house.

To my amazement, however, now my daughter, her arms stretched out, was saying to her brother, "*oide, oide,*" instead of the normal "*irion.*"** As I stood there, dumbstruck, my daughter used gibberish again, this time addressing it to me.

"Papa, *osuwari, osuwari.*"

"Honey, what is she babbling now?" I asked my wife. "Has her tongue suddenly shriveled or what?"

---

* *Kudŭl (chang):* A piece of thin flat stone for flooring a traditional Korean room; used here as a pun to rhyme with "Botchang," a diminutive and endearing name for the dog. The effect might be comparable to taking a dog called "Cutie" and calling it "Shitty."

**Irion:* An abbreviation of the Korean "Iri onŏra," a command meaning "come here."

"My, don't you even understand that? Ah, ha, ha! You're dumber than the dog."

"What?!"

I nearly laid hands on that unmannered wife of mine. She must have seen that she had gone a little too far, for she shrunk back in embarrassment, and then showered me with smiles.

"No need to get so bent out of shape over a little joke. My, you're so upset your face has flared up in red and blue. Why, you scare me. I say, you are a true Botchang."

"There you go again harping about that goddamn dog!"

My wife explained that *oide* and *osuwari* in Japanese mean "come here" and "sit down," respectively. That mutt Botchang responded only to Japanese, so the first thing the Korean-Japanese guest did was to give Chŏl's family a little lesson in Japanese language so they could give commands to the dog.

My wife went on to say that, thanks to Chŏl, these Japanese phrases had quickly spread among the kids in the alley, and now all the children were showing off by repeating them. Hearing this, my mood soured. My wife started to serve dinner. I felt as if I had drunk dirty dishwater.

At the sight of the meal table, our two-year-old rushed up and started to play with the food with his fingers.

Seeing this, my daughter shouted at the boy, "*Ikenai,** *ikenai.*"

My wife, too, blurted out, "*Ikenai*" as she took the baby away.

"Good gracious!" I threw down my spoon, a long-stifled rage rising inside me. Then, instead of striking my wife, I grabbed my five-year-old daughter, pulled down her pants, and slapped her bare behind mercilessly. Not knowing what she had done wrong, the little one screamed aloud as if she had been burnt.

"Don't you ever say that again, never! Wait and see what happens if you ever do it again."

I got out of breath as I went on spanking her. I kept on until my wife snatched her from my hands. The child's tender skin was red and welted from my hands by that time.

"My god, how would this little one know any better, and even if she

---

**Ikenai:* A Japanese expression of general disapproval, used here to mean "Don't do that," or "Stop that."

did, how could you beat your own flesh and blood like that? Christ, what kind of a heartless man are you?"

Tears welled up in my wife's eyes as she soothed our little girl's bottom. There and then, I was smitten with regret for having hit my child, and the anguish in my heart hurt me at least as much as the spanking had hurt her.

The kids in our neighborhood usually play outside in the alley, for few of the houses have yards. On Sundays the alley is so noisy you can't even take a nap. The alley is too narrow for cars to drive in, so despite the racket there's no danger to speak of, and the grown-ups tend to shoo their children away from their houses, saying, "Go play outside, go play outside," as if the alley were a grand playground of some kind.

On one lazy Sunday I was trying to take a nap, very much annoyed by the noise of the kids in the alley, when the sounds reaching my ears grew more and more unpleasant.

It seemed the boys were playing marbles or jacks or something, but as they counted, instead of counting, "*Hana, dul, set*" in Korean they were saying, "*Ichi, ni, san*" in Japanese. And the little girls, seemingly bickering over something, were using heavy-duty profanity, quite unseemly for them, with each curse followed without fail by "*Konoyaro, bakayaro.*"

They say a single mudfish can make the water of a whole river murky, don't they? A single mutt rolling into our alley from out of the blue had spoiled the speech of our cute children just like that. Granted, the kids were too young to know any better, but even my wife was playing the same tune. Listening to the kids using Japanese out in the alley, I got so furious that I said, "I wonder if the dog days of summer are far off. Sure would taste good if somebody took that Japanese mutt and made dog stew out of him."

My wife almost had a fit.

"Dear, what do you mean calling Botchang a mutt? It's a purebred Japanese dog. You have no idea how smart Botchang is. They tried to give him meat soup, but he never touches Korean food, and eats only the canned dog food brought from Japan. As for the language, too, he understands Japanese so perfectly, and does precisely what he is told. By now Chŏl's mother must have mastered basic Japanese just from looking after Botchang."

Even a dog would laugh, they say. But if our pure Korean mutts ever happen to hear of this, I'll bet they would not laugh but weep. And not only the mutts. I felt lousy, and I was afraid that no laughter or tears would ever relieve me from that feeling.

Day by day Chŏl's parents grew nobler and more aloof until they no longer belonged to the folks in our alley. At the mouth of the alley where the shit truck stopped, each morning a fancy leased sedan appeared and waited to pick up Chŏl's mother. All dressed up, with Botchang in her arms, she slithered away in the company of their mouse-faced nisei guest, whose kisser was always half-covered by huge sunglasses. According to my wife, they went out sightseeing and shopping everyday.

I could almost endure watching my wife as she practically drooled over the scene, but the spectacle she made of herself giggling and petting Botchang as he lay in the arms of Chŏl's mother, cooing "Botchang *ohayo*, Botchang *ohayo*" — I simply couldn't stomach that.

Even humans, when traveling in foreign countries, are known to make an effort to learn a few polite words of greeting in the local tongue. What, then, was this arrogance in this bastard of a Japanese dog? I trembled with an urge to force open the mouth of that shit dog, to stuff in a nice big lump of cooked barley soaked in soybean soup, all the while showering over the precious Botchang the many curses with which our nation is so richly endowed.

Still more painful for me was the fact that ever since that goddamn Botchang came on the scene my constipation had gotten worse and worse. Squatting in the outhouse mornings, I could clearly hear every word Chŏl's mom said as she coaxed that little mutt. The houses in our alley were shamelessly crammed on top of each other.

"*Saa*, Botchang, *undo-o shimasho-ne, ichi, ni, san, ichi, ni, san.*"

God only knows what she was making the dog do, but the voice was so tender and gentle, as she kept repeating "*ichi, ni, san*," that it was inconceivable that this was the very woman renowned as a cutthroat haggler over the number of shit barrels. Listening to this sound, my anus became so tense, as if sealed with wax, that the waste matter within me defied gravity and seemed to thrust upward. This caused a pain not to be sneered at. It had grown so excruciating that, in the depths of despair one hot and humid day, I feared I'd soon end up standing on my head in the outhouse in order to relieve myself through the mouth. But my wife rescued me with a news flash that was indeed refreshing and full of hope.

"Honey, that nisei guest at the Chŏl's house has gone, I hear. But then, what a conniving crook he turned out to be! All this while, he was being fed to his heart's content, he was being taken all over for sightseeing, and he pretended to be ready to launch some new business at any minute. He was tantalizing Chŏl's father with false hopes and blowing hot air into Chŏl's mom's head, but then all of a sudden he just took off without a word of explanation. I'm told Chŏl's parents spent an astronomical amount of money on that nisei relative of theirs. Highway robber is more like it. Money to renovate the house, money for sightseeing day-in, day-out, and even the expense of entertaining prospective business partners, it was all paid by Chŏl's family. 'When the company is formed, who else but you should be the president?' Well, that's what that slimy nisei said, so, you tell me, who wouldn't fall for it? And now, all that money thrown away without thinking twice! You see, that wasn't their own but borrowed money. God, what kind of a lunatic is she, anyway?"

"Dear, enough of your gossiping, and tell me, that nisei guest, I suppose he's taken that mutt of his, Botchang or whatever his name is, right?"

That was what I wanted to know first and foremost. But I was disappointed at my wife's answer.

"Ha, ha, ha! He took all his belongings with him, clean as a whistle, down to a shoehorn and a fingernail clipper, but can you believe it? He left Botchang behind! He told Chŏl's mom that since she loved the dog so much he just didn't have the heart to take him away from her."

"What? He left without Botchang?"

My disappointment knew no bounds. However, I didn't hear Chŏl's mother's "*ichi, ni, san*" anymore in our outhouse. That alone was enough to make my life bearable.

For several days, not a peep was heard from Chŏl's house. No one seemed to be living there. But suddenly, one day when I was in the outhouse, trying to alleviate my constipation by reading an article about a third-rate actress's bedroom escapades, I heard piercing curses from Chŏl's mother, followed by pitiable yelps from Botchang.

"Goddamn dog, you ought to be decapitated! You, shit of a dog! Let's see, between you and me, who wins!"

It seemed ages since I had heard Chŏl's mother's real voice, so filled with life! It was the same vibrant voice she had always used when arguing with the shit truck crew over the count of shit barrels.

Something like a knot of indigestion dissolved inside me, and I had the most satisfying discharge I had experienced in a long, long time. I felt as though I could actually fly.

Since then we've heard the cursing and the yelps often enough. It seems Chŏl's mother is still having a hard time controlling that tiny Japanese dog. But the day will surely come when she masters the task.

Children learn to mimic easily, but they also forget easily. We no longer hear *oide, osuwari,* and *ichi, ni, san* in the alley or in our house.

One day when the din of swearing and yelping coming over the fence into our house was unusually loud, my wife eagerly went back to gossiping about Chŏl's mother.

"She can't help it, you know. Buried under the debts they piled up, the family's going through hell these days. But then, honey, they say that even when the sky falls, there'll always be a hole to get out. You see, that Botchang, that little thing is not a Japanese breed after all, but some rare Western breed with a pure pedigree. And if you put him on the market, you can get two hundred thousand won on the spot. I tell you, two hundred thousand won is nothing to sneer at for a household like theirs. Why she doesn't sell it right now and pocket the cash is a mystery to me. Instead, she goes on beating the shit out of him every day — what if he drops dead, that means two hundred thousand won down the drain, right? Oh, I hate that sound. So cruel to animals, how barbaric!"

Chŏl's mother, when she upgraded her outhouse to a flush toilet, called those of us with old-fashioned outhouses "barbaric." And now, my wife calls Chŏl's mother "barbaric" for her transgressions against the spirit of the humane society. For some reason, it makes me laugh to hear my wife use the word "barbaric" that way. I don't see how people think they can prove they are not barbaric by installing a flush toilet or joining a humane society. No wonder it is next to impossible for them to grasp what a hard thing it is to get beyond barbarism — barbarians are not living in the jungle but swaggering down city streets with a dog wearing ribbons in their arms. Barbarians are wearing not grass skirts around their waists but suits fitted by first-class tailors. They are relieving themselves in flush toilets and riding escalators to coffee shops.

Today Chŏl's mother is still swearing and still beating Botchang.

I know she's not going to sell the dog that easily. What she needs now more than money is an object to vent her rage on. An object to be treated cruelly, an object that will groan and moan in pain under her merciless whipping.

Such behavior, as my wife says, is barbaric. But I'd prefer to understand Chŏl's mother by believing that the target of her cruelty is not just Botchang, but herself as well. Beneath the shrill yelps of that dog, I think I can make out the groans of her own dull pain.

I find myself wondering when the day will come, the day when Botchang grasps the Korean phrase "shove it" and acquires a taste for cooked barley in soybean soup, and when Chŏl's mother, likewise, is freed at last from the delusions of grandeur that once enthralled her. If her sadistic treatment of Botchang these days bespeaks a desperate need to be freed from herself, then her cruelty will also end when the day comes. Whether she gets a hundred thousand or two hundred thousand won, it won't be too late to sell the dog on that day.

Thanks to Botchang's yelps and the lively curses from Chŏl's mother, lately I've been free of constipation. Still, I go on waiting for the day when Chŏl's mom masters Botchang and masters herself so that Chŏl's family can once again regain its peace and harmony.

I, too, want to determine whether my liberation from constipation is permanent or only temporary.

translated by Chun Kyung-Ja

Encounter at the Airport

The travel bag slung over my shoulder was small but containing several stone *Harubang** statuettes. It was heavy enough to skew my posture. Besides this, in each hand I carried a box packed with just over four kilos of Cheju tangerines.

Laughing ironically to myself as I realized how flagrantly my appearance broadcast that I had just returned from Cheju Island, I staggered toward the taxi queue. I stopped short, however, suddenly thinking I might head over to the international lounge for a cup of coffee and a bit of rest before moving on.

Had rest been all I desired, the domestic lounge was quite a bit quieter than the international, and the coffee there certainly was no worse, but I had already made up my mind. In point of fact, I cannot tell good coffee from bad, nor did I have that day a particularly strong craving for a cup of either.

Unable to cope with the suffocating effects of daily drudgery, I had long plotted an escape to some far-away place; I had actually gotten no farther than the end of this country — so close to the border that by merely falling forward my nose might have reached it. I had succeeded in acquiring and retrieving yet another contribution to my sense of suffocation. And it was this stifled heart that compelled me to linger here, if only to catch the scent of a truly distant place, peeping into Korea's one and only — and tiny — window opening onto the world outside.

Still tottering under the burden of the baggage dangling off me in clusters, I felt too unsteady to brave the escalator and so grunted my way up the stairs. Before I even looked for a coffee shop, I first

---

**Harubang:* Cheju Island dialect for *haraböji*, or grandfather; these statuettes made from the island's volcanic rock are a popular souvenir.

dropped my burdens on an empty chair in the waiting room, then proceeded to sit down myself.

From my vantage point the exit was clearly visible and with it all those people who, having said their final farewells to wellwishers and shown their passports to the officials, were departing from the country.

The area around the exit teemed with technicians clad in blue work suits emblazoned with the logo of a well-known construction company. They mingled and milled with their families in all the disarray of an open-air marketplace. Even amid such confusion one frantic family stood out, shoving all others aside so that they alone might unite for an unobstructed commemorative photo. The deeply wrinkled old mother handed one of these mysterious one-minute family portraits to her departing son and held onto a second picture for herself as she raised her handkerchief to mop the swollen area under her eyes.

Yet another mother could be seen struggling to close the recalcitrant zipper of her son's carry-on bag after surreptitiously stowing a box lunch inside it as he rubbed his young child's cheek and talked with his wife.

"You have only two hours in Hong Kong. Only two hours, so . . . "

A bit farther away a burly man who appeared to be a crew leader for some other construction company had huddled his charges in a ring to give them instructions. The two spread fingers he held high to stress they had only two hours looked like a V, and the man seemed at ease in his role. His listeners, however, wore distracted and decidedly sour expressions, far from content at having to endure such preaching in this the hour of their departure — a time at which every minute was as precious as gold. Rather, it was their families, now gathered off to one side, who were listening most intently. The families resembled parents at the opening-day ceremony of a village school: dressed in their finest clothes, anxious lest they miss a single word, proud with no real reason, and filled with boundless expectation.

As soon as the sermon ended, each man was mobbed by ten or more farewell wishers. The whole crowd proceeded to throng about the exit. Failure to cling at such a critical juncture might lead to a forfeiture of their family qualifications as wife or mother, and so every last one of them latched on most desperately.

A young couple came and sat down in chairs near me. To be more precise, the woman dragged the man there against his will.

The woman seemed to be faced with some grave crisis requiring that she monopolize the man's attention, if only for a moment. Sunk deep behind eyelashes propped up straight and stiff as stakes with mascara, her eyes shone with the savagery of a kidnapper.

"What is it? Why are you acting like this?" the man asked vacantly, his neck still craning toward the exit and the crowd thronging there. He seemed worried that the rest of his family, suddenly deprived of the object of their rally, might flock around the wrong person. I, redundantly, was struck with that same worry.

The man was of average build, wore a uniform bearing his company's logo, and looked both earnest and able-bodied.

"You said if you work hard for a year you'll get a month's vacation and be able to come home, right?"

"Yes, we've already been over this."

The man was still preoccupied. The departure time must have been drawing near. His co-workers were passing in turns out the exit.

"Don't come back." The woman closed her eyes resolutely and spoke cruelly.

"What?" Only now did the man ignore the scene at the exit and turn to face the woman squarely as he spoke. But he seemed not to comprehend her message.

"I've heard you can also choose not to take your vacation."

"Yeah, but if they're giving vacations, why wouldn't I take one?"

"They say if you don't take it and stay on site you can send back close to a million won extra. Where else would we ever see a million won?"

"What do you want me to say? You're telling me that for a lousy million I should stay and work while everyone else is taking a vacation?"

The indulgent-looking man was rather more nonplussed than angry.

"Oh my, look at you. Haven't earned a cent yet and already rich enough to talk about 'a lousy million.' I won't have it. I'll be working hard at saving, so you have to work hard at earning. Think for a moment what a rare opportunity this is."

"All right. Fine, but I will be taking that vacation," the man responded indulgently.

"You really don't get what I'm trying to say? Then go ahead and see. Even if you take that vacation and come home, I won't so much as look at you. Because you won't be touching a single hair on my body. Because you won't be able to get into our room. Because I'll chase you right out the front gate." The woman put teeth to lip and spoke in the tone of unveiled threat.

"Well, well. If it isn't the reincarnation of Shin Saimdang."*

The man still refused to take her seriously.

I vaguely recalled a pertinent fable involving Saimdang, but this woman's hardened countenance, caked-on makeup, and short hair permed into tight kinks made the allusion sound utterly preposterous. Fearing I might laugh out loud, I ground my molars together.

"Do you think I'm acting this way because I want to? Don't you know what a rare opportunity this is? It's going to be hard anyway, so you might as well just endure it a bit longer so we can start living like humans too." The woman's voice cracked. She then quickly pulled out a handkerchief and mopped up her thick, black tears.

The man said nothing, but his gestures suggested an urge to embrace her. Befitting the average Korean man, however, he never got beyond the gesture. I found this lamentable, something like watching the Korean TV version of a foreign movie from which all kissing scenes have been cut.

"What are you guys doing over here?"

An elderly woman, most likely his mother, materialized in front of them.

"When a man's heading off on a long journey, you should be thinking about putting a little something in his stomach, but all you do is whine and snivel. Tsk, tsk."

The old woman glared disapprovingly at her daughter-in-law. She pulled out a black log of *kimbap*,** appetizingly rolled nearly as thick as an arm, and jammed it into her son's mouth. He bit off only one mouthful, then handed it back to the old woman.

A yell came from somewhere near the exit, demanding to know what they were waiting for. The man rushed toward the exit. He produced and displayed a black appointment book, waved at his wife and his mother, then disappeared through the exit.

Once the technicians had gone, their families also gradually dispersed. The atmosphere of the lounge changed completely.

---

* Shin Saimdang (1504–1551): A poet, writer, and painter; perhaps best known as the mother of the famous neo-Confucian scholar Yulgok Yi I. She was celebrated both in her day and after her death as an exemplar of feminine virtue in her dual capacity as mother and wife.

**Kimbap:* A layer of rice, meat, and vegetables wrapped in dried laver, then rolled and sliced into bite-sized pieces.

People with skin a different color from ours began to take over the place — mixed with these foreigners were people who looked like ordinary Koreans, judging from their color, eyes, ears, noses, and mouths, but who appeared not to understand our language. Like a child peering in through the window of a mansion at guests gathered for a cocktail party inside, I studied these refined cosmopolitans with a due mix of distance and curiosity.

"Hey, you little *ssangnom-ŭi-saekki!*"*

Out of nowhere came the thundering and dauntless voice of a woman cursing. The same swearing could be heard on any street, but, perhaps because the outburst occurred in such an uncommonly urbane setting, the words sounded so crude that I involuntarily shuddered with disgust.

"Hey, you little *ssangnom-ŭi-saekki!*"

All eyes were on her by this time but the woman nonchalantly repeated her obscenities, sending hand signals as well. Three boys all about the same size gathered around her. She hadn't been cursing at anyone, she had just been mustering her scattered children.

The boys were blond and looked like Western kids. Despite their childish faces, all three were taller than the woman. The florid, bright-colored clothes she wore were enough to make one think otherwise at first glance, but the woman was rather old. She had not aged gracefully. Her wrinkles were ghastly, as if they had been hacked into her face, and no amount of makeup could conceal them. And this woman was one of us, a Korean.

She was of a type nearly extinct in our immediate environs — that is to say, she was a specimen of the absurdly arrogant and totally died-in-the-wool Korean, the sort who at the first sight of people with yellow hair calls them "fucking Yankees," who demeans all Japanese as "sawed-off Jap dwarves," and who feels obliged to berate all Chinese as "dirty Chinks."

It was precisely this woman's totally died-in-the-wool Koreanness that made the clothes she wore and the children she led appear so out of place.

Every time I had met this woman she had appeared somehow out of place. Owing to this out-of-placeness, she always had been the butt of

---

*Ssangnon-ŭi-saekki: A common pejorative appellation combining the word for a commoner (*ssangnom*) with the word for the offspring of animals (*saekki*), thus having both a meaning and force similar to the English "son of a bitch."

jokes by those around her, but I knew just how much blind passion she poured into sustaining this very out-of-placeness.

Eager to renew my acquaintance with the woman, I left my bags where they lay and hurried over to her.

"Aren't you Auntie Elastic?"

"Well, what have we here? If it isn't Missy Pak."

By calling each other by these names we managed easily to bridge the long span of time during which the two of us had neither seen nor heard from one another.

Back during the Korean War, I had worked for a time as a salesgirl in the U.S. Eighth Army PX. Auntie Elastic had been a cleaning lady there during that same period.

These days the relationship between a salesgirl and a cleaning lady at a department store seldom goes beyond matching names with faces, but back then we were co-conspirators and were indispensable to one another. Just getting PX goods out the door to sell on the open market was an operation sure to bring double, even triple your investment; the problem was how to get the stuff out.

I'm not even talking about stolen goods here, just items we could lay hands on legitimately, things undeniably bought and paid for with dollars, but which we were forbidden to possess or to wear. The Yanks treated us like thieves, and if ever we were found with American products on us we were regarded as criminals caught in the act. In such cases we not only lost our goods but also had our base passes canceled. What's more, our names went onto a blacklist that barred our chances of future employment at any U.S. military facility.

At the PX the front door was for customers only; it was guarded by an MP who let no one but UN soldiers pass. Employees had to use a small door in the rear that was tended by a watchman who let employees out only after a procedure including a check of personal belongings, the emptying of pockets, and, of course, a full-body search or frisking. The watchman himself was watched by a constant rotation of MPs who stood there at all times. A Korean policewoman also was posted at the back door to pat down female staff. These policewomen were replaced often, but never often enough to keep them from coming over to our side.

It would have baffled the Yankees to discover that these police officers were in league with the very lawbreakers they were supposed to capture, but, from our perspective, it was extremely natural and hardly dishonorable in such hard times for people of common blood to ally themselves for survival in the face of starvation.

We salesgirls were expected to acquire dollars on the black market, and to use them to buy the PX items that could be resold most profitably. The role of the cleaning ladies was to smuggle the goods out of the PX and move them onto the open market. The policewomen saw to it that the cleaning ladies were cleared through the gates of the base without incident.

To share in the profits all you had to do was faithfully carry out your assigned task. The most strictly observed rule was that in case something went wrong the person apprehended would take the fall alone — there was to be absolutely no mention of accomplices.

The cleaning ladies had the riskiest job, which they facilitated by adopting a peculiar mode of dress. They wore seamless cotton skirts, stiffly starched and amply pleated, combined with roomy *chŏgori** jackets. Around their heads they wrapped towels in a turban. They also changed their gaits, affecting a slow, unstable shuffle. Some of the ladies even used various other ruses to avert suspicion. They pretended to be deaf, nearly blind, or not quite right in the head, so that the Yankees would think them incapable of mischief.

Each morning after the displays were arranged, a mountain of empty boxes was left piled up beside every counter. Among these boxes were always one or two that weren't empty, and the cleaning ladies, while pretending to throw them all out, had no real difficulty in spiriting the full ones into the bathroom reserved for female employees.

The Yankees had the nasty habit of presuming that each and every Korean working in the PX was a thief, but they also had a ridiculous sense of chivalry that under no circumstances would allow them to go snooping into the women's bathroom.

Concealment of purloined PX goods usually took place in the bathroom. Even in the most brutal midsummer heat the cleaning ladies were clad in long knit underwear. They rolled the underwear down to their ankles; loaded a ring of cigarettes, toothpaste, or chocolate around their legs, then covered the booty with the underwear and secured it with rubber bands. Successive loads were fixed in the same way from ankle to calf, calf to thigh, thigh to hips, hips to waist until

---

*Chŏgori: A traditional Korean top which is secured by a single tie across the chest.

an enormous heap of goods had completely vanished. Smaller items such as gum and razor blades were affixed to the upper body in like fashion.

Having thus donned their full-body armor of American goods, they donned their somewhat shabby but efficiently spacious Korean skirts and jackets, grabbed their brooms, and restlessly paced the floors until lunchtime — when they were allowed to go outside.

MPs guarded the exit, but making a stooge of any given MP was a snap. The women police officers, with a thoroughness even the MPs found excessive, a thoroughness born of fear they might be short-changed when payment for the load came in, felt every crack and crevice of each lady's body to try to ascertain the exact volume of outgoing goods. Invariably, these searches brought on little fits of tick-led writhing by the cleaning ladies. But this ticklishness was entirely a charade. If one of the cleaning ladies staged an unconvincing perfor-mance, acting in any way awkward, the MPs immediately grew suspi-cious, and whenever an MP showed the slightest hint of suspicion the female police officer quickly had to take his side: such was the pitiless functioning of the exit gate. All things fell under the jurisdiction of the day's luck.

On the outside, people thought that a job at the PX, even as the lowest menial laborer, promised great riches, but those who entered with an appreciation of the ephemeral nature of the position were easier to deal with than those in the thrall of sugar-coated dreams. Nearly every day somebody was fired, having been found guilty of this or that infraction. New employees in turn were brought in every day.

Whether you were nabbed wearing ten wristwatches up and down your arms or sneaking out a single pack of gum, being caught always meant the ax. Since punishment was the same in any case, all of us had the audacity to try for the big score. We wanted to make a fortune or at least to go down trying, but our schemes had a way of going awry. Maybe it was audacity that enabled us to live like there was no tomor-row, or maybe there truly was no tomorrow and we were bold out of the desperation of sheer need. In any case, what dominated our lives in those days, and not only with respect to that special place called the PX, was consciousness of tomorrow's uncertainty.

Auntie Elastic, though she betrayed not the slightest hint of the insecur-ity under which we all lived, was both the senior cleaning lady and the one who was best at the cleaning job. That said, she was no paragon of an upright cleaning lady; she was not content merely to pick up trash all day long until the days stretched into a month and she could collect her check while turning her back on the perilous but oh-so-sweet opportunities for profit in which her coworkers all took part.

On the contrary, it was she who was capable of hiding the largest quantity of goods on her person without divulging the slightest clue. Even when she loaded herself up with twice as much as the others, she craved just a little more. As if into a rubber pouch of limitless elasticity, an endless series of articles vanished under that woman's clothes. Her greed, too, was boundless. It was this uncanny ability to hide things — we never could foretell just how many items it would take before she would yield — that earned her the nickname "Auntie Elastic."

As for her age, there was no way really to guess how old she was. In those days she had no wrinkles on her face, but judging by the old style in which she wore her hair up, the stiffly starched black poplin skirt, and her walk, a slow, pigeon-toed shuffle that made it seem she had a chestnut stuck in her crotch, she was most certainly a semi-oldster whose body had already begun to decline.

Even when she worked unladen she walked and moved just as she did when fully loaded, thereby making all the Yankee employees and MPs who knew her believe that this was her natural gait.

But the fact that her luck had been so good up to then was not due solely to her strategy of subterfuge. She also possessed her own inimitable quality, a unique dignity that bordered on nobility. It was completely incongruous with her actual standing, and yet it could not be ignored.

No matter how seasoned, how brazen, a cleaning lady might be, if on the way out with a full load of goods she was unexpectedly ambushed by the sergeant, the man in charge of the whole store, the expression on her face would be the first thing to betray her, naturally. And so the saying "A guilty conscience needs no accuser" is both the most rudimentary common sense for catching criminals and an eternal truth, but Auntie Elastic was at all times and in all places consistently arrogant and impudent. She left no opening for Yankee suspicion.

But it was her insolent attitude toward her fellow workers, with whom she behaved as if she really were some sort of aristocrat to the bone, that was unbearable. She talked down to all of us, and indiscriminately swore at everyone.

After a month or two of PX life, even the lowest cleaning ladies would master the art of spicing up a "Good morning," "Hello," or "Hi" with a wink in order at least to appear friendly toward the Yankees they recognized, but Auntie Elastic's entire command of the English language consisted of a single curse.

It was her own version of "son of a bitch," a vulgar curse that even your average Yankee avoided, that she had altered into *ssangno'me bech'i*. She seemed to have blended the English to her taste with a similar Korean curse, *ssangnom-ŭi-saekki*, meaning "lowlife bastard."

At the end of every utterance and to whomever she pleased, Auntie Elastic recklessly applied *ssangno'me bech'i*. Inside the store the relationship between the salesgirls and the cleaning ladies was an equal one based on mutual exploitation. Still, since we salesgirls held the knife, we got a larger cut of the profits. The cleaning ladies were always near at hand waiting on us, trying to figure out just what we wanted, complimenting us occasionally on our clothes or makeup, and even trailing after us at lunchtime and paying for our meals.

But Auntie Elastic never even pretended to fawn upon us as the others did. On the contrary, she held us in contempt and often rebuked us. In particular she was hostile to salesgirls who had shacked up with Yankees and punctuated everything she said to them with either *ssangno'me bech'i* or "Yankee whore." Neither did that mean she was any gentler in dealing with the comparatively young and naive employees. Whoever was not a Yankee whore got a *ssangno'me bech'i*.

"Hey, you guys, you're real *ssangno'me bech'is*. Even if there is a war going on out there, why the hell would you work at the PX? You gotta think of your futures. You think any decent family would take in some bitch who used to work at the PX. It's too late for any of you to catch a good husband. This whole goddamn world is a *ssangno'me bech'i*."

Once in a while, when she was in a good mood, she would say, "Yeah, you guys. After all this, when things are peaceful again, you guys will all have the same problem. I'm talking about at last finding a man who suits you and a house you really want to marry into, only to have them turn you away because you worked at the PX. When it happens, don't hesitate to call me right away. Then I'll stand witness for you and swear you never once even glanced at a goddamn Yankee and how you all were good girls during your time at the PX. Shit, I don't know what kinda goddamn world can go on and on being such a *ssangno'me bech'i*."

And Auntie Elastic had reason enough to worry about us. We paraded around much too gaudily for the poverty-stricken Seoul of that time. More than a few of us salesgirls actually were living with Yankees, so the public image of girls who worked at the PX was extremely bad.

It was so bad that when we got off work in the evening the beggars and shoeshine boys who surrounded the base sometimes fell upon us like a swarm of bees and sang, to the tune of a popular children's song, "Yankee whore, shit whore, where you off to? Shaking your ass, where you off to? Walking alone in the back alleys at night, how much for one go? Off to sell your you know what." They continually dogged us with this chorus. What was worse, the truly vile beggars, putting a sinister twist on their already gnarled faces, would brandish buckets of excrement, screeching, "Hey, shit whore, gimme some money or I'll throw shit all over your clothes." What could we do but give them money?

Auntie Elastic knew what was what. Her superiority complex was what allowed her to scorn us all, to take pity on us from time to time, and even to strut around in front of the Yankees. Upon closer inspection, however, this superiority complex of hers stemmed from something completely preposterous.

This was Auntie Elastic's belief that her husband was a soldier of the Republic of Korea. She proclaimed this in a most reverential and elevated manner. But she was at a loss to give his rank or to say where he might be fighting at present. During the massive retreat of January 4 all able-bodied men under age forty had been drafted by the ROK. She simply reckoned that her husband, who had disappeared about that time and had not been heard from since, must have become a soldier and must now be fighting on the front line.

Therefore she loathed nobody more than those Korean soldiers who worked in the rear pressing uniforms and shining boots. "*Ssangno'me bech'is,* what time do they think it is? If you're soldiers, ought to be stomping the battlefield. What the hell are they doing in the streets of Seoul? *Ssangno'me bech'is.*"

We humored the foul-mouthed and haughty Auntie Elastic for so long partly because of her elastic talents, of course, but also because we were almost overwhelmed by her preposterous pride. Back then a truly proud person was precious. There was no way around the fact that the woman's unfettered arrogance, even though it struck one at first as something hateful, in time came to seem gemlike, a thing to envy.

But the day came when Auntie Elastic too was fired. She didn't go down like the other cleaning ladies, caught leaving with a load of goods, then crying and begging for just one more chance. No, she departed in the manner that best suited her — with dignity.

The electricity situation in Seoul back then was abysmal beyond description. The PX was given priority, but still there were frequent blackouts. Auntie Elastic's downfall happened not long after a new snackbar opened in the basement.

On a steamy summer day, the electricity was out all day, starting in the morning. The following day strange rumors began to spread, one on the tail of another. In the first place, rumor had it that all the meat and eggs stored in the giant refrigerator in the snackbar would be tossed into the Han River. The word out also was that the meat and eggs wouldn't all fit into just one truck.

The Yankees had a rule that absolutely forbade them to eat anything in the refrigerator once the power had been out past a certain fixed amount of time, and yesterday the blackout had gone just beyond that limit.

But according to the Koreans working there, the meat had been frozen so hard to begin with that it was now thawed perfectly for eating, and it would have had to go without refrigeration a lot longer before it would spoil.

This was an era when many Koreans had never even seen what an electric refrigerator looked like. An era in which even the butcher shops were called sanitary if they just stored meat in a thick wooden box on sawdust between a few blocks of ice. And an era in which slop made by scrounging scraps thrown out at the U.S. Army base and boiling them all together was the most nutritious meal a citizen of Seoul could hope to have.

"If they can't eat it, then why not be generous and give it to us? What could they possibly gain by loading it up and dumping it into the waters of the Han? No matter how full-bellied, a people must not lose their fear of heaven. Men have been struck down for far less."

We Koreans whispered such things around the base, and, just as knives are whetted by rubbing them together, we brought together our animosity toward the Yankees both to affirm it and to sharpen its edge. But who could brandish that blade in their faces? We knew too well just how futile this so-called blade of ours would be against their ironclad rules and regulations.

The closest we came was when one Korean working at the snackbar, who had befriended his Yankee boss, asked whether he might not take some of the spoiled meat home to his dog. Of course, for his troubles he received only a rebuke.

His supervisor said, "A dog's life deserves as much respect as a man's. How could you think we would give food too rotten for humans to eat to a dog?" Never mind that the Korean's wanting to feed the meat to his dog had been a lie in the first place.

At that time we knew the Yankees were obsessed with hygiene beyond our imagination, and we also knew that this "hygiene" business was supposed to be in people's best interest, but now, in actual practice, it brought a result so inhumane we were shocked and confused. Still, we dared not betray this and so just went on cursing them out of their hearing.

Even if they had given us the meat and eggs we probably still would have cursed them: "Telling us to eat stuff you won't? To experiment on us to see whether we die or only get sick? But we won't die or get sick. I'm telling you, if nothing else our stomachs have been subdued by all the red pepper." Throughout all this, of course, our genuine urge to gorge ourselves with their meat and eggs would have brought us all to the brink of madness.

At lunchtime on that same day, Auntie Elastic was in line waiting to be searched before going outside. As always, her profile brought to mind a hefty tree and her bearing was defiantly haughty. Whether she was carrying a load was for the policewoman who had patted her down to know — no one else could even venture a guess.

She passed safely through the search and slipped through the gate. In the back alley outside the main gate, there was a small iron door used only when local provisions were delivered to the snackbar. It happened that this door was wide open and the sergeant in charge of the snackbar was leading workers as they carried out boxes and slung them up onto a waiting truck. Assisting the sergeant were MPs who formed a solid line between the iron door and the truck, safeguarding the procession against any possible leak.

We all guessed that they were loading up the meat and eggs to be dumped into the Han River. They were guarding the cargo as closely as if they were transporting bombs. The whole thing was quite a spectacle. We all stopped in our tracks, grimacing derisively, and looked on. But we also knew that if they showed the slightest sign of carelessness, there was no way their cargo would move intact to meet its destiny as fish food in the waters of the Han.

Suddenly we heard a familiar curse.

"*Ssangno 'me bech 'i!*"

With a scream of rage that reverberated with a blood-curdling echo, Auntie Elastic, quick as a panther, sprang upon the sergeant. Hanging from his arm, which was as hairy as that of an orangutan, she sank her teeth deeply and with a sickening crunch into the appendage. The sergeant, dancing in pain, let out a howl. Until the MPs rushed upon her and removed her by force, she kept her teeth silently and resolutely in that arm and her eyes wide open. In her eyes, like those of a beast on the brink of extinction, shone absolute isolation. And it was the *ssangno 'me bech 'i* of that day which still stands out, against the background of countless others.

If on that day she truly was a wild beast, then we were no better than a gutless bunch of rabbits and squirrels, forsaking her to save our own skins.

Auntie Elastic was promptly dragged away by the MPs. The sergeant, after first aid was administered to his bleeding arm, was whisked off to the hospital as though he had sustained a critical injury. Fortunately for Auntie Elastic, the incident ended with her dismissal.

Even after she was fired, she was not the least bit hesitant to loudly let us know how she felt.

"Hey, you guys, why did I have to be loaded down then, of all times? It was awful being dragged off by the MPs in that state. You guys know the idiotic amount of stuff I take on when I'm taking a load out. So I said, 'Fuck it, there's no way out,' and I wanted to pull everything out before they found it. So I just lifted my skirt all the way up and began pulling out the things strapped to my midsection. You guys know how I load up, so there was no way everything was going to come pouring out all at once. And taking the things out one by one made it seem there was even more. Just the stuff I took out of my bottoms made a small mountain. When I went to unload my top, the MP suddenly gasped for air, yelling, 'Stop! Stop!' before his eyes rolled back in his head and he fainted. I'm telling you only the frames on those Yanks are big, their lily-livers are awfully tiny."

For her finale she made us laugh with this outlandish lie, and then she was fired. Later I heard a rumor that, all alone, she had been feeding about ten of her in-laws. For a while I puzzled over how, in such dire straits, she could have pulled off such a preposterous protest, but before long I forgot about her.

Not long after that incident, a truce was signed. As soon as the government returned to Seoul I quit the PX and got married. It was just after I had my first child, I think, when by chance I ran into Auntie Elastic on the street. If she hadn't yelled "Missy Pak! Missy Pak!" and been so glad to see me, I would never have recognized her, for she was thin and wore normal clothes that fit her well. Her walk, too, was that of a young woman.

We sat down facing each other in a bakery. It was there that I first learned she was only three years older than me and had been widowed very young.

"Oh dear, was he killed in the war?"

I asked this recalling how proud she had been of her husband the soldier.

"Killed in action would've been fine, but he died on the road. Either starved or froze to death, take your pick."

Her husband had been ten years older than she and suffered from an unusually feeble constitution and a weak heart. Like others drafted out of militia reserves as the enemy approached, he had joined in the big retreat, and only later was he found unfit for military service. He endured terrible hardships struggling to get back, but he met his end in some far-off place on the way home. Auntie Elastic wept constantly as she spoke of her husband.

"No matter when a man dies, he only dies once. If only he had died in battle I wouldn't have come to this. That poor, poor man. When he was drafted I'm the one who danced with joy, thinking the war would make a man out of him at last. Who could know he'd die in such disgrace?"

Then I realized that at first I had failed to recognize Auntie Elastic not because she was thin but because she was dispirited. Auntie Elastic without the starch was like a red pepper without the heat.

Since I had admired her, back when she was unaccountably haughty, I urged her to pull herself together and think about remarrying. I told her things had gotten better and it was still not too late for her to enjoy life.

"It's because I pulled myself together that I've managed this much. When I learned of his death my first impulse was to follow him to the grave. I may not look it now but you know me — if I say I'm going to do something I do it. For a week I took no food, not even a spoonful of rice, and lay wasting away. As you'd expect, in time my mind began to

falter and drift between this world and the next; as time spent in the
next world slowly increased, I knew my day of death was drawing
near. I was not scared in the least bit, nor was I in pain, in fact, I could
not have felt more relaxed. If they would have just let me be I could
have closed my eyes in peace, but somehow my mother got wind of it
and came bawling and begging me not to go through with it. When
even my mother's hysterics could not produce in me the slightest desire to live on, I realized that before people die they first make stones
of their hearts. But, and I'm not sure what she was thinking, mother
headed for the kitchen and began making rice. Before long the aroma
of perfectly cooked rice wafted in through a hole in the door, and the
strangest thing happened. My mind was still dark and I could not move
a muscle, but inside my stomach something began to stir. Before long
it began to tremble like a furious beast and I could control it no longer.
Looking back on it later, I saw that the damned beast was probably
life. Until then I had believed a person's mind and a person's life were
one and the same thing, but now I know it isn't so. Mind is one thing
and life is another. So, like a woman possessed, I shoveled down the
rice mother had made. Hell, not only did I not starve to death, that rice
was so damn good that had there been ten of us eating and had nine
died in the process I'd have been none the wiser. Still I almost did die,
but that was from the indigestion I got from eating so much."

It had been ages since the last time she made me laugh like that.

After that another ten years or more passed.

A friend came over to our house for lunch, after which instead of
complimenting me on the food she teased me about the sorry state of
my dishes. She mentioned a black-market dealer in American-made
goods who lived in Itaewon and whose house was piled high with the
best foreign-made dishes, asking if I wouldn't like to go and have a
look sometime.

By that time I was through having kids and things had gotten a little
better financially, so it was not hard for her to get a rise out of me with
that suggestion. It wasn't only me; almost everyone around me was
doing well enough to stop worrying about having enough to eat and to
start worrying about the kind of dishes on which they ate.

I went with my friend to see this dealer, who lived in a cozy,
two-story house in Itaewon. She was an attractive widow who had put
a kitchen and bathroom in each of several rooms to rent them out to
"Yankee brides," girls who were living with U.S. soldiers. The combi-

nation of rent and profits from trading in foreign goods afforded her a rather nice double income.

In that house there certainly were a lot of truly gorgeous dishes, and I wanted to buy every one of them. My own style of cooking, which had always placed the flavor of the food before the dish's appearance, now seemed simple-minded and embarrassing. But the prices she quoted were outrageous.

"If you compare the cost to the prices of domestic goods, you'll never buy first-rate goods like these. You have to compare the quality. Once you know how to judge quality, then you'll know that no matter how high the price, it's still a good deal."

Thus the foreign goods dealer lectured me, in a scornful tone.

Just then, from upstairs, came the sound of lots of glasses simultaneously shattering. This was followed by the sound of wood cracking. Then came the frog-croaks of children blubbering. Finally came a woman's voice, "*Ssangno'me bech'i. Ssangno'me bech'i.*"

I held my breath. Amid the rising noise of children crying and the low, unintelligible murmur of some man, the phrase *ssangno'me bech'i* had surged forth with dizzying speed and depth.

"They're at it again. Can't go three days without this kind of craziness. It's so shameful . . . I'm very sorry, ma'am," the foreign goods dealer apologized.

Accompanied by a thud, an old and worthless-looking Yankee came tumbling down the stairs, got back to his feet with some difficulty, and, flashing a grin, went out. A woman followed him about halfway down the stairs, yelling, "*Ssangno'me bech'i, ssangno'me bech'i.*" Then, as if weary of it all, she clasped her hands behind her back and sighed.

As soon as I heard *ssangno'me bech'i,* Auntie Elastic had sprung to mind; still, I was shocked when the woman standing there with her hands behind her back actually turned out to be her. The years had not been kind to her. Even pitifully heavy makeup could not conceal her considerable decline. Still, perhaps because she had won the fight, she seemed her old self, unreserved in her pride. Totally oblivious to our watching her, she returned to the second floor. In her hands, clasped behind her back, she held a club.

The building regained its quiet. The foreign goods dealer, overly concerned about the goings-on in her house, rambled on with answers to questions I had never asked.

"Some people think living with a goddamn Yankee means a life of luxury, but it's not like that at all. Those goddamn Yankees can be some of the worst characters imaginable. You think some of them don't beat their women every three days, some don't go on drunken rampages, some don't gamble, some don't fool around? That woman on the second floor is the exception: She gives all the beatings and takes none. Can you imagine? Even if her husband is a goddamn Yankee, can you imagine how bad things must be for a woman to raise a hand toward her husband? He is a perfectly good-for-nothing bum. A bum who never lifts a finger, a parasite who lives comfortably off his woman's labor, gambling and even chasing other women . . . "

"Isn't the man a soldier?"

"When they began living together he was a soldier. And the woman didn't start out as a Yankee bride either. She was working as a maid or something in the house of some other Yankee bride. I don't know if she fell for that guy or was raped by him or what, but before anyone knew it she had squeezed out a little half-breed kid. After that, it came time for him to go back home. And maybe he thought his little brat was wonderful, or maybe he really cared for her, anyway he told her he planned to come back and marry her as soon as he was discharged. But no one believed him. Hard to find anybody in these parts who'd believe such empty Yankee promises. But he really did come back and they're living together. Why, they say he even officially registered the marriage. I'd say he planned from the beginning to get himself a naive Korean woman and leech off her for the rest of his life. Being completely ignorant, she still hasn't figured it out and acts like living with a goddamn Yankee is a mark of success. I can't tell you how arrogantly that woman behaves. I guess living with a goddamn Yankee does at least take care of the problem of earning money, and if someone wanted to call that success I couldn't argue, but . . . "

"How does living with a goddamn Yankee solve money problems?"

"Because you are free to come and go as you please at the Commissary and the PX, buying things with dollars. But I hear that woman way overdid it and has been caught too many times. Even after she was caught and released, the sight of her shameless blustering was beyond words."

"Blustering? How?"

"She swaggered about yelling things like 'Do you think I'm doing this shit so I can eat? I'm doing this shit to support a fucking American. You fuckers think all thirty million of us are sponging off of you, but I'm telling you there are goddamn Americans who are not starving to death thanks to Koreans. And you're looking at a Korean who's keeping a fucking American alive and that American is my husband.' But who would believe her?"

"Why, don't you believe her?" I asked, intimating that I wanted an explanation.

"How would a woman that ignorant have said something so long and complicated in English? You know they've already popped out three kids and lived together for over ten years. Even to that husband of hers all she ever says when they fight is *ssangno'me bech'i* and maybe, when things are really good, "I love you." I'm telling you, the kids only look like half-breeds. They can't speak a word of proper English."

What she said made sense. I could believe Auntie Elastic had said such things. And that they weren't able to understand her was of no consequence. I bet she said all of it in Korean. There really are thirty million of us benefiting from the Yankees; she alone went against the grain and supported a single Yankee — an outrageous and friendless undertaking indeed. But, in her case, one that was possible.

As I saw in my mind's eye how absolutely isolated she had looked on that day so long ago when she sunk her teeth into the arm of the Sergeant from the snackbar, as if she was ready to take onto her own shoulders the sole responsibility of retaliating for the needless suffering of her starving countrymen, I believed it all was true.

But I offered no such explanation to the foreign goods dealer.

Thereafter, because I had used the pretext that I was afraid of being caught with contraband instead of saying the dishes were too expensive, for a while the foreign goods dealer came often to my house. But, though I often considered buying foreign dishes, I never committed, at most buying trifles such as black pepper or hand lotion, and the foreign good dealer came around less and less often. Still, through her, I occasionally heard news of Auntie Elastic. I heard she had been evicted from that house for fighting too much, and had moved to another house in the same area and was making out all right. The last word I had, after which the foreign goods dealer stopped visiting me, was that the Yankee, a hopeless drunk, had just dropped dead one day, leaving Auntie Elastic a widow once again.

And now we had run into each other here at the airport.

"Where are you headed?"

I asked casually, as if speaking to a neighbor I had met on the way to the market.

"America, because I got to find some way to make these *ssangnom-ŭi-saekki* into decent people."

"Auntie, why '*ssangnom-ŭi-saekki*'? What happened to '*ssangno'me bech'i*'?" Not knowing my place, I attempted to correct what she had said.

"Naw, you just wait till I get to America. I'll never use those damned curly-tongued American curses anymore. I'll be using my country's language to curse my country to my satisfaction."

She spoke in a hopeful voice, as if her goal in going to America was to swear to her heart's content. I merely nodded in silence.

If not for her curses, how would she cope with the phobias she was bound to suffer all alone among those people who say "Excuse me" when it is their foot that has been stepped on, people civilized to the point of deceit.

For Auntie Elastic, who was to suffer in a foreign country, her only resource these lonely curses that nobody would understand and that would connect with not a soul, I felt it was a blessing that Korean is so rich and varied in its profanity.

At last she took her three kids and headed for the exit. Even after she was gone I stood there in a daze.

I thought about how over the years I had sent so many relatives and friends through that exit. To study, to get degrees, to earn dollars, to see the sights, to throw themselves upon the mercy of the Statue of Liberty — so many had left and I had seen them off.

But no matter how close those friends and classmates had been, sending them off had never left me feeling as empty as this.

translated by John M. Frankl

Granny Flowers in Those Heartless Days

I

Gentlefolk indeed were the villagers of Dallae.

They held land of their own, and spared neither sweat nor tears in heeding the will of heaven. Hunger held no fear for them as long as they tilled the earth. They lived in harmony, observing those few rules human creatures ought to follow without fail, whether anyone is watching or not.

But one day the roar of artillery came even to this gentle village, nestled snugly in the surrounding hills, shattering its serenity. In time the region would grow famous for the intensity of its fighting, but Dallae itself suffered little from the war. The villagers never endured an actual battle and no bombs fell. Tales of houses incinerated in the blink of an eye and of playing children hacked into a thousand pieces were but rumors from afar.

The villagers ascribed their good luck to the wondrous powers of the mountain spirit. They housed this deity in a shrine on the slope of Dallae Mountain, and with the utmost devotion they offered him sacrifices on the first day of the tenth month by the lunar calendar.

Still, the casualties they suffered were scarcely fewer than those of neighboring villages where bombs had fallen. As the battlefront shifted, control of territory changed hands as easily and as often as if the flip of a coin determined boundaries. With each change of government, the villagers repeated the madness of massacring those accused of having taken the wrong side.

Most young men of Dallae had already volunteered for the army of the Republic of Korea or else had been drafted by the Communists. Refugees fleeing south, and others dragged north, had depleted the village's population further. Whatever their reasons for leaving, those missing from each household were men. Only women remained in the village: widows and possible widows, whether young or old, unmarried maidens, and old women. Except for suckling babies, there was not a single male to be seen, not even a boy. All males old enough to walk had been sent along with fathers, uncles, or even distant kin to find refuge in the south.

Males were a sacred breed responsible for continuing the family line, and for the women protection of these holy beings was a duty. In a world turned topsy-turvy, human ties and morality likewise were turned upside down, inside out, and at times were obliterated, but this bond between women and men became all the clearer and remained beyond question.

With only women left in the village, the slandering and the slaughtering of the innocent ceased. The impulse that drove the men to malign and murder one another emanated from the school at the entrance to the village. When Communist forces seized the building from the ROK Army, the impulse shifted as well from an urge to denounce neighbors as Reds to a desire to stone one another as "counterrevolutionaries."

The women, for their part, cared little who took over the school building. It did not matter which side held the already decimated village; hardly a whisper of life was astir. Nothing was left to be destroyed, and no benefits flowed from the occupying presence.

The women's only concern was to survive somehow until peace came and the men returned home.

Spring was far off and food was running low in every house, but the women had nowhere to turn. The school changed hands, but the vacuum in village government persisted. One day a rumor circulated that the new tenants of the school building were neither the ROK Army nor the North Korean People's Army, but big-nosed Yanks from across the sea.

Soon, big-nosed foreigners did appear, snooping around the village in twos and threes, and chomping on wads of gum.

"*Saeksi* have, yes? *Saeksi* have, yes?" they said whenever they encountered a female, making suggestive gestures that sent the women scurrying inside their homes. The naked sensuality that dripped like dog oil from the skin of these big-nosed barbarians evoked an instinctive shudder in the village women.

In asking after *saeksi* the Yanks seemed eager to locate prostitutes who would service foreigners, but there was nobody like that in a rural hamlet like Dallae.

The whole community became a crucible of fear. As dusk fell, women gathered one by one at the biggest house, afraid to face the darkness of night alone. This house, in addition to being the largest, belonged to an old woman respected by all as the matriarch of the village. The cruel times may have led villagers to slander and kill one another, but like other hamlets spread over the countryside, Dallae had its roots in the bonds of kinship.

As night fell, the big-nosed Yanks' cries of "*Saeksi* have, yes? *Saeksi* have, yes?" took on a desperate, menacing quality, like the lowing of beasts in rut.

Young brides and unmarried maidens quaked like leaves as they sat wide-eyed in a ring around the old woman, sleepless the whole night long. Nor was there any sign the following day that the big-nosed Yanks in the school building would be moving on.

Night fell again. The foreigners knocked on each and every gate, wailing ominously. "*Saeksi* have, yes? *Saeksi* have, yes?"

"We'll have no peace tonight, I guess," the old woman rasped.

"I'd rather bite off my tongue and die than have that happen to me," avowed one young woman, straightening her thin shoulder blades. She had married into the village from a nearby hamlet, but the war had erupted only a few days after her wedding. Within days she had lost her husband to the ROK Army as an "honorable volunteer."

"I'd die first, too. I'll hang myself from a rafter . . . "

"Me, too. I'll jump into the well . . . "

Each one eagerly declared she would choose death, as though failure to express such resolve would brand her as a slut with a secret lust for the big-nosed foreigners.

The old matriarch smiled faintly.

"So young, with your whole lives ahead of you. Don't be stupid."

The cries of "Hello? *Saeksi* have, yes? *Saeksi* have, yes?" came closer and closer.

"I suppose I'll just have to play *saeksi* to the big-noses," the old woman rasped slowly.

"You?"

The young brides and maidens had been wearing solemn, stony expressions as they vowed to guard their honor with their lives. At this remark, however, they all doubled up in loud giggles.

"Okhi, bring me your makeup case." Far from laughing, the old woman spoke severely. Okhi, her young granddaughter, had been engaged shortly before the war, but her fiancé was away in the ROK Army.

"Oh, Grandma, you are getting senile!"

Okhi poked the old woman's side and flashed a sidelong look of embarrassment at the others.

"I'm not senile yet. I told you to bring me the makeup case."

When the old woman spoke like this, with authority, she seemed a totally different person.

In more peaceful times, the village's biggest festival came on the day when offerings were made to the mountain spirit. On those occasions, the men butchered a sow and the women cooked rice cakes. And this old woman, the eldest lady in the village, was the one who oversaw the women's work.

With astonishing acuity she could sense out those who were having their period, or young women who had been with their husbands the night before, and whom custom thus excluded from the rituals. At such times, the old woman emitted an air of infallible authority. It almost seemed as though the welfare of the entire village for the coming year depended on her.

The women sitting in a circle around the old matriarch stared at her now as she radiated that same fearless authority. They grew somber. Finally, one of the older among them spoke up.

"We know you're doing your best to keep the young ones from being violated, but think about your age. Your age. I mean, those Yanks aren't blind, are they? Makeup can only go so far . . . "

Before finishing her sentence she broke into laughter, echoed in half-stifled giggles from around the room.

"Shut up and bring me the makeup case, I said," the old woman's calm, dry voice commanded silent obedience. Okhi finally fetched the case, and curiosity lit up the faces of her audience. The makeup, bought as a wedding gift for Okhi, was not of the best quality, but at least it contained all that was needed.

"Now, make me up."

The old woman handed the case to a young woman with a pretty face. She had money to spend and before the war had been regarded as the village's most fashionable woman.

"Oh, Grandma, you're crazy," she said, searching the other women's faces for approval of her refusal.

"I guess you want to be the unfortunate one, then." The old woman had suddenly turned malicious.

"Oh, you are senile, aren't you?" said the young woman, appalled. She began applying makeup to the matriarch's face with precise strokes.

"*Saeksi* have, yes?" The cries grew more insistent. The light dimmed as the oil in the lamp dwindled.

Giving herself up to the expert hands of the young woman, the older one murmured, as if to herself, "Can you tell how old a big-nose is from his looks? It's the same for them when they try to tell our age. Different races age differently. And no matter where, east or west, everybody does it in the dark. Yes, of course, they do it in the dark . . . "

Her remarks were intended more for her own reassurance than for the ears of the other women.

At last, the old woman's face was all made up. She looked into a mirror and grinned in satisfaction. Her gruesomely coquettish smile, issuing not from any natural feeling but from sheer desperation, sent shivers down the women's spines.

"*Saeksi* have, yes?" The cries finally came to a halt outside the gate of the house. The big-nosed Yanks seemed to sense a human presence within; they shook the gate in a fury.

"Okhi, lend me your clothes, too."

The old woman changed into a red skirt and a yellow blouse. She wrapped a brightly striped scarf around her head.

"*Saeksi* have, yes?!" The cries had become screams and the gate seemed about to burst under the Yanks' violent kicks.

"I'm ready now. Open the gate and let them know there is a *saeksi* for them," the old woman ordered in her raspy, cracking voice that sounded like an oak branch splitting.

Someone removed the crossbar. The gate swung wide open. The women shuddered with a blend of shame and relief akin to that one feels when urinating after holding back for a long time. They hid themselves in the darkness.

A single *saeksi* stood there in the light. A big-nose in the very front, of gargantuan stature, lifted the *saeksi* effortlessly in his arms. Sensing that he was being watched from every dark corner, he did not take her on the spot, but with long strides went out through the gate with the *saeksi* in his arms.

"Come on!"

The other big-noses followed him. Not far away stood a jeep. They climbed in and the *saeksi* sat, slight and meek as a baby, on the big-nose's lap.

In the blink of an eye, the jeep arrived at the school. It was completely dark outside, but when the big-noses opened a glass door and then a rickety wooden one, blinding light poured out on the old woman. Simultaneously, she heard loud cheers and hoots. She curled up like a shrimp in the arms of the big-nosed foreigner, and covered her face with her hands.

Before she knew it, she was thrown onto a bed. Even then, the old woman peeked out at the room through her fingers. She wanted to see how many men she would have to deal with before the night was through. Luckily, she told herself, it seemed there were not more than five or six.

The big Yank who had carried her in started undressing her.

"My word, how filthy!" she thought. "He may be a barbarian who knows nothing of propriety, but to carry on this way when it's brighter in here than broad daylight!?"

The old woman and her husband had been a loving couple and had had seven children. In fact, they had made love well into their sixties, but they had never done it except in the dark, not even in dim lamp-light. For them, the only illumination had been the moon shining through the paper windows.

The old woman struggled desperately to keep the ties that held her blouse closed, and the belt of her skirt. How her face might appear in the light had become a minor problem by now. In the hands of the big-nosed Yank, her feeble struggles were like the flailing of a newborn.

The big-nose effortlessly peeled off each layer of her clothing as if he were husking an ear of corn. She supposed he would at least put out the lights before removing her inmost layer, but goodness no, the ghastly spectacle of her nakedness was exposed under the shining light.

Breasts sucked dry by seven children and long since so sunken that the nipples clung to her ribs. A belly with cracked leathery skin, that showed marks of each of the seven children who had stretched her to the bursting point. Skin resembling the parched bed of a stream — all this was exposed under a light brighter than the noonday sun.

The old woman gave up her resistance and began to cry weakly. A mosquito-like drone issued forth through the hands hiding her face.

Though she had stopped resisting, her gray underpants — the last bit of covering — descended no further, but just clung to her gaunt hipbones, which jutted up like steep hills in a desert of red sand.

Letting out a thin, high-pitched whine, the old woman told herself, "Once the last piece is stripped off and that is exposed, what can I do but bite my tongue and die? Ah, but what a hard, hard thing suicide is! Why bother going any further?" she even thought. "By now they must know they've been deceived; I wish they'd just shoot me dead and be done with it."

But suddenly there was merry laughter. Perhaps because she was hearing it in a wretched, suicidal state, the old woman thought that laughter the most innocent and jovial she had ever heard. Before the war, there had been both happy times and sad in the village; young people often got angry, but they laughed just as frequently. But no matter how joyful they were, dregs of sorrow always lay at the bottom of the laughter, and in its wake came lingering traces of a sigh. Only a child could laugh such unclouded, gleeful laughter.

Dire though her predicament was, the old woman began to steal glances at the big-nosed foreigners. Every one of them had fallen off his chair and was rolling with laughter on the bare floor.

There was nothing in the empty room besides her that could be responsible for their outburst. Lest she be swept along in their laughter, the old woman raised the volume of her whimpering.

Finally the laughter subsided. Someone set her upright, picked up her garments off the floor one by one, and brought them to her. When she had finished dressing, they led her into the darkness outside. The thought that they would probably shoot her dead terrified the old woman.

But the Yanks put her in the jeep, loaded it with boxes and drove her back to the big house where she had been picked up. Upon arrival, they unloaded the jeep.

Pointing to the boxes, the big-nosed Yanks smacked their lips and made gestures of eating to the bewildered woman. "Mama-san, chow chow. Mama-san, chow chow, okay?"

The Yanks got back in the vehicle and drove off toward the school.

The women all ran out of the house the moment they heard the jeep leave. The old woman quickly recovered her authority and ordered them to bring the boxes into the house.

Every box was filled with things to eat: canned fruit, tinned meat, jam, fruits, milk, a fragrant powder that was sour and yet sweet, chocolates in shining silver foil, candy, jelly, chewy cookies, and crispy biscuits in boxes bedecked with ornate pictures.

The women were bedazzled and breathless.

In accordance with the dictates of age, the old woman regained her composure first. After recounting in relative calm the ordeal she had just endured, she concluded, "It's because they were Yanks that I came back alive, and with so much food. If they had been Japs, they'd have shot me dead the minute they found out they were tricked. And if they had been not Japs, but Russians, they wouldn't have cared how old I am. They'd have jumped on top of me and I would have been done for. They wouldn't even have wasted a bullet; they'd just have done me until they crushed me to death."

The women listening agreed wholeheartedly with the old woman's pronouncements. They all shuddered.

Neither the old woman nor anyone else in the village had ever been abroad, of course, and they had never before encountered Yanks, Japs, Russians or the like in their own village. This was their first run in with foreigners. Even so, the old woman asserted her views confidently, and none of her listeners made the slightest objection. True or not, that much insight into national character was basic knowledge shared by anyone born in Korea.

II

All was quiet on the front. A major battle was expected in a few days. For the green recruits who never had seen fighting before, the calm on the eve of the storm was unbearable. What was more, a very queer rumor was circulating: that enemy bullets were attracted to virgin soldiers and that death was unusually common among them.

This rumor was nothing more than a fairy tale someone had cooked up as a diversion from the razor-edge suspense of the "calm before the storm," yet the virgins in the ranks had grown so uneasy that they were readily discernible among the other soldiers. Upon learning that the rumor was unsettling his company, the commander allowed his men one-hour leaves to go to one of the nearby villages if they wished.

The commander knew, of course, that the villages had been completely evacuated. "But you never know, there's always a chance to get lucky," he thought. "A clever fellow can feast on pickled shrimp even at a Buddhist monastery, no? What can I do but give them a chance?" He remained skeptical, however.

Darkness was already falling as Private Kim wandered alone into the village. He had strayed from his group of virgin recruits. Not a single house showed smoke from the chimney, and no lamps were lit. Without scouting further he knew the village had been evacuated. All his fellow soldiers had gone in search of inhabited villages, but Private Kim somehow found himself drawn to this one.

Something about it reminded him of Hyesuk's village. Private Kim recalled the day he had gone to her village to say goodbye. Before the war he and Hyesuk, college classmates, had been in love with each other. Everyone knew the two of them planned to get engaged upon graduation.

The war broke out right after their senior year began; Hyesuk returned home, while Kim stayed in Seoul. Luckily, he escaped harm when the city fell, but after it was retaken by the ROK Army, Kim had been drafted. Before reporting for duty, Kim had gone to the country looking for Hyesuk.

It was early evening and smoke was rising from every chimney. Maybe because there was no breeze, or because the chimneys were so low, the dense purplish smoke crawled along the ground. The thatched straw roofs floated amiably in the smoke, a cluster of friendly islands on the sea.

The smoke turned color by degrees — from purple to a deeper purple to a dark gray. Soon night fell.

"So," Kim had thought back then, "in the countryside twilight rises out of the chimneys." Hyesuk, facing their long separation, had been wretched and pitiable that day.

They left the village, by then submerged in darkness, and climbed a hill to the rear of the dwellings. Along the slope were many tombs. Some graves lay side by side, some lay isolated off by themselves, and still others in clusters.

They sat in front of one of the graves, leaning back against a stone altar set before it for the conduct of ancestral rites.

"Whose tombs are all these?" asked Kim.

"My ancestors."

"Wow, so many ancestors dead and gone!"

Kim grinned feebly at the stupidity of his words.

"Don't die. I don't want you to," Hyesuk sobbed desperately as she clung to his chest.

"Silly, why would I die? I'm not going to die. I love you. I love you," Kim said, rolling to the ground with Hyesuk in his arms. The grassy hillside was soft and dry beneath them.

The couple's relationship had been no secret on campus, but never before had they kissed as intensely as they did now.

In fact, had he wanted to, Kim could have had her right there and then, for Hyesuk wanted it too. But he restrained himself. He lifted her fevered body, brushed the grass off her clothes, and sent her home.

He had sworn he would return alive, but still he sought to ease Hyesuk's sadness in case he was killed.

Was I right then or not? Can it be true that virgins attract enemy bullets? Pondering these thoughts in solitude, Private Kim made a full circle around the village.

No smoke rose from the chimneys, but darkness was rapidly descending over the empty village. As he left it, he looked back again and again, remembering the country road where he had bid Hyesuk farewell. Suddenly, his eyes detected a wisp of smoke that seemed to rise out of nowhere. It was faint but definitely a different shade from the night sky.

Kim's heart raced as a peculiar illusion suddenly engulfed him. It seemed he was back in Hyesuk's village and that she was somewhere nearby, all alone and waiting for him. He was drawn in the direction of the faint smoke.

The house was the smallest and the shabbiest in the village. The brushwood door would give way at the slightest push.

"Anybody home?" Kim's mouth was dry and his voice trembled.

"Who is it?"

Opening the door and emerging from inside was an old woman. She looked relatively healthy and spry, but her voice too was trembling.

"I'm a soldier. Army of the Republic," the private said in a gentle tone to reassure her.

A look of delight shone on the old woman's face. As if starved for company, she eagerly led Kim inside.

The stone floor, heated from below by a well-stoked fire, was warm. Kim could see that the old woman was having supper alone.

"How did you come to be left alone like this?"

"My husband was paralyzed by a stroke. I couldn't leave, you know, with or without him . . . "

"And your children?"

"Only one son. He's in the ROK Army."

"I see. And your husband?" Kim scanned the room for a paralyzed old man.

"He passed away."

"When?"

"Just a few days ago. Unlucky old man, would've been better if he had died before the war, or else lived to see better times than these."

"Then you took care of his funeral by yourself?"

"Not much of a funeral to speak of. I buried him, that's all."

"By yourself?"

"Of course. Who was here to help me?"

"That's very admirable indeed."

"No, not admirable. Just desperate. There's nothing a person pressed to the wall can't do."

"Still . . . "

"I may look old, but I'm still healthy and strong. With the old man laid up like that, I did all the farming myself. I was dead set on sending that son of mine to school no matter what. Anyway, it isn't much of a farm we have here."

"I see."

Kim found himself increasingly moved by her tale. He took a liking to the old woman, and soon he was telling stories himself — how he had left Hyesuk behind and the circumstances that had brought him there. To explain his presence, he mentioned the rumor that virgins were the first to fall to gunfire.

"Oh, no! My son's a virgin too, I think. In fact, I'm sure he is."

Deep worry clouded the old woman's face.

"Oh, grandmother, don't worry too much about it. It's just an old wives' tale somebody spread to have fun at the expense of us inexperienced soldiers. A superstition. And who believes such things these days, what with the whole world so civilized?"

After a while, Kim rose. He was about to leave when the old woman grabbed at the crotch of his pants.

"Son, don't you want to lose your virginity before you go?"

"Pardon me?"

"So what if it's a rumor or a superstition? If it might do you some good, why not do it? Life's a precious thing. Especially for you. You said you have a girl waiting for you."

"If I could, why wouldn't I? But there's nobody around to do it with."

"Yes, you can. I'll let you."

"What?" Kim was appalled.

"Why so shocked? No need to be so shocked. Now, come on. Let's turn off the light. I'm still quite able, you know."

The old woman turned the lamp off and led Kim to the bedding that was spread on the warmer part of the stone floor. Surprisingly enough, she still had an ample bust and soft skin, and her hands were more than exquisite; they were artful. In the dark, the old woman had become just a woman. As if under a goblin's spell, Kim lost his virginity naturally, almost without trying.

When the light was turned on again, however, the old woman was still an old woman. Turning his back on her, Kim was about to flee when she spoke.

"Please visit again."

What did she mean, please visit again? Did lust still burn in a body as old as hers? Did she still long for the pleasures of sex?

Gratitude for kindness received turned into anger at having been hoodwinked somehow. Kim now looked at her with a different attitude; on her face he thought he saw rapture and satisfaction.

As he left, Kim shuddered to shake off a feeling of pollution. He felt as if he had been drenched from head to toe with dirty dishwater. For a long while afterward he could not shake off that feeling, and it turned to disgust and, ultimately, to an absolute loathing for women.

Kim survived many battles unscathed, perhaps because he was no longer a virgin. He left the military a year after the armistice was signed.

He returned to Hyesuk's village, but she was not there. She had married and set up house somewhere far away.

"Dirty bitch."

Kim disposed of all his feelings toward Hyesuk with that single phrase.

The lust inside a woman over sixty had been strong enough to make her lure a young man her son's age into her bed, while her late husband was still warm in his grave. How then, he reasoned, could he have thought Hyesuk, so young, would wait so long for him? He thought back to their burning embrace on the grass by the tomb.

Kim's view of women remained fixed in this way. He had, of course, no way of knowing that his many letters to Hyesuk had been intercepted by her parents and destroyed.

Days passed. Kim earned money enough and fell into a life of dissipation. He no longer shuddered when he recalled the satisfied expression on the old woman's face as she had said, "Please visit again." In those days he had been an innocent. Now he was a suave, worldly man. Whenever he thought of that old woman, his confidence in his masculinity soared. He made women into his playthings.

His conceit that his manliness had to be extraordinary to rekindle the fire in a sixty-year-old woman may have been outrageous, but it fueled his lasciviousness, which in turn made his rakish inclinations even more striking.

More time passed. His dissipated lifestyle had sapped his strength, but in the end he married a good woman, had children, and settled down to the regular routine of a family man. People said that he had finally matured.

From time to time, he still thought of the old woman. His original notion that he had caused her to reach the height of ecstasy gradually altered. When the old woman received him inside her, her flesh had been dry and loose, like the pocket of his mother's sweater into which he would put his hand as a child. And so it remained the whole time, not a place where sensations of pleasure seemed likely.

How, then, to explain that satisfied look of rapture on her face as she told him to visit again? "Could she have meant she would welcome other virgin soldiers seeking help?" Kim wondered. The pleasure she felt must have come from the notion that her sexuality could still bring joy to a man.

Countless days have passed. Kim, now a successful businessman, is nearing fifty. Every so often he thinks of the old woman. He is old enough now to be able to see the sincere compassion in the favor she bestowed upon him. The look of satisfaction that had so disgusted him as a young man now strikes him as the smile of a true humanitarian. He thinks now that growing old is not the sad, lonesome thing people believe it to be.

translated by Ryu Youngju

Three Days in That Autumn

---

1. Three Days Left

Only three days left.

Autumn fills the window. Each day the sun peers through this south window into the farthest corners of the room. The velvet chair beneath the window is a soft gray, but when you brush the fabric against the grain it turns a subtle shade of olive. Originally, the velvet was a dark forest green. It is a totally useless chair. For thirty years it has stood in that same spot, doing nothing but fading in the sunlight to a dull gray. From the beginning it has been there and from the beginning it had no use.

In the spring of 1953, the war was still on. With rumors of a ceasefire circulating, Seoul took on a decidedly bustling look. The city's population visibly was swelling day by day, but the government had not yet returned. I was twenty-seven years old then, an unmarried woman. Without trepidation I had come back to Seoul alone in search of a suitable place to open my medical practice. Despite my childlike face, I was perfectly qualified to found my own practice. I graduated from a women's medical school before the war, and during the fighting I nursed casualties fresh from the front. Then, as a refugee in the countryside, I worked for a college acquaintance who had set up a thriving clinic but was shorthanded after the Army drafted her husband as a medic. In those days the system of medical specialization was far less rigid than now, and my qualifications to set up a private practice were in no way lacking. I was free to choose whatever specialization I wanted.

Given that the government was yet to return, I could have set up practice almost anywhere, even in the city's center. But I had to be mindful of my means and show some foresight. To avoid areas where rents might soon skyrocket seemed wise. Before long, a deluge of renowned specialists with university degrees would surely accompany the returning government, driving me out of business if I dared to compete.

I thought about infiltrating one of the obscure residential districts in the suburbs. After looking mainly in the outlying parts of the city, I came upon this space for rent on the second floor of the Kyŏngsŏng Company building. Back then, this street was an eastern approach to the capital, and just beyond the railroad tracks lay the stinking, nightsoil-drenched farms of Yangju county.

"Kyŏngsŏng" in Chinese characters on the company sign was an old name for Seoul. Despite its imposing name, the place sold farm implements, and the rustic store befit its squalid surroundings. Still, the old-fashioned name had an endearing echo, affording a sense of relief at having finally reached Seoul, something like the relief felt by Yangju peasants who left home before dawn to drive their ox-carts laden high with firewood to market in the city.

An old broker from a real estate office in the neighborhood showed me the second floor of the Kyŏngsŏng building. A sign reading "Kyŏngsŏng Photo Studio" hung outside the window. The studio had stood vacant since the photographer vanished during the war. By now everything remotely useful had been stolen, and the place, in a shambles, was used as a playground by neighborhood kids. A plywood partition and door that once separated the studio from the space used for sleeping had been ripped down, and the pieces lay strewn on the floor. The black curtain that once hung in front of the darkroom was a tattered rag. The door to the staircase was entirely gone and not a single pane of window glass was intact. In this desolation and disorder, the velvet chair seemed singularly precious, like the prince of a peaceful kingdom taken hostage by barbarians.

Only later did it dawn on me that even if it were rescued from its chaotic surroundings, that velvet chair would have looked garish and extravagant, conspicuously out of place anywhere you might put it. That chair was not for sitting and resting, and never would it match any ensemble of furniture: its sole function was to serve as a prop for taking pictures. In old-fashioned portraits taken at photo studios, it is common to see one subject posed sitting in such a chair and another standing beside him, or a lone subject standing stiffly behind an empty chair with arms resting lightly on its back. Also, for the customary one-hundredth-day celebration portrait of a precious first-born son, an elegant yet comfortable chair must have been needed in which the naked baby could sit by itself, propped against the back. As though designed especially for such uses, the velvet chair was opulent to the point of absurdity. Images of phoenixes were carved into the wood framing its high, velvet-upholstered back. The armrests were in the form of writhing dragons. I was so amazed that I stood dumbstruck in the middle of that abandoned, debris-cluttered studio.

The old man showing me the place seemed to read my silence as a sign of satisfaction with the space. He headed downstairs, assuring me, as if doing me a great favor, that he would negotiate the rent and costs of repair with the owner on my behalf. The landlord was, and still is, the owner of Kyŏngsŏng Company. Left alone, I gingerly sat down on the chair, acting on the same curiosity felt by children left on their own whose hearts pound with a sudden urge to try on the clothes of grown-ups. Even then, the chair stood by the south-facing window.

The area across the street, which since has been redeveloped as an apartment complex, back then was the site of an agricultural school that had been commandeered by American troops for their use. In the spacious research garden adjoining the school, scores of quonset huts had sprouted like so many mushrooms. Helmeted American MPs stood guard at the front gate. Upon entering the neighborhood one could see at a glance that it was little better than a slum, but thanks to this American army camp it exuded an air of impending prosperity, a hint of something good about to happen. Somehow, the district's shabbiness seemed less than pure: it was tainted by a strange wantonness.

Suddenly I sprang up from the chair, shaking my head as if to repel an unpleasant daydream. Feeling stifled as though already trapped, I restlessly paced to and fro. The wooden floor squeaked so loudly it seemed to scream. Absentmindedly, I began gathering trampled pictures scattered about on the floor: a photo of a girl student with bobbed hair, prudishly resting her chin on her palms; a first-birthday picture of a handsome baby; and a portrait of an elderly couple, looking simple and rustic as they sat a little apart from one another. It occurred to me that this last might have been a gift, paid for by the couple's children out of filial devotion. Stamp-sized ID photos showed an assortment of frozen, expressionless faces. Naturally, I recognized none of the faces in the pictures.

Yet, those faces all of a sudden seemed familiar to me as I reflected that every one of those people must have drawn a thick line between the time when those pictures were taken and the present. I, too, had such a line. The Korean War — that was the common line, the hurdle we had all shared. Confronted with that line, what outrageous deflections of fate had each one of us faced?

Vehemently shaking my head, as if trying to rid myself of something, I went back to gathering discarded pictures. I picked up a pornographic photo of nude male and female figures entwined in a knot of contorted flesh. Hands quaking, I quickly ripped it up and, retreating a couple of steps, flopped down into the chair. Just tearing the picture up was not enough to keep these people from springing to life in my body — the suffocating smell of armpits; the hairy chest brushing my face like a broom with each jolt; the limbs, long and tough like ropes, binding me in an unyielding yet tensile grip; the pain piercing my body's core . . .

Out of a fog like the stupefaction that overwhelmed me after the rape, obscuring all meaning, the old man reappeared, grinning. "Why is that old man smiling?" I merely wondered. I couldn't budge an inch.

The old man put his nicotine-reeking mouth to my ear and whispered: "Doctor, don't say a word and just do as I tell you, *ying?* Our neighborhood is about to get a clinic, so you can rest easy that I'll do nothing to your disadvantage, *ying?*" I did not mind the "*ying?*" ending each of his sentences, for it was more like an endearing habitual nod than dialect for "yes?" Soon Mr. Hwang of Kyŏngsŏng Company came upstairs and the old man unfolded the lease contract. I gave him my purse as a writing surface so he could finish the lease more easily. True to his word, the old broker took my side and doggedly bargained down the deposit and the rent by highlighting flaws in the former photo studio space. Hwang seemed taciturn by nature, or possibly he was upset at the moment. He spoke brusquely, but before long surrendered to the old man. With no real difficulty, the haggling ended just as the old man intended. In the end, the owner even agreed to replace the broken glass and the missing door, and to rebuild the partition. The old man wrote everything down in the lease in minute letters. Hwang and I read it quickly and took out our seals.

Only after the contract was signed and the brokerage commission paid did Hwang ask me what kinds of diseases I'd be treating. The old man, already used to speaking for me, interceded before I could speak:

"All and everything, didn't you say, doctor, *ying?*"

"No. I'll be doing obstetrics and gynecology," I said, rising abruptly from the velvet chair.

It was not a spontaneous decision. The dissolute atmosphere of the neighborhood had given me the idea, initially. Then I had made up my mind while in the throes of the nightmare set off by that pornographic photo. Only a woman who has had an unwanted baby growing in her own womb knows the agony of it. Sicknesses and pains all elicit pity, but that suffering attracts only accusations and contempt. If the dream of the healing arts was to free people from disease, my dream was to liberate women from that lonely agony, a suffering harder to endure than merely physical maladies.

"Just in case the business doesn't fare so well and she ends up taking off, please write something down so there's no disagreement over the cost of restoring the place. Something to the effect that the owner is not to be responsible," Hwang suggested to the old man. Contempt flashed across Hwang's face as he gave me a sidelong glance.

"Listen to yourself! Instead of wishing prosperity for her new business, what are you saying? The doctor must be disappointed. Doctor, this man here is not very good with words. But his heart is in the right place, so try to understand, *ying?*"

"You know what I mean. Women in these parts are having babies right and left with no problems at all. Why should a decent woman, one who hasn't suffered any curse to spoil the childbirth, need a women's clinic? What a shameful idea!"

"Uh-huh, look at you! When you should speak up, you act like a mute with a mouth full of honey, but what shouldn't be said at all you spit right out! Didn't I tell you she's going to treat everything? If you get rid of the sickles and hoes you've been hawking and start a drapery business or something you'll be in trouble, but the doctor here is an expert in curing people, so no need to worry she'll treat women's maladies only. Let's go, I'll buy you a drink with the commission I just earned." They went downstairs. The old man was almost shoving Hwang along. Alone, I reflected on their simple-minded, unschooled understanding of gynecology and smiled desolately to myself.

Preparations for the opening progressed quickly. As promised, Hwang hired a carpenter to fit a new door and the window glass was replaced. I hired a painter and a sign maker, and had the interior painted and a new sign made and hung. "Eastern Clinic" the sign said, and I even added the specialities "Obstetrics and Gynecology." Seoul back then offered plenty of cheap, used furniture. I selected desks, chairs, and a sofa. Visiting the other side of Han River a couple of

times, I bought a few essential medical instruments, items indispensable for my practice. Tiny mirrors for vaginal examinations, forceps,
measuring probes from size 1 to 15, curettes shaped like long
teaspoons — my cold heart grew even colder at the cool touch of the
metal instruments. I was unaccustomed to handling these tools, yet I
felt strangely at peace as though finally facing a preordained destiny. I
bought an examining table with stirrups designed to hold a woman's
pubis up near eye level. Before you lie down on such a table, it may
seem no more than a scientifically engineered convenience. Once you
are in place, however, you discover just what a demeaning instrument
of persecution it is to women. I shuddered, recalling my own unjustifi-
able torment.

All preparations were finished. The photo studio had been transformed almost overnight into a medical clinic. One vestige of the
studio days lingered, an eyesore marring the sense that the work was
done. The velvet chair remained. When Hwang cleaned the studio for
the first time, he set it aside, and the carpenters did the same. Even the
painter, instead of using it as a step stool, shielded it from stains with a
paper dropcloth. I knew very well that the chair had absolutely no use,
but somehow I couldn't give or throw it away. I ended up leaving it in
front of the south window, just where I found it.

Though all was finished, no patients came to the clinic. Hwang's
prediction had been right. I was not uneasy, though. At times I felt
preparations were still unfinished because that chair was so hopelessly
incongruous with the ambience of an examining room. When I came
back from shopping one day, a visitor awaited me. He was sitting on the
velvet chair before the south-facing window. My visitor was not a
patient but my own father. He was dressed in white and wore shiny,
pointy-toed, patent leather shoes. He even had grown a beard — all in
all, he looked like a person life had treated well. With my father loung-
ing comfortably in it, that kitschy chair all at once seemed dignified. I
was glad I hadn't tossed it out. But I wasn't so glad to see my father.

"How did you find this place?"

"I went to the hospital in Iri where you used to work, and they told
me."

"Wouldn't I be somewhere doing just fine? Why wander about
looking for me? Especially when your health isn't so good . . . "

In reality, I knew nothing about my father's health. Whenever they
broached the subject of my marriage, my brothers threatened me until

my ears stung: father wouldn't live forever and I ought to stop worrying him and just get married while he was still alive. So I had simply come to assume that my father wouldn't live too long. Well before that, I always felt I'd soon be an orphan because I was the youngest child and had lost my mother at an early age. Yet my father never directly told me he wanted me to marry before he died. He was not the kind of person to meddle selfishly with his children's destiny.

"It's a good location for a clinic." Once again, my father was granting his approval of something I had already begun.

"Not really, it's a slum." I concealed my grand design and feigned ignorance.

"A poor neighborhood is bound to have more sick people, eh? Don't ever think about making money with that hard-earned skill. Since ancient times, medicine has been considered a humanitarian art, so you must practice it with compassion."

I bit my lip to suppress the laugh surging up my throat. Not a soul would ever be able to guess my secret. Not that episode in the past, not my objectives for the future, not the anguish storming in my heart right now . . .

Soon my father was ready to leave.

"Wait a moment," I said, stopping him.

How he construed my stopping him I don't know, but he said not to trouble myself, for he didn't want to eat. I had not held him there to feed him. It was just that I immensely enjoyed the sight of him in that chair. At that moment, I thought I could understand why people took portraits of their children or their parents, and treasured them. I couldn't snap a picture of him just then, but even now I have that image vividly etched in my heart, the way he looked — a little tired but nonetheless dignified, his eyes profound and quiet.

My father sat there a little while longer. Looking shy as an adolescent, he took out a gift he had brought. Then he left, saying he had to make it to Taejŏn, where my eldest brother lived, that same day. The next time I saw my father he was on his deathbed.

The gift he gave me that day was a framed copy of the Hippocratic oath. When I opened it, the same sort of laughter I had stifled as my father sat in that chair spouting nonsense about medicine and humanitarianism burst out freely. I did not hang his gift on the wall, but I didn't have the heart to throw it out that same day and ended up sticking it in a closet. Over the intervening thirty years I have not moved even once, but the clinic has undergone major renovations five or six times, not to mention the semiannual cleanings, and I wonder whether it is still around. Apart from that one time when my father sat in it, the velvet chair has remained a useless eyesore. It did not and does not fit in. During renovations and cleanings, it has been a minor nuisance and has been treated as such. Maybe I haven't been able to get rid of it because I felt I'd have to hang up the Hippocratic Oath if the chair were no longer there.

As chance would have it, my first patient was the daughter of the landlord, Mr. Hwang. Until then, Hwang had lived by himself. From the clinic's north window, the inner yard of his house was plainly visible. Hwang would wash rice and do his laundry in the front yard framed by his shabby, L-shaped house with a tiled roof. The large living room and crock stand as well as the kitchenware were unmistakable signs he had once had a good-sized family. His wife was said to have been killed in an air raid during the war while coming back from her parent's house; both of his sons were captured and taken to the North; his aged mother had passed away from an illness; and his only daughter had taken refuge in the countryside and never returned.

Nobody knew when the daughter came back, but late one night Hwang came to my clinic asking for a house call. He was in a rush and his body shook violently. His house was right next door but I couldn't go out in my nightgown, so I quickly threw on some clothes. Even for that short wait, Hwang couldn't hide his impatience, constantly getting up and sitting back down, opening and closing the door, all the while muttering in a shaking voice, as if trying to explain.

"Doctor, can't you hurry, please? Her condition looks grave. I don't know what's wrong with her, but it's awful — her stomach is all bloated, she can't lie still, says the pain is too much — I think something terrible will happen soon. You said you treat all kinds of ailments, right? If people find out later an unmarried girl's been to a women's clinic, she'll be shamed, first of all . . . Damn bitch! Running away all alone, scared of nothing. Abandoning her father to save herself, and now the girl has picked up that awful disease, God knows where . . . Doctor, if I lose one more of my own flesh and blood, I'll surely die, too. Doctor, you do treat all kinds of diseases, right? Once the word gets out an unmarried girl has gone to a woman's hospital, . . . but doctor, I beg you, please, save my wretched daughter. If I lose one more of my own flesh and blood, it'll be the end of me."

He kept running his mouth, mumbling confusedly. I was itching to tease Hwang: there he was desperately depending on me; yet the fact that he was in a women's clinic was revolting to him, as if he was gripping a lifeline covered with shit. Old Hwang's daughter was my first patient, but I was not nervous at all. In fact I was quite calm. I dressed myself fully, even put on my white smock and scrubbed my hands.

Already packed in my bag were all the instruments needed for a delivery. Hwang snatched up the bag with his shaking hands and ran down the staircase. From his house came a woman's ghastly screams, like the shrieks of an animal having its throat slit.

The girl was writhing in the main bedroom, biting her already bruised lips relentlessly. She glared at me, clutching the waist of her drawers as if her life depended on it. Her sweat-drenched hair clung to her face and the eyes looking out from that face shone with a loneliness and pain too pure to be called human. Her water had broken some time before and her drawers were drenched. I pushed Hwang to her pillowside and pulled her drawers down. My mouth was so parched I couldn't speak.

After losing her drawers, the girl flailed her arms about a couple of times in the air and then clutched her father's trousers. Parturition was well advanced: her birth canal had opened uncontrollably, like an overripe chestnut.

Hwang hollered something unintelligible and collapsed onto the floor. The girl grabbed his waist and bellowed like a wild beast. The baby's head popped out, but then stopped coming. Shockingly, it opened its eyes amid the chaos. It was no fetus but a full-term baby. Startled by an enveloping sense of dread, I ordered the girl to push hard one more time. My voice sounded to me like a stranger's, fresh and imposing, heard for the first time.

The girl bellowed once more, and I proceeded to pull the baby out. I took care of the afterbirth skillfully and efficiently, like a veteran midwife. It was a textbook delivery, not so much thanks to my skill or experience, but more as though the birth proceeded smoothly under the guidance of some superior force. The baby was a boy.

Afterward, I went back to my place on the second floor and slept soundly until morning. I was cooking breakfast and singing by an open window when Hwang appeared. Overnight, he had visibly aged and his appearance was disheveled. His eyes were downcast and his shoulders seemed totally drained of energy.

"The mother and the baby are fine, right?"

"I've no courage to look you in the face."

"Now do you see? Why there should be women's clinics?"

"God was punishing me for bad-mouthing women's clinics."

"What do you mean 'punishing'? You have a grandson now! Some baby, too. His head was only half out and he gazed right at me with eyes wide open. Warrior material, he is. Just you wait and see."

I kept babbling, excited for no reason. Hwang raised his downcast eyes. They were like caverns, deeply recessed and devoid of spirit.

"What's to be done about this disgrace? Doctor, my daughter doesn't even know who the father is. No matter how much I scold her and vow to force the father, whoever he is, even if he's a snot-nosed degenerate, to marry her, she just keeps on weeping. Then, all of a sudden, she tells me she was raped. Raped . . . by some cur she can't even name!"

Hwang was trembling with fury and grief. I thought I caught a fleeting whiff of lust in his rage. Nauseated, I grimaced. All men are capable of rape. To me it didn't matter who the man was or what his name might be: All that mattered was that he was a man.

"Can there be such shame as this? My family already is in ruins, and this wretched daughter of mine somehow survives, but only to besmirch our family name. It's an outrage. . . ." He went on and on in this vein.

I knew nothing about how well-known his family may once have been. All I knew was that he seemed to care only about the stain on that invisible pedigree, and not at all about the living hell his daughter must have endured carrying an unwanted baby.

"Doctor, won't you help me, please?!"

With obsequiousness added to grief, he became even more unbearable.

"Sorry, but putting the baby back into the womb is beyond my power."

I was truly sorry I could come up with nothing more cruel to say to him.

"Doctor, even I know that much. What I meant was . . . "

He failed to finish his sentence, but a glint of mischief brightened his face. It struck me as quite incongruous, given his tactless manner and farmer-like attitude. It made me uneasy. Searching for the motive behind that glint, I locked my eyes onto his. He avoided my gaze as if it blinded him, and rubbed his hands together.

"That's not what I meant . . . Doctor, if you just pretend you know nothing about this, then there's a very good way out. I am going to trust you. It came out to live and I can't just choke it to death — that's not a thing for a man to do . . . "

"Mr. Hwang, what do you mean by a 'good way out'?"

"Of course, of course, I'll tell you! At least my wretched daughter knows what shame is and luckily she returned in the middle of the night. She hasn't met or seen anyone. So, what I'm saying is, we can just pretend she hasn't come back at all, and I'll adopt the baby as my son."

"Your son?"

I was at a loss to respond to this bizarre idea.

"Yes, I just need to raise a ruckus about adopting a foundling! My daughter can hide herself in the back of the house and then appear after she recovers. There'll be no need to explain anything. It'll just be as if she has returned from her refuge."

"Did your daughter agree to this?"

"Can a girl like that have any say in anything? Letting her and her son live is enough for her."

"But it's still your daughter's life we're talking about."

"What about the fact that the bitch is my daughter and this baby is my grandson?"

He protested like a schoolboy, insisting his way was the only thing to do. Realizing his predicament, he cowered again to beseech me to go along, unsure what to do next.

"What sort of unwanted hindrance am I to this spontaneous and perfect scheme of his?" I asked myself, feeling a little intimidated.

"If your daughter agrees, it seems a very good plan for dodging the dishonor you face."

So, I ended up consenting to his scheme.

"No matter what happened, how could I cook up something like this just to escape shame? In a family with no one to carry on its name, a newborn is like a blossom on an ancient tree. If I did adopt a foundling, who wouldn't regard it as a cause for celebration? And won't my daughter raise her child with devotion, whether she thinks of her son as her brother or her brother as her son? And once a respectable man comes along, and I marry her off, who'll know the inside story?"

He seemed intoxicated that he had cleverly managed to transform last night's nightmare into an incredible blessing. His face had a healthy glow, and he virtually beamed with gratitude at life's unfathomable capriciousness.

"If only you can close your eyes to everything . . . "

His eyes were downcast as he spoke, but I could see those eyes were not the same dens of despair as before. Also, I imagined he might strangle me if I refused to agree to "close my eyes to everything." He looked duplicitous rather than violent, but, mindful that men are capable of much in their quests for gratification, I reluctantly promised to close my eyes to everything. If the truth be told, there seemed no better way to cope with the situation for the baby and the mother, as well as for Hwang. Possibly their wily and neat reversal of fortune left me jealous.

Once I gave him my promise, Hwang, repeatedly kowtowing, took out a wad of cash.

"How can money possibly repay you for saving two lives last night? I'll try to repay you little by little over time, but for now, please accept this as a token of appreciation."

And he rushed from the room. I counted the money after he left. It was at least three times the normal fee for delivering a baby. It must have been intended as hush money, too. Once again, I felt an inexplicable sense of jealousy at their sudden change of luck. Then I spit on that money as merchants in the marketplace do on the first income they earn. It was my first pay, a handsome sum for my first day's work, but I had no plan to deliver babies ever again. From the outset I had counted on the wantonness of the neighborhood. Though I was setting up an obstetrics clinic, I hadn't even thought of installing a delivery bed and other necessary equipment. I had simply resolved to profit from the wantonness around me.

My intuitions upon first entering the neighborhood had not been wrong. Prostitutes catering to the American soldiers began to arrive one by one. Before long I was performing several abortions a day, and in time I became an expert in the field. If all the babies I prevented from emerging into this world had lived, would another good-sized elementary school have been needed? Perhaps they would populate a small town? Yet, almost never did I indulge in such pointless sentimentality. If any sentimentalism plagued me, it had to do with that velvet chair under the south window. I couldn't rid myself of it. As the chair gracefully aged, it clashed more and more with the atmosphere of the clinic. The nurses who came and went through the years clamored for it to be thrown away. I trusted these nurses enough to let them handle my household affairs, but that wish was one I couldn't grant them.

If I got rid of the chair, I would feel bound to hang the Hippocratic oath on the wall, but it had long since vanished. In truth, I could have discarded the chair without hanging up the Hippocratic oath. But if I had done this, no longer would I have been able to gaze at the chair to conjure up the image of my foppish father clad in white with his pointy-toed, shiny, black shoes. That chair belonged solely to my father. I could not get rid of the chair for a reason: I could not casually erase that sad face my father wore as he looked at his daughter who, instead of becoming a doctor, had become a kind of a medical technician using her skills in the service of decadence. For me, the chair aroused feelings that went beyond the fondness one feels toward a dead father.

Almost thirty years passed while I repeated the same routine in the same place. The neighborhood changed a lot during that time. Now it was more urban than suburban, and the prostitutes who had serviced the military camp were long gone. The air of wantonness that first drew me to the neighborhood persisted for quite a while, even after the prostitutes moved on.

For two or three years after the government's return to Seoul, the agricultural school remained a military camp. After the school reverted to its normal function, the sleaziness of the area deepened, thanks to another, bigger military base in the vicinity. Even after the American troop presence was dramatically reduced, the dissolute atmosphere was not easily lifted; instead it lingered in the form of a cheap red-light district. Due to recent police crackdowns on prostitution in residential areas, my customers were more dispersed, but even from afar they continued to visit me and their loyalty generated other customers. Moreover, with the population control policy encouraging families to limit the number of children to two regardless of gender, hardly any of the housewives in the neighborhood were not in my debt.

The agricultural school across the street shut down and sold its land to a construction company. An apartment complex now stands in its place. For some reason, no new customers have come to my clinic from that densely populated area. Whether I liked it or not, my clientele mainly came from the old neighborhood behind the Kyŏngsŏng building. Among these humble housewives and among pimps and prostitutes scattered about the city, I acquired a reputation as a reliable and affordable doctor. This reputation of mine is well deserved, because in all those years not once did I encounter any grave mishaps. The class of women who required my service on a regular basis naturally sought value for their money, preferring dependability and affordability over pompous academic degrees or luxurious facilities.

To say I experienced not a single mishap that was my fault perhaps bends the truth slightly. If there were a few accidents, I took care of them quickly before anyone noticed, smoothing them over as if nothing had gone amiss. And fortunately, all problems were settled according to my expectations, without escalating into anything unmanageable.

On my hand are three big calluses, deeply rooted, at the spots where I grip the curette and mirror. These calluses are tangible proof of my having killed enough people to populate a town. Even after I was experienced enough to perform the procedure with my eyes closed, I kept on making one mistake after another. More than ten times, I've committed what doctors consider the most horrendous mistake — puncturing the uterus. The source of the problem was the very fact that I could perform the procedure with my eyes closed. In truth, the procedure does not require a doctor's eyes. Even the best physicians cannot visualize the miraculous intricacies within a human body designed by life itself. What needs eyes is the curette. To keep the curette's eyes open, the doctor holding it must stay alert at all times. If the doctor's mind wanders, the curette goes blind.

Like someone accidentally puncturing a ripe cherry, you say, "Oh no!" as you feel the instrument take an unexpected plunge, and your mind rushes back to where it should have been all along. You lose awareness of your mind when it's elsewhere, but when it returns it momentarily becomes tangible like an object. This fleeting but cruel physicality often made me feel hateful. Yes, that's how it's been. I've done my job, driven by malicious hatred. To finish the procedure successfully, not even for an instant can I do without my hatred, not only for the woman lying there on the table holding her foul-smelling vagina up in front of me like a face, but also for the unwanted life within. This hatred was necessary, too, for me to handle mistakes quickly and efficiently. Once my mind returned and took perfect control, I dealt with each mistake promptly and coldly. Outwardly, I showed no sign of disturbance. My face neither blushed nor grew pale. Still more calmly than usual I would finish up the abortion, give the patient an injection of antibiotics, feed her some medicine to aid contraction, and help her relax by describing the procedure: "The scraping was difficult because the womb is deeper than usual. You may experience some pain, but try to tolerate it," and so forth. There is always plenty to say. A uterus is as easily punctured as an overripe cherry, but a human body is not a picked fruit. It heals itself naturally. So far, not even one of the punctured wombs has developed peritonitis or other serious complications. In the end, there was never any evidence of anything having gone awry.

However, I was weak enough to suffer symptoms of overexhaustion afterward. Whenever such mishaps occurred, for a time I lost all will to go on working. But I always came back to the job, telling myself I had to keep at it until I turned fifty-five. The age fifty-five had no special significance. I guess I just unconsciously adopted the retirement age mandated for government officials or bank clerks.

Three days from now, I turn fifty-five. As it happens, the Kyŏngsŏng building is set to be demolished not later than that same day pursuant to the urban renewal laws. For thirty years I've faithfully saved my earnings. Now I can retire to a comfortable and abundant life, perhaps even do some leisurely traveling around the world. Unlike government jobs, my profession has no mandatory retirement age, and I signed no contract requiring retirement at age fifty-five. Even so, I have no intention of prolonging my career. A pretty house with a big yard in a quiet residential neighborhood has already been renovated and is waiting for me to move in. I have rental income from buildings I own. My retirement annuities are all paid up, and I can expect a nice annual income from that source. I own stocks and bonds. From here on out, I don't need to make any more money, I only need to figure out how to spend what I have before I die.

Be that as it may, I feel hopelessly agitated by the fact that only three days of work are left. There is one thing I've been wanting to do before retiring. I want to deliver another baby. My first patient was a woman in labor. Since then, I've not delivered a single live baby. In the early days I purposely avoided delivering babies and so became known as an abortionist. Back then, women did drop in from time to time for advice on childbearing and I even referred them to a midwife in the neighborhood, but such requests came less and less often and finally ceased. Now there is no chance any woman will ask me to deliver her baby.

For two months now, nevertheless, I've been counting down the time: sixty days, fifty days ... ten days, nine days, all the while nervously waiting for the impossible to transpire. Now only three days are left. The more I tell myself it will never happen, the more uncontrollable my wish becomes, driving me almost mad. When I recall my first patient and the baby she successfully delivered with my aid, I realize how utterly inexperienced I was, a neophyte compared to what

I am today. But still I see myself back then as my ideal self, the self that's always ahead of me, that I may never again reach even if I keep moving onward until the end of my life. Maybe I'm already senile: Time is playing tricks on my mind . . .

Only three days left. Only three days . . .

The desperate wish to deliver a baby, which I've entertained from the moment I saw that Manduk's wife was in her last month of pregnancy, remains unfulfilled. Only three days are left in which to fulfill it.

Manduk is Mr. Hwang's grandson, the first and the only baby I ever delivered. After imploring me to keep my mouth shut, Hwang went around spreading a story that the baby was a foundling. The nameless infant at first was known to intrigued neighbors only as "the foundling." Later, it was generally agreed that it would be best for Hwang to adopt him formally, making him a legal heir to carry on the family name. Hwang, who all along had planned to do so, adopted the child after hesitating with feigned misgivings, and gave him the name "Manduk," meaning "late-begotten son." He beseeched everyone never again to utter the word "foundling." Soon after Hwang adopted Manduk, the daughter reappeared, ostensibly returning from her refuge in the countryside. Although she could not nurse the baby, she reared her new "brother" devotedly, earning praise from the neighbors. After raising the boy for five years, she was thought to be at risk of becoming an old maid, and so Hwang quickly married her off to a childless widower. She now has sons and daughters and lives happily. Thus, everything went according to Hwang's scenario. What was my role in Mr. Hwang's play? Asking myself this, at times I felt like moving away, as Hwang no doubt wished I would, but my clinic was prospering more and more with each passing day.

Mr. Hwang grew old, turning into a stubborn, stingy, and always suspicious old man, nicknamed "Miser Hwang." Manduk grew up to be a tall, extravagant, and often profligate young man. Meanwhile, neighbors came and went, and these days nobody doubts that Manduk is Hwang's own son, raised by a father whose elderly wife died shortly after giving birth.

It may have been because I knew the inside story, but to me the alternating love and hate Hwang showed toward Manduk as he was growing up were too extreme. He was too indulgent in regard to Manduk's bad habits, which should have been corrected early on — eating between meals, complaining about food, an ill-mannered way of speaking. Hwang never reproached the boy for such bad behavior, but if Manduk brought home a test scored 100, Hwang would try to beat a confession out of him that he had cheated. On the other hand, when Manduk showed improvement on his report card, Hwang would accuse him of forging the grades, reducing the child to tears. More than once, Manduk even ran away from home for a few days. When such things happened, Hwang's daughter would come back from her in-laws' place, surreptitiously rant and cry for a while, then return to her husband. Old Hwang appeared to be torturing himself by seeing in Manduk first his daughter's blood and then the blood of his daughter's rapist. The Mr. Hwang whom I first met, had seemed healthy and kind-hearted, deteriorated into a suspicious, miserly, and melancholy man. His reversal of fortune had not been perfect. Even I, once so jealous of his good luck, felt sympathy.

Even as a child Manduk was wasteful, and it hardly helped that his mother, unable to reveal that she was his mother, expressed her love by spoiling him with lots of pocket money. When he grew up, completed his military service, and started working, he became even more of a spendthrift. Instead of telling people how much he himself earned per year, Manduk bragged about the annual exports of the company that employed him. As if he were not an entry-level clerk, but the principal shareholder of the company, Manduk gloated over the company's profits, seeming to think they justified his personal spending. Hwang not only showed contempt for Manduk, but watched him like a thief. The old man himself lived like a penniless vagrant, saving money by skimping on food and clothes, and refusing to recognize that the human body has its limits. When he looked at the grown-up Manduk, his eyes no longer displayed any trace of affection. Old Hwang now seemed to see Manduk only as the offspring of the lowlife who raped his daughter.

Hwang's twisted outlook did not end with Manduk. If Manduk boasted that his company's annual export sales amounted to several hundred thousand dollars, old Hwang disdainfully quoted a multiple of the figure as the company's foreign debt. He kept informed about many things, perusing daily newspapers borrowed from my clinic, but somehow he always knew more about foreign loans than about export revenues, and more about why some people were poor and miserable than about why others lived well. He always knew more shady news than sunny news. He fastened on the dark side of everything, not just Manduk, and he grew old like that, gloomy and grim.

It was only natural, consequently, for Manduk to leave his father's house as soon as he was old enough to support himself. Nobody could tell whether Manduk's departure was a shock to old Hwang. By that point, it seemed impossible for Hwang to be any more miserable than he already was.

Two months ago, Manduk came back home with a woman in the last month of pregnancy. Old Hwang neither welcomed them nor shooed them away. He wanted to know just one thing: Were the two of them married?

"Dad, I may be an undutiful son, but do you think I could have had a wedding ceremony without inviting you? Gosh, do you really take me for such an ungrateful, damnable creature? Yes, I am really hurt you think so badly of me."

Manduk played dumb and did his best to look dejected. Hwang must not have forgotten the shock his daughter gave him when she appeared with that ripe chestnut of a swollen belly, nearly spilling the baby on the spot, for he hastened to make marriage arrangements. About his future daughter-in-law — her family background, age, occupation, etc. — he asked no questions. He just booked space in a dilapidated wedding hall on the second floor of a supermarket and then rented a yellowed wedding gown for the bride-to-be. Manduk insisted he wanted a big wedding at a fancy hotel after the child was born, with both families and all the friends in attendance, but he could not prevail over old Hwang's obstinacy. Only a few neighbors who knew the story behind the marriage were invited.

The wedding hall seemed cavernously big and cold. Above all, the bride's wedding gown was a spectacle too embarrassing to behold. Hwang had rented the largest size that was available, but the zipper in the back could not be pulled all the way up. The gown was held together with a safety pin, but a gap wider than a hand revealed the bride's slip underneath. Even by old Hwang's abysmal standards, the fiasco of a wedding was botched. Cheerful and affable, Manduk nevertheless humored the guests, saying it was only a warm-up and they could expect the main event soon.

"Such insolent scum! If you can't mind your mouth, you should at least mind your prick, and if you can't mind your prick, then at least mind your mouth. Doesn't he know he's shamed us because his prick and his mouth both are indiscreet? Tut, tut, it's a sure sign our family's headed for ruin."

Listening to old Hwang's abuse, I began wondering if the whole wedding had not been staged just to embarrass Manduk. In any case, it was a rare spectacle, one of a kind. Everybody giggled and gossiped. But when I saw the bride's swollen belly nearly bursting the waist dart of the gown, my heart fluttered with a sudden longing to deliver that baby with my own hands. Even when the wedding ended, this notion stayed with me the rest of the day. My heart was in the grip of this longing, this desire to see the clear and innocent eyes of a newborn baby stare at me again.

Even though I had done nothing but abortions for the past thirty years, I thought old Hwang would let me deliver the baby if only I asked. I even considered offering to do it for free or for less than my usual fee, given his stinginess. But when I mentioned it, Hwang flatly refused, and even aimed an unspeakably cruel remark my way.

"Stop talking nonsense, will you? However desperate I get, do you think I'd rely on a butcher of humans to deliver my first grandchild?"

As if that were not enough, he grimaced repulsively. He looked like he wanted to throw salt at me. If you're in my line of work for long, the pimps who escort their girls to the clinic begin to treat you like a close chum. They say "Hey, you," slapping you on the back, instead of addressing you as "doctor." They seemed to think I was in the same business they were, making a living by trafficking in women's sex. Still, I didn't really mind their attitude. I was as friendly to them as they were to me. But for old Hwang to call me a butcher of humans hurt like a spike hammered into my heart.

Three days after the wedding, Manduk's wife gave birth to a healthy boy at a general hospital. Despite the painful insult from old Hwang, I went to see the baby once the mother and child came home from the hospital. The boy was the spitting image of the first baby I delivered. I was fiercely envious of the nameless and faceless physician who had delivered him. I felt the burning desire to deliver a baby, which had been briefly suppressed by old Hwang's insult, revive in me stronger than ever. Manduk's baby was not the only baby in the world; surely I would deliver another baby before quitting this job. So I told myself.

That was when my countdown began; but back then more than sixty days were left. It seemed impossible that not even one woman would surface wanting her baby delivered. Sixty days, fifty days . . . ten days, nine days . . . and now only three days left.

The third-from-last day is like any other day. I have had three abortion patients and two venereal disease patients today — and that's it. I go downstairs. The old Kyŏngsŏng Company that once sold farm implements is now a grocery store. The sign still reads "Kyŏngsŏng Company," but the old Chinese characters have been rewritten in Korean, due to a ban on the use of Chinese for signs. The words "Seoul Grocery" written in Roman letters under the Korean name seem to bespeak Manduk's playful touch. This makes me smile.

"Give me a yogurt."

Old Hwang glances up briefly from the newspaper he is reading and hands me a large yogurt from the refrigerator. I do not much care for yogurt, but the easiest way to reach the Hwangs' house out back is to go through the store, so I buy it as a toll and drink up. Old Hwang is sitting sideways. The veins in his neck are hideously prominent, and white stubble frosts his chin. I feel a lump of pity in my heart as I note that he has aged a lot recently. This lump is a cluster of both disaffection and fondness accumulated over thirty years, the inevitable bond I feel with someone who has shared the same building with me for so long.

Old Hwang, sitting sideways, murmurs, "It's the end of the world, the end of the world," without lifting his eyes from the newspaper. For him, not a day passes that doesn't foreshadow the end of the world. He sees the apocalypse everywhere and always: He sees not his daughter but his daughter's rapist in Manduk; he knows import figures better than export figures; he is an authority on increases in our national debt rather than on improvements in our living standards; and he sees only the shadows in the hearts that drive our lives.

This peculiar attitude of old Hwang does make him seem more formidable and more principled than his thoughtless neighbors, who start dancing whenever they hear a drum, without a clue as to what the drumbeat meant. But just as I cannot claim to know more about the nature of women than others do because I know more about their sex than their faces, old Hwang's focus on the dark side of life does not necessarily mean he knows more about the world than anybody else. I try to empathize with old Hwang, even contriving this ridiculous logic to excuse him.

"The baby's getting big now, right?"

Signaling that I am going in to see the baby, I head to the back of the building where his house is. Manduk's wife is the kind of woman who smiles easily. She flashes grins while boasting about her baby, while complaining about her husband, and even while talking about her irksome father-in-law. Perhaps because of the mother, the baby, too, smiles easily. His lips loosen and part in a smile whenever he makes eye contact. I have come there to assuage my longing to deliver a baby, but the visit only makes it worse. If I retired without satisfying this wish, I would be miserable the rest of my life. But after today, only two more days are left. Only two more days.

2. Two Days Left

A horrid dream. The calluses on my hand become malignant, and tumors spread all over my skin. As I struggle to wake from this nightmare, I think I hear a legion of midsummer night frogs croaking in a chorus. It is the same croaking I had heard as I struggled, long ago, to break free from the overwhelming smell of armpits, the thick chest hair, the long and muscular limbs binding me, and the bulk of a massive body pressing down on me like a boulder — the assault had come from all sides at once. At that moment, the sound of frogs croaking was so peaceful, so detached from the war waged by men, that it made what was happening to me seem unreal, driving my consciousness into a dreamlike haze of oblivion.

Today, unlike that time, I awake gradually due to the croaking I hear in the twilight between dreaming and waking. First, to reassure myself I've only had a bad dream, I check the calluses on my hand and run my hand down my breasts, stomach, and thighs under the nightgown. This is the body of a woman who has borne no children in her fifty-five years: The plump, aging flesh is soft and without resilience, but not coarse or unpleasant to the touch. Those calluses . . . they are only calluses, and will vanish in a few months once I stop working. Still I am uneasy. A ridiculous thought haunts me, suffocates me. Maybe the calluses that in the dream became tumors pervading my whole body are not the calluses on my hand, but calluses rooted in my heart. I open the bedroom window, driven by an old habit. The faint croaking of the frogs suddenly grows louder, as though amplified through a speaker, and floods into the room.

It is the wailing of people attending an early morning service at a new church nearby. The people at that church wail like that every day. Whenever I hear it, I feel in my heart a longing to howl mournfully, but at the same time I am certain not a single tear will issue from my eyes. It's still before dawn. The neighborhood around the Kyŏngsŏng Company is submerged in ultramarine darkness.

Only two more days left. Only two days . . . my first thought, once I fully awake, is that only two days remain before I'll be moving. The chance to deliver a breathing baby is now limited to two days.

Facing the south window with the velvet chair are my living quarters and a consultation room that doubles as a surgery room. Both from my living quarters and from the consultation room, I can readily look out on the L-shaped and rectangular roofs cluttering the dilapidated neighborhood. The dazzling development of Seoul is now a cliché that nobody with eyes to see and ears to hear can dispute, but somehow this neighborhood, where my patients have moved in and out, has not changed much since I first opened my clinic. The flimsy tile-roofed houses, built late in the Japanese occupation when good materials were very scarce, are neither Korean nor Western in style. Nowadays they look so run down, overcrowded, and squalid that not even renters who own little in the way of furnishings are likely to envy their owners. Nor is that all. Because the neighborhood slopes down a grade from a street lined with two- and three-story buildings like Kyŏngsŏng toward a filthy sewer that was left open until only ten years ago, the area almost always floods during the summer rains.

It is not possible to get a permit to raze and rebuild dwellings because the lots are so small, less than thirty *p'yŏng** each. Anyone who amasses a bit of money promptly moves out of the neighborhood. Of course, it would be possible to demolish several adjacent houses and build a large house on the merged lot, but what would be the point of constructing a nice villa in a seamy shantytown? Nobody feels enough of an attachment to the neighborhood to do something so foolish. And so, in this neighborhood, talk of the affluence and abundance of the rest of Korea is little more than hearsay. But how fortunate to be able to hear such rumors.

Outwardly, everyone appears to be living a comfortable enough life. Having heard the hearsay, each knows how to simulate a life of comfort. Just as Manduk justifies his lavish spending by quoting his company's export revenues, and just as some people dance at the first sound of a drum without caring why it is beating, they all live well with no practical worries. First and foremost, just noticing that the underclothes and private parts of housewives have become as clean as

---

**P'yŏng:* One *p'yŏng* is equal to 3.3 square meters.

those of prostitutes makes me realize how much the standard of living has improved over the years.

A chaste woman may be appalled at having her sex compared to that of a whore, but I am only talking here about outward appearances. Common sense dictates that a chaste woman's sex is clean and a prostitute's dirty, but your eyes and your nose will tell you the opposite on close examination. The sex of some prostitutes is as clean and virginal as an idiot's face. On the other hand, the more virtuous a woman believes herself to be, the more shameless she is about the unhygienic condition of her sex. Perhaps there is an analogy to the fact that the living room is the cleanest part of any house.

With the decline of prostitution in the neighborhood, the most conspicuous change has been the growth in the number of churches. It is true that the neighborhood is densely populated. The local district office is so crowded one normally has to stand in line to do anything, but the area represented is not that large. There are at least seven new churches in the neighborhood. When I first settled here, there was not a single church. As soon as one church is established, others follow and they develop rapidly in size and in number of members. The only prosperity in our district that is more than hearsay is that of the churches. Although all seven churches evidently uphold the same Jesus Christ, they seem to be of distinct denominations, with different signs and symbols. Members seem to transfer back and forth among the churches, but none of the seven seem to suffer from a lack of parishioners. I don't know the denomination of the newest church, but people gather there at dawn each day, begin by mourning in a great collective wail, then clap their hands and sing hymns in ecstatic voices, praising the glory of God in unison before the service ends. This must be the ritual for that denomination. From the point of view of non-Christian neighbors, it is not exactly a desirable way to conduct a service. Yet, the collective wailing at daybreak has been getting louder day by day, so the membership of that church certainly seems to be growing steadily. More than half are women. So they are my clients as well. What is it that they yearn for when they cry like that? Whence springs all that tedious wailing day in and day out? When they come to me, pregnant with an unwanted baby, most wear a face of absolute despair, like someone wanting to drop dead. After the fetus is safely and absolutely eliminated, all at once their faces become carefree and refreshed. My ability to excise their agony without leaving even the smallest residue is truly miraculous. I can do this only because I harbor in my own heart the deepest loathing for such pain imposed on women. I am the savior who frees them from that agony.

But every single morning they disturb my sleep with their anguished laments. What in the name of God is the further agony that makes them cry like that? Not even God can be as skillful as I, who pluck out their agony and show it to them. Even so, churches proliferate and flourish.

Once I asked one of my steady clients, who went from one church to another, what was the source of these churches' prosperity. I didn't mean to embarrass her; I just hoped she could tell me something about the distinctiveness of the denominations. She said she had gone to the previous church hoping to cure herself of chronic neuralgia, after hearing a rumor that the church could cure various diseases. She had then moved to her current church hoping her husband would earn more money because, as rumor had it, this church improved your luck and brought you wealth. If this is typical, then what sort of promise does the church where people wail hold out to those people who lament each morning?

"Dear heavenly Father, though they swear a hundred times to believe in You, do not believe them. They mouth their longing for You, saying dear God, my Father, but I know what their lower half longs for and what sins they have committed."

I even have the temerity to brag to the one they beseech with their loud cries. Still, that sunrise wailing of theirs makes me think there may be a hard, encrusted lump of lamentation in the deep recesses of my own heart.

As the early morning darkness gradually lifts like a curtain, the first things to reveal themselves here and there are church steeples. The houses are still submerged in the milky fog of darkness. The view from the window is like a misty ocean and the church steeples look like the masts of sinking ships. The lamentation turns into a desperate bickering. It is the noise of passengers on those sinking ships fighting each other to climb to the top of the mast. Yet there is no one at the top of the mast. All the fighting must be preventing anyone from claiming the top. Whether or not the passengers reach the top, the outcome will be no different. The ship will sink just the same.

The darkness is fading, revealing hazy outlines of the L-shaped and rectangular roofs hovering in the brightening sky. I think I see a person atop one of the masts, but it is only a cross.

Only two days left. The second to last day brightens rapidly.

My first customer is a prostitute named Hwa Yŏng who routinely comes for VD treatment. She doesn't live in my neighborhood, but I still have quite a few prostitutes as patients, women who are steered to my clinic by their pimps.

Madame Chun, a procuress I've long known, has come along with the prostitute on this day. Madame Chun has aged a lot, unlike old Hwang. Her aging has left her badly blotched and wrinkled, and I feel pity and embarrassment at her appearance. Outwardly, however, I am unfeeling and brusque.

After telling Hwa Yŏng to lie down on the examination table, I stick my head into the waiting room and bluntly call out to Madame Chun, "My, my, what brings you here, Madame Chun? Gee, girls must be getting awfully scarce. Looks like Hwa Yŏng is your best bet for a cash register nowadays?"

"No. You don't think I came here out of curiosity about that bitch's cunt? Doctor, I heard you're closing down this business of yours tomorrow."

"Yes. And that saddens you, does it?"

"Why, yes, I'm no wooden statue like you. Sad, but I envy you, too. When will I be able to quit this damn business and have an easy life?"

Madame Chun is smoking. She lets out a deep sigh. The purple nail polish on her fleshy hands looks unclean and pathetic.

"What have you done with all your money, to be crying now?"

I spit out those words and slam the waiting room door. Madame Chun is a prostitute turned procuress who has been my steady customer since the old days when the agricultural school was a camp for American troops. She is indebted to me in many ways, and all along has sent her girls to me faithfully regardless of where they lived. A longtime customer, she still addresses me with respect as "doctor" instead of using more familiar speech, but unmistakable in the way she calls her work and mine alike "this business" is her conviction that we are both in the same line of work.

After the examination and treatment, Hwa Yŏng asks how soon she can resume "business."

"You can start working again tomorrow, but shall I use this as an excuse for you to rest a few more days?"

"No, no, can't do that. I'm loyal. As it is, I'm really sorry to have missed work for so many days, for Mother's sake."

"Is that so? Then why not be loyal to your Mother and start working again tomorrow?"

My words spew out as if I am spitting.

"Doctor, a Mother like mine is hard to find."

She defends the pimp as she pulls her panties up her slim legs. She wears gaudy makeup, but her natural face is plain. The way she takes off her underwear and spreads her legs wide on the examination table is extremely refined: it exudes a gracefulness found only in professionals. I think of her as beautiful.

When the three of us gather in the waiting room, a kind of family ambience is created.

"They say the street out front will be doubled in width — what luck for this neighborhood!"

"Of course. Say, Madame Chun, if you'd held onto that house, you'd be rich!"

"Well, why bring up ancient history? It's not the first time I've missed a chance to get rich."

"Mother lost a lot this time, too, Doctor."

"She must have given in to useless greed again."

"Doctor, when have you seen me look sideways at another business? Even when I dig just one well, however it goes, I keep running into trouble. Fate must be warning me to get out of this racket, but it's not like I have any savings."

"What made you so dejected?"

"Well, nothing really. It happens all the time. I put a lot of money into a girl, and she ran off without paying her debt."

"You'll find her eventually; she may even come crawling back to you."

"I could try to find her if I wanted to. If someone whisked her away, I wouldn't just sit still and take it — my nature wouldn't accept that, but she ran away with the one she's been dating as if there's no tomorrow. I have a soft heart, I guess. I can only wish her happiness now."

"You might reach heaven yet, Madame Chun"

"Doctor, you know very well, too, that I have a soft spot for true love . . ." Madame Chun smiles a lonely smile.

"Hwa Yŏng, you'll have to start dating soon . . . just to keep from being left out."

"I can't date because I don't want to be left out."

Though I always feel reluctant at first to join in the sort of family-like banter that is developing, this time I give in and relax. I've known them for so long it is almost inevitable.

"It's not fair to people whose places are to be demolished. If Kyŏngsŏng Company wasn't slated for demolition, doctor, you could keep this business going for ten more years at least."

"No, no, it's not that. I'm calling it quits at just the right time. Since I've already fixed the last day, I don't think I could go on another day even if it kills me to stop it."

"Where is old Hwang planning to go? He's such a miser, he must have a big hoard saved up somewhere . . . "

"His lot is the biggest around here, so he must have gotten a pretty hefty sum when the property was condemned. I hear he's buying a nice house with a storefront and moving everything there as is."

"Well, then. I'll see you again sometime. Now that you're folding up shop, I feel like I'm losing an arm. Draw me a map to your new house. It's all right for me to come and visit you, right?"

"Nope, I'm moving to a respectable neighborhood — you wouldn't have any reason to visit me." Even as I say this, I draw a map.

"I'm in the habit of going where I'm not wanted . . . " Unwilling to give up, Madame Chun replies with a witty rejoinder. She pays for the treatment and leaves with the map.

Only two days left. But the only people who come into my clinic want either a VD treatment or an abortion. Nothing unusual about that. Such is the path I myself treaded and polished bright. It is too late to change the course of destiny. Only two days left. Still I am unable to abandon the hope of delivering a baby with my own hands.

As if to mock that hope of mine, the remnants from the three abortions I have performed on this day are all small fetuses, less than three months old, perfectly preserved in their curled-up forms. Most times, a scraped-out fetus is badly damaged, but this day is strange. The mothers themselves probably do not even know that their fetuses, about the size of fingernails, already have developed most of the features of humans. Only the proportions of the body parts differs from those of a fully developed person: the fetus's head is much larger relative to the body. Surprisingly, even when the head is the size of a pea, two eyes are clearly embedded in it. Perhaps it is so striking because the eyelids have not yet formed and the eyes are open and staring, resembling two flower seeds.

The eyes I have put to death, the seed-sized eyes that never lit up with a thought and never will light up with a thought, all of a sudden gaze piercingly through my past and present, and I shudder. Illumined in minute detail by those staring eyes, my life is more pathetic than a beggar's, and blood is smeared on my hands. How could I fail to understand old Hwang's refusal to let me deliver his grandson?

Do those unliving eyes have an infinite field of vision? They are intruding upon my past, present, and future, upsetting all the beliefs and ideas on which I've relied. A summer night filled with bombs exploding in the distance and the deafening croaks of nearby frogs. The disgrace I endured that night in a weed-choked field is my only excuse for my arrogant self, for having lived well and comfortably without loving any man. The fetuses' eyes mock me now, as though I were no better than a half-wit. Suddenly they transform what I have achieved in this life into an immense loss. As if that were not enough, they belittle my knowledge and my skills: "You're not even a healer, let alone a doctor." For I deal not with patients' suffering, but with my own sense of impurity.

The tiny eyes see through everything — the unforgettable torment in my youth that resurrects itself every time I perform an abortion, and even the secret ecstasy of retaliation I allow myself by avenging that torment with another torment.

In the pleasantly decorated consulting-waiting room, the velvet chair still sits there under the south window. It is as much a thorn in my side today as it has always been. When I brush the now gray and faded velvet against the grain, a bright olive color springs to life, a feeble echo of the dark forest green of thirty years ago. That chair has never fit in my clinic, not when it was dark green, and not now that it has turned olive and gray. Never apart from that one time when my father sat there, that is.

What did my father say as he sat there? "Since ancient times, medicine has been considered a humanitarian art, so you must practice it with compassion." I had to suppress a surge of laughter when he 'said that. Even now, I can hardly keep from smiling. Back then, when my father visited me, I was already planning to use my skill for profit. From time to time I have conjured up the image of my father by staring at that chair, but I've never been troubled by what he said. I have always done as I wished. Still, at times I've suddenly felt that chair had my soul in its grip. Not the soul that has hatred as its essence, but another kind of soul.

184 • PAK WANSŎ

Perhaps that is why I cannot get rid of or even mistreat the useless chair that clashes with the rest of the furniture, and have simply kept it there under the south window. I have decided not to take any of the furniture with me to my new house, but as I stare at that chair, I find myself visualizing the south window in the new house with this chair beneath it.

Only two days left. But for today it is too late to hope for my wish to be fulfilled. Indifferent to my desperate longing, the autumn sun is fading already. As I pace around from room to room, biting my lips for no reason, I find an appalling thing on the table in the examination room. Preserved in a bottle filled with formalin are the three fetuses aborted that day, looking like peas with little sprouting tails. Outraged, I quickly summon the nurse, Miss Choi.

"Miss Choi, what is the meaning of this? Why did you do such a thing? Why?" I demand to know this in a shaking voice. I feel and sound a little afraid, like an easily frightened child.

"Doctor, I didn't do that. Why, it was you who did it a while ago," Miss Choi protests, her eyes widening as if she doubts my sanity.

Miss Choi is not the kind of person who would lie for no reason or indulge in a practical joke. Thinking again, I realize I may indeed have done it. Why? I cannot understand myself. Though it is fascinating to scrutinize an extracted fetus, this is by no means the first time I have performed the surgery. Why did I do it? On the other hand, I recall seeing at a friend's clinic a row of glass jars containing specimen fetuses from each month of pregnancy. It turned my stomach, as though the jars held pickled humans. Now, I am the one who has pickled human beings in my clinic.

"Doctor, should I just throw it away?" Miss Choi asks, lifting up the jar.

"No, no, don't throw it away!" Nearly shouting, I snatch the jar away from her. I have no intention of keeping it or of doing anything in particular with it. I simply do not want to throw it away while fully aware that I am doing so. Until then, I had routinely disposed of aborted fetuses along with ordinary garbage, without realizing I had cast them into the trash. They had been discarded unconsciously, never materializing in my mind as anything but refuse. Why have I made such a preposterous move today? As I place the jar back on the table, I secretly hope that Miss Choi will dispose of it later when I am not looking.

Meantime, self-doubt engulfs me. Why do I get more upset when I do things I myself cannot understand? Perhaps, since the day of that ridiculous wedding when I first felt the urge to deliver a living baby, I've begun breaking away from myself, turning into something not even I myself can comprehend. I resolve to leave myself alone as much as possible. I fear that I may shatter asunder, like mercury that keeps dividing into more globules the more you disturb it.

"Doctor, later can I call that woman from the boutique and the wife of the hardware store owner and let them have this?" Miss Choi asks, studying my face. On a plastic plate she holds are long glistening red strands of something that resembles roe of pollack.

"What's that?"

"Doctor, you sure are acting odd today. What else? Umbilical cords from the abortions you did today."

I see distrust flash across Miss Choi's face. I can bear it when I myself think that I am strange, but I cannot stand having other people think me odd.

"Oh, yes, sure. Those women asked for that, didn't they? Call them. Now, if you want."

I feign a cheerful generosity as I grant Miss Choi's wish. An old wives' tale that umbilical cords are a beauty elixir that slows aging is current among the women in the neighborhood. As a doctor, I cannot say it is a totally unfounded belief, but of course I do not believe that umbilical cords have any of the rumored miraculous effects. Given that youth and beauty largely depend on one's state of mind, I suppose it might help rejuvenation in that respect.

The women who had spread their legs in front of me often enough were uneasy telling me directly about their urge to eat umbilical cords, and so most of them approached Miss Choi instead. Miss Choi would ask me, and then I let them eat the umbilical cords in Miss Choi's room. If they snuck around behind my back with this business, the cords might have spoiled before they could get to them. Also, I wanted to keep money from changing hands. The ones who felt comfortable enough to ask Miss Choi for umbilical cords already had longstanding relationships with me, and they came without hesitation or embarrassment. Those who could not manage to swallow the cord by itself would bring a bottle of *soju* with them, using the liquor to wash it down as if it were raw fish. Ready to try anything to combat aging, these women were bold and shameless even when sober; with a little liquor down the hatch, they soon ended up trading all kinds of vulgar stories.

Through the years, observing those women, I had felt a cruel satisfaction, as if I were witnessing the vileness of women reach a new pinnacle, a loathsomeness different from the way they looked as they lay before me on the examination table, their sex propped up like faces. Feeding them fetal umbilical cords and hearing them spew lewd gossip from their gore-filled mouths was yet another way for me to torment women. No means is more natural than persecution in carrying out a mission of hatred. I had sought to ease my own suffering by passing along to others, by all possible means, the memory of the agony I had had to bear because I was a woman. But my suffering had never diminished. The more I made others vile and wretched, the more vile and wretched I myself became.

Today the eyes of the hardware store owner's wife are as pink as peach blossoms after she washes down her exotic snack with a few shots of liquor. She babbles nonsense for a while, then wobbles into the waiting room and starts to plop down in the velvet chair. Ashen-faced, I steer her toward the sofa instead. The boutique manager soon follows, and the two ladies sit there side by side. The awkward expressions on their faces tell me they are looking for a way to take their leave.

"It's the day after tomorrow, right?" The boutique manager, cautious and not a drinker, asks first.

"Doctor, are you really closing the clinic? We're truly sorry to see you go."

"You might feel like quitting now, but wait and see. You can't just walk away from a trade you've gotten so accustomed to. Take a break for a while. When we give you a spot in the new building we're going to build, you mustn't refuse it, you must come back. If you don't, I guess we'll just have to gang up and drag you back here."

The owners of the hardware store and the boutiques in the neighborhood are excited at the prospect of a new building going up, even though the urban renewal project will leave them homeless. The chance of other lots being greatly improved is slim, but the area is zoned for residential use, so at long last the neighborhood at least may change for the better.

"Even if it's at your home, I hope you'll go on treating your old patients. I don't know about other specialties, but for gynecology the doctor you're used to is best."

"True. The thought of opening my legs in front of another man is not that bad, but the thought of doing it in front of a different doctor is something else. Meanwhile, doctor, how can I keep from getting pregnant?"

"Don't fuck." I say, grinning, as I get up. They giggle, thinking I am continuing the dirty jokes they've been swapping. In my younger days, I used to give serious advice to patients about birth control methods, handing out contraceptives, leaflets, and charts. But however many times I teach them, the neighborhood women go on repeating the same mistakes like illiterate morons. They scorn anything needing close attention, and are not about to sacrifice their physical pleasure in any way, so the only advice left for me to give was — no fucking. Knowing it is the only answer they will get from me, still they keep on asking over and over. No doubt they enjoy the profanity of my reply. I, too, find it refreshing, as if I have just spat on them.

"We ate well, doctor."

"Thank you, Miss Choi."

I listen as the two women depart like well-fed guests leaving a feast. Then I sit by the window in my room, watching the lights come on one by one in the neighborhood below.

Below, old Hwang's front yard is visible like an outstretched palm. Even the yard is lit up, and the family are packing. Old Hwang's daughter did not arrive until yesterday, but I can see her now: she must have come to help her father pack. She, too, has aged quite a bit. Holding Manduk's baby, she's only supervising, not actually doing any work. Occasionally, she rubs her cheek against the baby's and talks. Maybe the baby is smiling, but Hwang's daughter is loudly bossing the busy movers around as she proudly parades the baby about. As though love is flooding her heart, her face is blissful. She cannot help it, for even if people take her for an aunt, in actuality she's the grandmother. Mesmerized, I follow old Hwang's daughter's movements in the chaotic scene unfolding beneath me. Emptiness gnaws at me more and more, until I feel nothing is left of my body but skin.

I used to think old Hwang's daughter was at my mercy because of the part I played in her private nightmare, but that was not the case. She freed herself from me long ago, and she now belongs to a world I can neither reach nor understand. It is not she but I who remain trapped in that nightmare.

Abandoning myself to a reverie about the two days I have left, which are sinking from view faster and faster, I ponder many things: that a woman living with others is more beautiful than a woman living alone; that a woman who bears three or four children despite a series of abortions is even more beautiful; that more beautiful still is a whore whose last wish, after sleeping with innumerable men, is to go on a date and fall in love; and that most beautiful of all is an old madam who decides not to chase down one of her whores who has run off with a customer she fell in love with. I build my thoughts in reverse brick by brick out of the rubble of lifelong prejudices.

Now the night is deep. I count the number of church steeples in the night below me — one, two, three . . . seven.

Dear God, how obscene I would be if I were to say now that I want to find a man to love. I'd be an object of derision. God, don't make me so abominable. Instead, I pray you'll give me just one more chance to deliver a baby alive. Don't ask why I want to do it so much. I don't even know that myself. What's important to me now is not the why but the fact that I desperately want to do it. Don't deny me this one wish.

Finding myself praying for the first time in my life, I suddenly burst into lonely laughter.

3. The Last Day

I am in the front yard of my new house. From here I can see pretty houses, their grassy green yards bursting with all sorts of flowers. Only my yard is empty and surfaced with concrete. My pocket is full of flower seeds; I stomp on the concrete and I try to dig holes with my fingernails but it's no use. I have no tools but my own hands and feet. I'm irritated at not having any tools, yet glad I brought none with me. Even in my dreams the tools I left behind are not shovels or hoes but vaginal mirrors and curettes.

Reluctantly, I scatter the seeds on the concrete by hand. Then I realize that they are rose moss seeds. The little rose moss seeds can bore through the concrete and into the earth below. Before long, the concrete fractures into powdery clumps. The little seeds sprout and soon a myriad of colorful flowers bloom. Red, yellow, pink, purple . . . my yard becomes a rose moss garden. Then the flowers begin quarreling among themselves. They cry, shriek, and scream, sounding uncannily like children's voices. Soon the blossoms develop faces with eyes, mouths, and noses, looking more and more like babies. My yard is no longer a flowerbed. It is a living hell, with the heads of countless babies jutting out of the concrete, incessantly squalling their dreadful and repulsive wails. Stop, stop crying, stop right now. Stop before I scrape you away with a bulldozer and pour fresh concrete over you. Stop, enough, no more . . .

Another nightmare. I am now awake, but the wailing persists, though it's a little more distant. Out of habit, I open the window. The distant cries suddenly flood into the room, extremely loud, as if amplified electronically. It is the sound of people attending an early service at the church. It is barely daybreak. The church steeple looks like the mast of a sinking ship and the desperate wails are like the last pleas for help as the ship capsizes. The clash between my longing to surrender to despair and the conviction that I cannot shed even a single tear is worse than ever today.

Today is the last day. With zero on the countdown imminent yet unable to relinquish that desperate wish, I feel squeezed between tightening fetters.

Already I know it will not happen today. Nevertheless, I can't stop waiting for it. Though I told Miss Choi that work would continue as usual through today, she is out of uniform and has been packing her things since early morning. Demolition has already begun down the street. Like a dusty mirage in spring, the air outside is hazy. From time to time, I hear shoddy houses collapsing to the ground. What is there about this pathetic neighborhood that has kept me here till this ghastly final day?

Old Hwang; Manduk; the women who covet umbilical cords for their mysterious power of rejuvenation and who themselves are the source; whores whose sex is clean and pure as a virgin's and the pimps they call "Mother." I always told myself I could simply walk away, free of regrets, from all of them, people I've never respected. Never did I doubt that I was their benefactor and they the beneficiaries of my good will. But now that I think of it, I am the one who is indebted to them. Time and again, I will miss the "kinship" linking us, based on closeness developed over the years. From now on, I will have nothing but them to think about, but they will soon forget me.

"I doubt we'll have any patients today," remarks Miss Choi.

Evidently, she hopes to be released a day early. I've already given her a substantial bonus as severance pay and arranged for her to start a new job after a few days of rest. We have already decided to leave together the next morning. It would have been a nice gesture to let her go a day early as she wishes, but I cannot bring myself to do that.

"Miss Choi, have you ever seen a day without patients at this clinic?" Coarsely, like a merchant, I shout her down.

Just then, the face of a young girl, not even twenty years old yet, peeks in from the staircase. Refusing to climb up to the top of the staircase, she comes high enough to reveal only her shoulders. She looks as though she wants to reconnoiter before entering. When I catch her eyes, uncertain and anxious like those of a criminal, she grimaces as if about to cry. Then she stays completely still. She is in such obvious agony over whether to advance or retreat that I almost pitied her. I wish she would turn tail and walk out. A girl that age coming to a women's clinic on the verge of tears can mean only one thing. On my very last day I don't want to perform another abortion. Miss Choi hurriedly dons her smock and helps the girl, still standing riveted halfway up the stairs, into the office. Perhaps Miss Choi is mocking my utterly mercenary nature.

My heart begins to beat faster when the girl emerges at the head of the staircase. Contrary to my expectations, I can see that her belly is quite swollen. She stands with her rear jutting out to make her stomach seem flatter, but she cannot fool me. She looks to be close to full term. Maybe the girl is in labor and has come to give birth. But if that were so her parent or guardian would be with her, and the girl standing alone before me is quivering, with her eyes full of tears. Whether it is fear or shame that makes her tremble so is impossible to say. First, I have to calm her down.

"You're pregnant? No need to be so terrified. You do look a little young to be having a baby, but if you're old enough to get pregnant, you can surely deliver and raise the baby. Come in, rest your heart and tell me what happened."

I speak in a kindly tone and pick up a chart. I'm notorious for being blunt and abrupt, and to hear such an ingratiating voice come out of me is almost uncanny.

"No, doctor, no. I'm not pregnant. Who said that? Who said I am pregnant?" The girl shakes her head violently and replies in an unexpectedly sharp and clear voice.

"Really? I am sorry . . . I just assumed. Why did you come here, then?"

"To, to get a diagnosis . . ."

"This is an obstetrics clinic, and you came here knowing what kind of things we diagnose here?" It occurs to me that the girl might be retarded or mentally unbalanced, so I speak to her gently as though she were a mere child.

"Yes, I know," the girl says, looking directly at me. On the chart, I perfunctorily write down her name, date of birth, address, and the other usual items, then inquire about her symptoms.

She can't recall the exact date, but sometime in spring her menstruation had stopped and her belly had begun to swell little by little. More than two months ago something began to kick and twitch in her belly. Such were her symptoms. She is being cute. No telling what her reasons are, but it seems she wants to make a fool out of me. By now her tears are dry, and her face wears a shameless, bold expression.

Without losing my temper, I say to her, in a dignified manner, "I need to take a look at you before I can say anything for sure, but my opinion now is that you are pregnant. I am ninety percent sure."

"I never slept with a man," the girl protests in a sharp voice.

"I was under the impression that you were much younger, but your identification says you are twenty years old. At that age, it's better to skip the transparent lies. Miss Choi, prepare the patient for an examination."

The girl merely keeps her mouth locked shut and glares vehemently at me. Nearly dragging her, Miss Choi leads her into the examination room. When I go in, after putting on my smock, the struggle between Miss Choi and the girl is at its height. The girl stubbornly refuses to lie down on the table in the position necessary for examination as Miss Choi has asked her to. Glancing at her swollen belly, I let her simply lie down on the table. She does not object when I run my hand down her belly. It is plain even to the naked eye that the baby is playing well inside, and its position is very good.

"You're pregnant. Seven or eight months now . . . "

"No! I told you I didn't sleep with any man!" the girl hollers, sitting up abruptly. Then, on her own, she takes off her clothes. As she gets back onto the table, she says, "No, there must be some mistake. There's no way this can be true. Take a look again, carefully."

There is something desperate and frantic in her manner. I almost hesitate, so cruel does it seem to pronounce her pregnant again after the second examination.

"It's not true, right? Doctor, I am dying, right?" the girl asks. By this time she is standing rigidly erect with nothing on.

As though I were under investigation for malpractice, I mumble abashedly, "Dying? Nonsense. Both you and the baby are healthy. You'll soon be a mother."

The girl collapses into my arms.

"That cannot be, no, never. I am dying, I am going to die. I cannot live, I must die, there's no other way . . . "

The girl is writhing violently. Tears stream down her face, and her shoulders and bosom convulse fitfully. Her arms are locked around my neck, and her tears dampen my collar.

"Doctor, what should I do? What should I do? I have to die. Doctor, doctor. . . ."

I hug the girl, trying to soothe and comfort her, but she squirmed even more violently in my arms.

"Sis, what can be done? What should I do? There's no way out but to kill myself. Sis, I am just going to die right now."

When I found out an unwanted baby was growing inside of me, I had gone to an older friend — a doctor in Iri — and wept violently in front of her. Holding this girl in my arms, I feel my own hellish suffering spring back alive. Never before or since had the urge to kill myself been more sincere than at that time. Against the man who put this girl in this state, I feel an outrage bordering on murderousness. Tears well up in my own eyes, and I am so livid and mortified I feel every part of my flesh tremble. My intense rage no longer stems from compassion for the girl; it is heart-searing fury from my own long-repressed past, accumulated and feeding on itself.

"Miss Choi, bring a tranquilizer, a tranquilizer!"

Miss Choi brings in a tranquilizer and gives it to the girl. She takes it, sobbing.

"Miss Choi, one more dose . . . "

After I too have swallowed a tranquilizer, I take the girl into my consulting room, supporting her. Maybe her tranquilizer has worked, or maybe such a high pitch of emotion cannot survive for long. For whatever reason, the girl stops crying and tells me her history in an orderly fashion. She had been raised by a single mother. The family were not well off, but she and her two siblings had grown up in a fairly stable and happy household. After her mother died of some nameless disease before they could even take her to a hospital, the three siblings split up, going to live with aunts and uncles. The girl, being the oldest, chose the poorest of their relations, an aunt, to live with. This aunt was eking out a living by running a cheap boarding house, so the girl naturally had to get used to helping out with this and that, like a servant. The girl was thinking she should at least earn some money by hiring herself out as a maid and was looking for an opportunity to do so when it happened. It is understandable that the girl insisted she never slept with a man, because she always slept with a cousin, the aunt's daughter. It happened one night when the cousin was away on a school trip. She remembers waking up that night with a heavy weight pressing down her entire body, but because she fought with all her might, for a long time she told herself it could not have happened. She could not believe a girl could get pregnant that easily. She could not guess who it was because it happened in a boarding house at night when she was asleep.

"Anyway, what would be the use in figuring out who it was?" she asks.

She says that if she could guess the father, she might stab him to death and then kill herself, too. Beyond that, any relationship with that person is unthinkable. When I merely hint at the possibility of marrying the father, she nearly relapses into the fit that had only just been soothed.

"What can I do, doctor? Now that pregnancy's certain, how can I go on living? The shame is not the main thing. I just want to die. No, I want to kill that thing inside of me. I'm going to kill that thing. After I kill it, I am going to die."

The girl violently shakes her head and looks up resolutely. Even without tears, her eyes glisten with an unmistakably murderous glint. If the epitome of hatred is murder, then the most heartless and savage of all murderous intents is against a being inside you — that much I know from my own experience. More than likely, I would have chosen death if I hadn't been freed from the thing inside of me at my friend's hospital. Shame would not have been the reason. I would have chosen death because killing myself seemed the only way to eliminate that thing growing inside me. All murderous designs leave a way for the murderer to live, but the urge to murder something living inside yourself is so extreme you will end your own life too if the goal can be achieved no other way.

"I can't let the girl die," I tell myself. I need to do for her only what my doctor friend did for me. Moreover, am I not far more skilled at this than my friend was? But I swear I have never before aborted a baby big enough to cry at birth. It isn't that I don't know how common such killings are around the country; it's just that I have never gone that far, not because anyone has watched me or prevented me from doing it, but by my own decision. Of all days, today, my last day, I find myself at a loss to face this boundary. Because it is my last day, I want to finish without transgressing that boundary, but on the other hand, what can possibly happen, I ask myself, if I sneak across the line just once on this last day? Still, I feel I would be stigmatized as a "butcher of humans" for the rest of my life even if I did it just this once. The reason I have been able to stay on good terms with old Hwang even after he slandered me, saying he'd never let a butcher deliver his first grandson, is that I have not taken it as anything more than a vicious turn of speech. I was able to placate my own conscience because I knew I had never actually killed a late-term baby. Now that I am about to cross this line, old Hwang's labeling of me as a butcher of humans is paralyzingly offensive all over again.

The hellish agony of being pregnant with an unwanted baby does not belong to the girl, but to me, resurrected from the deepest, darkest recesses of my heart. Without exaggerating a bit, I am turning this girl's torment into my own. No, the girl aside, I alone am whetting the blade of my own murderous thoughts.

I have no need to heed old Hwang. Until now I have lived as I pleased. I have never let others judge me. Already I have racked my brains, unsuccessfully looking for even the remotest possibility of saving the baby, so why should I hesitate?

I harden my resolve, and agree to take care of the girl's problem. She weeps tears of relief and gratitude. As I realize that the girl had been wanting this from the start, the tempest of indecision that was roiling my heart begins to subside. Already the object of my hatred is not the girl, but the unwanted baby, the baby conceived not to be born but to become a fountainhead of troubles.

I begin to work, expecting it to go slowly because it is the girl's first time. I decide to insert several probes into her uterus and check the progress, while letting the girl rest comfortably. Surprisingly enough, by that evening the cervix is already dilating. For a girl who has never had a baby before, things are moving quickly. The baby's position is good as well. Inducing labor by pressing the womb, I begin injecting a stimulant. The delivery is being induced without a hitch. The girl complains of pain as contractions come at shorter intervals and with growing vehemence.

I comfort her, trying to help her endure the pain, but I am waiting for her to scream insanely. At last the girl starts hollering like a beast. I don't know what time it is, but outside the window the night is deep and dark. The window becomes a black mirror and my sunken eyes shine ferociously from the sweaty and glistening face reflected in it. It is the face of a torturer. The cruelest of all torturers, who has avenged one torture with another, again and again for thirty years, is finally tottering on the brink of madness.

As the girl emits a ghastly, hellish scream, I too can feel a burning hatred flaring up from the bottom of my heart. At that very instant, the baby is born. The afterbirth follows without any difficulty.

Except for the odor of blood, my abortion clinic is instantly transformed into a perfect maternity ward, as peaceful as though all that had happened was but a dream. The girl, sleeping deeply as though the world did not exist, seems totally innocent. Miss Choi, who has been there all along, yawns and staggers. Though my exhausted body feels like it was melting into a pulpy mass, an inexplicable sense of emptiness keeps me alert.

I check the clock more than a few times, but I still cannot be sure if it is today or the next day. I leave the room, hoping for a breath of fresh air unpolluted by the smell of blood. But the smell has permeated everywhere. It is exasperating to be unable to eliminate that odor of blood from the feeling of liberation I feel now, for the first time perhaps. I pace restlessly back and forth. I can hear a feeble yet unmistakable sound coming from nowhere. At first I imagine it is coming from outside, but that is not the case. Like the rusty sound of heavy wooden gates closing, it seems distant and faint, but without a doubt, it is issuing from somewhere nearby.

My heart is racing. I have a strange hunch and turn on the light in the waiting room. The velvet chair is the first thing I set eyes on. The sound is coming from that chair. On the chair is the premature baby I just delivered, wrapped in a blanket, letting the world know it is alive, with that queer sound.

"Miss Choi, Miss Choi, what have you done here? Who told you to do this?"

I summoned Miss Choi in a loud voice. In the middle of buttoning her pajama top, Miss Choi rushes out and gazes quizzically at me.

"Doctor, you've been acting very oddly lately. You did it yourself. You left all the after work to me, and you took the baby."

Me? Did I really do that? For an aborted baby, there is no need to follow the normal procedures usually performed after delivery. I've heard of doctors who leave the baby in water to drown or lay it on its stomach to suffocate, but even without such extreme measures, aborted babies do eventually die — it is their ephemeral destiny. But the girl's premature baby is alive. What I have done, without knowing it, is to give it the kind of tender care a perfect newborn baby receives. The navel has been properly bandaged, and the baby has even been diapered.

Ah, I no longer need to hide anything. The truth is I've been wanting to have a baby myself. A baby I can raise with love. My inexplicable desire to deliver a living baby for one last time is only a facade masking my longing for a baby. I feel my honest wish bursting forth vividly, ripping off the mask and shredding the shroud under which it lay hidden.

I rush down the stairs and out the door like a mad woman, holding the yelping baby in my arms. Behind me Miss Choi shouts something in a shaken voice. The city is drowned in a deep sleep, locked up for the night. A big hospital, a hospital with an incubator . . . Baby in my arms, I race forward like an arrow. The big hospital with incubators is far, far away.

Out of nowhere, a night watchman appears and grabs me. The noise of whistles blowing envelops me from all sides.

Revealing the baby in my arms, I weep pathetically, repeating, "My baby, my baby, I have to save my baby."

"Mad bitch, just leave her alone," hisses the night watchman.

The noise of whistles shatters everything asunder and the road in front of me is clear again. But the hospital with incubators is still far, far away. And the strand of hope I have for saving this baby's life is even further away, even fainter.

The big hospital is still far away, but already I am mentally throwing myself at the doctor's feet asking him please to save my baby.

"Doctor, please save my baby. It's my baby. It's my one and only child. It was born just a few minutes ago, prematurely . . . I've been punished. I didn't want the baby at first. But I don't feel that way anymore. Please save this baby, please . . .

"No, he wouldn't believe me, I mean the doctor. Look at me, I am wretchedly old. Anyone can see I'm nothing but a barren old hag. Then I'll say it's my grandson. I might as well say he's a fifth-generation only son.

"Doctor, please save my only grandson. I'll be in your debt till the day I die. Save him, save him please . . . "

An endless cascade of tears runs down my cheeks, and my throat burns and chokes. But when I finally reach the hospital and take the baby out in front of the doctor, I can say nothing.

The baby in my arms is dead. I see flit across the doctor's face a certain kind of pity, not unlike that of the night watchman who said, "Mad bitch, just leave her alone." I turn back from the hospital, holding the precious infant against my breast. A taxi with red headlights slowly passes by. The city, freed from the curfew, is waking up, rubbing its eyes and stretching. The baby was born yesterday and died today. Yesterday was the last day I was able to dream of delivering a baby alive. That wish was granted and today is a new day. I finally realize my wish has been granted.

Slowly, but without pausing to rest, I head toward the district where my new house is, carrying the baby in my arms. Today I move into my new house. I am going to move into my house with my baby. I am going to put the baby to sleep in the sunny front yard of my new house. How could my baby die? . . . But I think a woman with at least a grave of a baby is more beautiful than a woman who has never had a baby at all. I am going to plant rose moss in the yard where my baby sleeps. Rose moss, tiny flowers like the eyes of the innumerable babies I have killed, eyes that never had a chance to develop a conscience and never will.

I don't know how far I've come, but I begin to hear churchgoers wailing. This neighborhood, too, seems to have a church where the congregation gathers early to attend a tearful service. The parishioners are steadily assembling. From nowhere, people carrying little bibles with tears in their hearts emerge to form an endless procession.

Without thinking, I now become a part of this procession, entering the church with the others, holding in my bosom a dead baby and a lament mighty enough to overwhelm all the other cries.

No longer is the grief in my heart a hardened mass, unable to produce even a single teardrop. It is merely holding back, as though biting its lips under torture, until I reach a place where it can freely flood forth.

translated by Ryu Sukhee

My Very Last Possession

Hello? Yes, it's me now. So, what's up? What led you to call me, I wonder? I'm always the one who picks up the phone first, right? And I do all the talking and you just listen. So much so I can't help wondering at times whether you haven't softly set the receiver down on a table and gone off to do something else while I babble on. At those times I'd shut my mouth, glue the receiver to my ear, and wait. With you, my sister-in-law, such a refined, gracious lady and all, it was only natural that I heard not a sound. You're awful, my dear. How could you possibly listen to someone in such perfect silence? I'll bet you have no idea what it's like to sense that void on the other end of the line. It's like a cliff. I mean, like a cliff where you should jump off or else somebody pushes you down. True. You're not the sort of person, I know, who'd ever do such a thing. If you really couldn't stand any more of my prattle, you'd just say, "That's enough, dear." When your mind's twisted, it's easy to toy with all kinds of weird notions, I'm afraid. But what I heard from the beyond the deathly stillness of that cliff was anything but tender.

"Go on, I'm listening."

Whenever I hear your voice, without the least trace of feeling, like the voice of some mighty queen in a historical drama, I feel such pity for Chang-sŏk's wife. To hear you talk, you've done a great favor for your eldest daughter-in-law just by letting her keep her job. But can you imagine how hard it is to wait on a mother-in-law like you? I'm sure you don't believe you ever made her wait on you, and not even once have you given her an earful. Oh, but silence can be deadly. And a puffed up, affected tone can be anything but bearable, you know. Sister, are you irritated at me? Right, you called so you must have something to tell me, and here I am yacking away again. The day before yesterday was the great-grandmother's anniversary, you say? My, my, it just slipped my mind. You forgot, too? Well, since you and I both failed to remember the date, we couldn't do the ancestral ceremony. Couldn't, or didn't, I don't know. No way for Chang-sŏk's wife to recall and remind you. That's your fault, since you've kept your daughter-in-law at arms length from such matters. With these girls today, sister, even when you set them clear tasks, they seldom shoulder responsibilities. You trained her from the start as if she needn't bother about formalities, so why complain now? You know as well as I do that Chang-sŏk's wife has circled lots of dates on the calendar in their room, dates of all the big and small events of her own family right down to the birthdays of her nieces and nephews. I doubt she circled them just for looks, so she must have observed each and every one of them, don't you think? I'm sorry, sister. Why I'm going on with this outburst is beyond me. Now I'm even badmouthing my own niece-in-law. But I tell you, sister, if you feel like picking on her, go right ahead. And stop making me feel ashamed of myself.

Anyway, sister, it all worked out for the best. From here on, why don't you, once and for all, cut the ceremonies down to two generations of ancestors? They may be great-grandparents for us, but now that Chang-sŏk has become the chief mourner, for him they're great-great-grandparents. As I understand it, even the Compendium of Family Ritual Standards only calls for ancestral rites to be observed for two generations. It's quite reasonable to carry out the rituals only for ancestors the living can actually remember, don't you think? But then again, since you had to change the soiled clothes of your husband's bedridden great-grandmother, I'm sure you remember her well enough. Three months was all, but what a three months! By the time she passed away, nothing at all was kept private from her great-granddaughter-in-law. And afterward, every year without fail, food for her ancestral offering was prepared by the same hands with utmost care and attention. Well, I'd say she's lounged in the lap of luxury, don't you agree? By the way, sister, are there really spirits, do you think? If so, she might feel a bit wistful, but she wouldn't hold it against you. My guess is nowadays you're not likely to find too many spirits four generations gone who are still being honored with feasts. If spirits are indulged too lavishly for too long, they might end up being hated by the other spirits, you never know. No need to worry that she'll go hungry. I've never once seen a spirit make a dent in the ceremonial offerings. And if she needs to eat, well, I daresay she'll find food somewhere. In your neighbor-hood, there's even an alley they call "Let's Eat." Everybody in Seoul's heard of it. So on her way to your apartment she could have paused for a snack. Who knows? Maybe she ate her fill of earthly food around the corner before even reaching your place and, shaking her head, just headed back. Sure, even I know that. Yes, they do say spirits only consume food offered on the ceremonial altar. I know, too, that you didn't really call me because you were so troubled by our missing the ancestral ceremony, you called to reproach me. I don't deny it, I was always the one, year in and year out, who reminded you of ceremony dates. But, honestly, it never occurred to me that you, dear sister, would forget those dates without my reminders. I just developed the habit of contacting you a few days ahead of time, to check with you on when I should drop by to help make radish *kimchi* for the ceremony, and willy-nilly, that made me seem to you to be keeper of the ritual calendar. And now, to think that all along you were relying on me! From now on, sister, don't you ever rely on me.

Why, I hate memorizing things. Especially numbers. That's im-possible for me. A few days ago while I was out I had occasion to call home. After inserting the phone card I was about to press the buttons when I realized I couldn't remember my home number, you know. I was dumbfounded. Night was falling. Cars sped by with headlights on, and neon signs were beginning to be switched on in the shops across the street. I stood there in a stupor with the receiver in hand. A young man waiting in line urged me to hurry up. He didn't look like he had short temper or bad manners. After he waited a while, his patience just ran out, I suppose. Just because time had stopped for me didn't mean it had for others, I guess. I looked back over my shoulder at the young man and said, "Would you give me my home number, please?" He staggered backward, spun around, and ran for his life. While my head refused to recall anything, my whole body felt powerless, like it was totally empty, nothing but a shell. But then, what was it, I wonder, that made the young man so frightened of an old woman? I tell you, sister, it was an eerie feeling. You see, it was hard to believe I was alive. How can you say you're alive when your memory has been wiped out? It seemed as if people passing by on the street were mere phantoms and the enigmatically dancing lights existed only in my eyes. The outlines of buildings and cars were erased and the lights they sent off were merging this way and that, as though in spirit everything was freely interpenetrating in a sympathetic harmony. I felt relief and sorrow at once. Wouldn't this be how we must feel as we depart from this world, glancing back at our lives filled with vanity, only vanity? Though I felt relieved, somehow I longed to be consoled.

Sister, do you know where I found the clue for consoling myself that day? Out of the blue, a certain radio DJ I'd seen on TV not long before popped into my mind. She's very famous, so famous even you would recognize her if I gave her name. I hear she'd been a DJ for twenty years, so however old she is, she's at most ten years younger than us, if that. Must have always taken care of herself, for she didn't even look like she was pushing forty. Still, she rarely showed her face in public and had made her name through her voice alone. She was telling stories about her experience as a DJ and offered an anecdote about an incident when she couldn't remember her own name. She wasn't trying to be funny, you know; she was very serious, in fact. Over twenty years of presenting mainly music programs in a calm, collected voice, she always began and ended the program by giving her name. So, she said, you wouldn't easily find a person in Korea who'd pronounced his or her own name as many times as she had. But then one day, at the close of a live broadcast, when the moment came for her to say, "It's been such-and-such with so-and-so," she just couldn't remember her own name. Veteran DJ that she was, she revealed no bewilderment. Guess what she said. Instead, she said, "The name, I'll tell you this time tomorrow." That day, when I thought of her story, I felt a little less uneasy for not recalling my home telephone number.

Considering that I'd gone so far as rehashing a trivial anecdote to console myself, I must have been terrified of losing my mind. My mind is something I don't really understand, either. I thought I was enjoying the insane state of my mind, but in fact it must have scared me. I don't remember how long I was there like that. I never managed to make the call, but I did make my way home late that night. You're asking if I didn't forget my apartment number? Ever heard of a man finding his home by the address? You get home in spite of yourself; your legs just carry you there. I can't distinguish between the things remembered by your mind and by your body. At any rate, I wonder if spirits really exist.

The children scolded me for being so late without calling home. Our family is reversed. They're the grown-ups, I'm telling you, and I'm the little child by the water. That day, after going to a hotel buffet on account of a friend's sixtieth birthday, followed by a chat over tea, it occurred to me that it was getting a bit late, so I meant to call home just to check in. That's how it all happened. These children, you see, they've trained me to do that. They must think I'm a schoolgirl or something; whenever I leave the house, they make sure to clarify the destination and the time of return. When I'm out, if for whatever reason I can't make it back by the designated hour, then I must call home without fail, etc., etc. I suppose it's a way of making the point that they don't want to worry about me needlessly, you know. I didn't mention to them that I'd forgotten the telephone number. Instead I accepted the loud reprimand from my daughters in silence and went to my room, but I must have seemed not my usual self. For they did something out of the ordinary. Chang-hee followed me into my room and pried. You know how she is. Compared to her elder sister, Chang-hee's fuse is short and her temper is fiery.

"Mom, you've gone too far. You've got to stop it now. It's already seven years since brother died. Was he your only child? Daughters don't count? Do you know why my sister is still unmarried? She's been trying to find a man who'll live in the same house with you, and all the good men have slipped away. You don't even realize that, I'll bet. How could you when you don't even care? I'd be forever satisfied if I heard just one word, one single word of concern from your mouth about your daughter becoming an old maid. There's no other mother like you in the world. Do you even know how old she is? Probably not. Because brother gets no older, maybe you think we're still twenty-three and twenty-one, right? But then, I guess even time, faced with a solid rock wall like you, has no choice but to stand still. I can't be a dutiful daughter like my sister is, always putting you first, but I've tried to be good to you. I'm worn out now. Sister will wear out too, before long. Being good to you is like pouring water into a bottomless pot. On the rare occasions when you devote some attention to us, what do you do? You gaze at us with an expression that says, 'If I'd lost one of you two girls instead of him, I wouldn't have been so heartbroken.' That expression makes my skin crawl, I mean it. Mom, you're making us feel guilty for being alive. We have only one life, too. Must you do this to us? Mom, you've gone too far."

Well, that's how she rained on me. Sister, don't forget this; they tell me Chang-sook hasn't been able to marry all this time because of her mom. Well, that should be enough to let her be advertised as the world's most filial daughter, don't you think? True, I'm not living my life constantly crossing t's and dotting i's about my daughters' ages, but I've never, not even in my wildest dream, thought of living off them. The very idea leaves me speechless, you know. It's useless to say so now, but I meant even to let Chang-hwan set up a separate household as soon as he got married and never entertained the thought of living with him. What do you mean, why? Didn't you, sister, have more than your share of life under the in-laws? Three years had barely passed since you'd freed yourself from your mother-in-law's yoke when you became a widow and a mother-in-law yourself, so you wouldn't know the pleasure shared by a man and wife living alone, the taste of that liberty, would you?

Well, at the time there was no other choice for living arrangements. Still, thanks to your genteel parents-in-law, your years with the in-laws didn't seem so bad. When I was trudging to the market or cooking in the kitchen with my baby strapped on my back, your children were nestled in the arms of their grandmother and grandfather like treasured jewels. Their backs never touched the floor, and you know very well how much I envied that, don't you? Whenever I breathed an envious remark, you'd say in a voice tinged with sighs, "I'd give anything if I could just cook in my own house with my baby on my back."

They weren't false protests, were they? My intuition told me those words revealed your innermost heartfelt yearning. I knew it wasn't yours alone, but your husband's, too, very likely. Without a couple sharing that hardship, how could the wife play the part of a perfect daughter-in-law as you did? Then again, when you dropped in at our house and saw the helter-skelter of life with three children, you'd grow envious and say, "Compared to your life, mine's only half a life." I didn't want my Chang-hwan to live half a life when he wed. I wanted to give him the whole world. Indeed, I was bound to give him the entire world and nothing less. I never thought of living with my own son, so, you see, why on earth would I ever have dreamed of living with one of my daughters?

Had I had nothing to live on, it would have been a different story. A man's life is hard and rowdy; I can't rightly say I'd never live off my children, you never know. Now I can afford to bluster this way, thanks to the pension my man left behind. You're saying, all the same I should be grateful for what my child said, even if they're only words? I see, well, I didn't find anything to be grateful about, but I wasn't going to condemn her. But what she said next was abominable, don't you think? You couldn't thrust a sharper knife into a mother's heart, sister. How could she breathe such things out loud? I never once compared Chang-hwan's life to those of the girls, nor thought of replacing his with theirs, I swear. That wasn't at all the same as an artificial vow to treat sons and daughters fair and equal. Chang-hwan for me was the one and only Chang-hwan, so exceptional, defying comparison with anybody.

But then, what do I gain by berating my daughter? Since I lost Chang-hwan, I know that my relatives and friends, everyone who's brought up their sons in one piece, feel apologetic to me for no logical reason, I know that. They brag about their sons, but clam up in my presence. When their sons get married, they're hesitant and indecisive about sending me an invitation, fearing I might feel jealous and hurt. Well, I know that, too. You know Myung-ae, don't you? My friend from high school, who lived next door to us in Sŏngbuk-dong and even shared pancakes with us over the fence — remember her? Her son and Chang-hwan were classmates from grammar school all the way through middle school. We knew each other's lives inside out and always understood one another completely, with no secrets untold, so much so that I was a whole lot closer to her than to you, sister. You see, no matter how close relatives are, somehow there's always a limit to how close you can be to the in-law side. You just can't help dealing with in-laws with a sort of second skin, you know? After Chang-hwan was killed in such a way, no relative of mine could have been more shocked or pained than Myung-ae was. When I wailed in grief, she wailed along with me. When I jumped high and low, so did she; and when I was bedridden, she made gruel and brought it to me every day without fail. You say, you've also done it yourself? Why, you feign as if you weren't listening, but then you simply can't let a single slight slip by, can you? Even Myung-ae, too, was avoiding me when she married off her own son. On the wedding day I learned about it from one of our alumnae. That friend who approached me to find the way to the wedding, which was held in a small neighborhood church somewhere on the outskirts of the city, couldn't believe at first I hadn't been invited or even informed, but later she apologized to me for not having been as considerate as Myung-ae and begged me to ignore what she'd said.

Sister, what have I done so wrong to be ostracized like this? It's as if Chang-hwan's death were something for me to be ashamed of. But that I could never allow. Then and there I leapt up, got ready in a flash, and hurried off to the wedding with a bright smile on my face. Myung-ae was at a loss how to react, but I carried myself with dignity and congratulated her from the bottom of my heart. Really, I felt not the least tinge of envy at Myung-ae's son getting married. Her son could never compare with my Chang-hwan. Even to get into that sorry college it took him three years of repeating the exams, and he shows no trace of ambition, let alone lofty ideals. About all he's developed is a taste for pleasures of the flesh; every day he's got a different girl in tow. Now it looks like one of them finally showed up with a bloated belly. Otherwise, a boy without rich parents wouldn't be rushing to get married even before graduating, would he? How can such a guy be compared to Chang-hwan? Don't be absurd. Still, don't you be imagining that my heart shatters whenever I see somebody else's splendid son. You, too, have heard the story about my nephew? Remember? Neither my folks nor yours ever had a relative make a big success in the world, but when I'm in a boasting mood he's the one I crow about. I mean the one who passed the state judicial examination even before finishing college. That's right, you actually saw him a few times at my house. Not just bright, a fine-looking one he is. By the time he got married, almost a year had passed since I lost Chang-hwan, but even then I could sense that the whole family shared a hope that I, his only paternal aunt, would stay away from the wedding. It made me sick, no lie. Did they actually think I'd care so much about his being a high and mighty judge, or was it a prosecutor? In the time since I lost Chang-hwan, the mothers of Minkahyup, the association of relatives of political prisoners, made me more socially aware, so that for me my dead son is a thousand times more splendid than any judge alive. So why in the world would attending my nephew's wedding make me feel timid or envious? What's more, just a few days before, I'd gone with the Minkahyup mothers to watch a trial of fighters for democracy, and we hissed and even spat as the judge mumbled through a nonsensical set of criminal charges. That young, green judge was pathetic, nobody to envy, that's for sure. Thanks to the Minkahyup mothers, I made it through that day without any unpleasantness and courageously discharged my role as aunt.

Sister, it's not Mingkyehep, it's pronounced Minkahyup. You say everything else crisply enough, I don't understand why you mangle this particular word. Are you doing it on purpose? To show your disdain, putting me and the group in the same basket? My, you startled me! Why did what I said make you so angry? I must have hit a sore spot, really. You spent less than a month at your daughter's place in America, and when you got back, didn't you go around saying "battery" like an American instead of using the Korean pronunciation "bba-ta-ri"? A tongue so talented at mimicry shouldn't find it hard to say Minkahyup, should it now? Maybe calling it disdain is too much, but it still seems to me that you do it deliberately to show you don't approve. At any rate, it grates on my ears. I don't want to hear it anymore. So you say I'm harassing you with trivia like you were my daughter-in-law? Well, the wife of your husband's younger brother is an in-law, too, you know. Sister, don't you think you've given me the daughter-in-law treatment yourself often enough?

Where was I when I got off track? Ah, right, I was saying that everybody tries to shun me when their sons get married. And you say it's paranoia? That's possible, I guess. You think being shunned is the only thing that makes me sick. People can be too nice, too, and I hate that. Either way, it boils down to the same thing. You, for instance, remember how you doted on me when your Chang-sŏk was married? And thanks to that, Chang-sŏk's would-be in-laws ended up bearing the awful burden. I can well imagine how much grudge the bride's family must have borne when they presented me with the ceremonial presents exactly the same as those they brought to you. You told me that since they didn't have to do it for the father-in-law, they'd probably done it for me instead, but no matter how many times you said it I do know that they didn't do it on their own. By the time Chang-sŏk got married, Chang-hwan had been dead for more than five years, and you still had to worry about me so much, right?

When the newlyweds made a ceremonial bow, you had me sit next to you as if I were your husband. At first I held back, feeling it awkward for a set of widows sitting side by side to receive the ceremonial bow, but in the end I gave in. I could detect that the people present were in a sinking mood somehow. I didn't want them to think I was sulking at the thought of my Chang-hwan. Because that wasn't true. You see, I wasn't the least bit envious when Chang-sŏk got married, for I wasn't at all inclined to compare my Chang-hwan with your Chang-sŏk. On that occasion, with the absence of your husband as a pretext, ever so persistently you dragged me down right next to you, but I bet you'd have done the same even if your husband were alive. You probably wouldn't have cared if some mistook me for your husband's concubine. You went right ahead and made your new daughter-in-law bow to me just like to her parents-in-law. You do admit that, after your husband's death, my husband put his own children aside to take better care of his nephews and nieces. Even so, he barely outlived his elder brother by the difference in their ages. Those husbands of ours didn't live very long compared to most heads of household, but that was about their only fault. We may have married through matchmakers, you and I, but we hooked up with pretty decent husbands, didn't we? Mine departed this world before reaching sixty, but I sure have no regrets about it. He took off without much ado, never suspecting that Chang-hwan would soon follow. Such a lucky man, how I envy him. At times I even resent him. He's the only one I envy, in fact, him and him alone. Sometimes when I lie awake in bed I wish so much that I could've traded places with him. My heart aches, and the pain keeps me awake the whole night through. But that is nothing like coveting somebody else's living son. I don't deny Chang-sŏk is a fine, faultless young lad, but you can't compare him with my Chang-hwan. They're two very different sorts.

Well, sister, the whole world knows how well you've brought up your son. He never caused his parents a moment's worry, and it was a snap for him to get into a first-class university. Big corporations were recruiting him even before he graduated, and his boss thought so highly of him that he went out of his way to find him a bride from a family of reputation. But, sister, what year was it when Chang-sŏk entered college? 1980, wasn't it? A university student in 1980 and he did nothing but study, caring nothing about how the world around him rolled by? Well, the way I look at it, you have to wonder about the integrity, the human side, of a boy like that. How could he be that way? Would a decent man act like that? When Chang-hwan entered the same university three years after Chang-sŏk, at first he, too, did nothing but study, just like Chang-sŏk. But the clouds of tear gas hanging over the campus made my Chang-hwan suffer. You say that was true for Chang-sŏk as well? I don't doubt it. Even the passersby were suffering, jumping high and low with tears streaming down and noses running. Chang-sŏk's suffering was only physical, but my Chang-hwan's heart was aching, too.

Right. Maybe you're right when you say Chang-hwan wasn't involved in the student movement. Not even I, his own mother, was aware of it, if he was. But who can say that for sure? That's probably why we have the old saying "Mothers give birth to a child's form, not its content." Anyhow, why does that matter so much? Every time we talk, you always bring that up, as if it nails everything down. At a time like this, I'm glad we're talking over the phone. That's not true, actually. Even on the phone, I can feel your gaze. I mean the unpleasant gaze someone who knows a great secret wears when looking at another who's ignorant of it. Whatever you may say, when all's said and done, you know no more than I do. We're both guessing Chang-hwan just happened to be there that day. But why's that so important? True, at first, I felt so wronged, indignant to the point of insanity. That damned steel pipe, I told myself, how could it have missed all those militant fighters leading the protest and landed on none other than my poor Chang-hwan? Yet death, after all, is an irrevocable fate, isn't it? And uniquely personal, to top it off. I was so terrified I wanted to escape it at all costs. The first and easiest way to escape the personal part of it all was to let myself be swept away in the crowd. Absorbed in the passion of the mass. You remember, too, don't you? That somber funeral procession for my Chang-hwan. A million college students exalted my Chang-hwan as a man of principle, a martyred patriot.

Sister, don't talk like that, please. The world was responsible when young people set themselves ablaze, using their own bodies as torches to guide the times, wasn't it? It was nothing so outrageous, seeking to use a dead life as a torch. You and I, maybe because we grew up as children in such unspeakable poverty, we couldn't believe this new world, with plenty of food and basic needs met, was not a dream but real. How we loved it, sister. But to the eyes of the young, how dark must this same world have appeared to make them try to light the way with their own bodies? What's important isn't so much whether Chang-hwan was active in the student movement, but that the time was so dark even deaths were inevitable, deaths made into torches to show the way, don't you think?

Yes, sister, you and I survived in a very heartless world, I realize that. How is it possible for such an unfeeling, cruel world actually to exist? But have we now left that cruel world behind? You may laugh at me, but if the world has changed, I think my Chang-hwan was part of the force that brought the change. It sounds absurd, I know, but I've experienced Chang-hwan's unending resurrection. Don't patronize me, please, as if I've been brainwashed by the Minkahyup mothers. Who's brainwashing whom, I ask you? After what happened to me, how else could I keep going, day after day, without becoming a walking dead woman myself? You have no idea of how you wounded me back then, at the time of the June 10 uprising, do you? It wasn't long after Chang-hwan's death, but that wasn't the only reason. Somehow I sensed that something unusual, an alarming event, was about to happen. So I pulled myself together and got out of bed. At that moment, do you know what you said to me? "Do you still love demonstrations so much, after a demonstration devoured your son?!" You screamed that at me. What do you mean, when? In 1987, at the time of the June 10 uprising, I said. Please, sister, don't ever confuse June 10 with June 29. You can't help mixing them up, you say? You may be confused about some things, but how can you mix those dates up? You confuse June 10 and June 29, can't tell April 13 from April 19, and May 16 and May 18 whirl around in your mind. Well, I really can't stand it anymore. At times I wonder if you're playing the fool in my presence. If that were so, I'd never speak to you again.

How can I recite those dates by heart when the date of our great-grandmother's ceremony so completely slipped my mind? Well, I knew you'd ask such a thing — you, a veteran at trying to corner others. All right, let me be frank. The ancestral rites for the great-grandmother are no longer of any importance to me, that's why I can forget the date. Want to know the biggest change in me since I lost Chang-hwan? Things I thought were important until then became trivial, and things I never thought important became very important. The great-grandmother's ceremony is one thing that no longer matters to me, but it certainly isn't the only one. I confess I surprised myself by changing like this. At first it was strange, as if I'd become someone else. I even wondered if I might be losing my mind. So, when I ran into other people, I did my best to act as I used to. Even after losing Chang-hwan, I kept on reminding you of the dates of the yearly rituals, but I was just pretending to be the old me, probably. If not, then it was just habit, a kind of inertia, I suppose. You feel such inertia, too, don't you? You pour your heart into setting up the ceremonial offering, but when it's a matter of keeping up with the dates, you got into the habit of relying entirely on me? That devil-may-care attitude of yours, isn't that inertia?

What else lost its importance besides the dates of annual rituals? Well, a lot. So many things I can't name them all, but I doubt you could understand. Not that I underestimate you, sister, but, you see, they're not the kind of things you can rattle off in sequence like dates on a calendar. For instance, what other people think of me used to be important, but now the way I think of myself and the way I see things are far more important. I don't want to deceive myself for the sake of others. Most of all, that's tiresome. I hate to exhaust myself with useless things. Sure, there's more. Before, acquiring things was important, but now throwing things away is more important. I wasn't as bad as you, but I had my share of greed for material things, remember? When I spotted a pretty plate or a fancy teacup at another's house, I'd ask if it wasn't an import, marvel at its superior quality. I'd spare no expense to buy whatever item I had my eye on. Well, that was the fun of living. Back in the 1960s, I suppose it was, I mean back in the days when you and I both retained a bit of the aura of newlyweds. In those days material goods were hard to come by, but we were like professional shoppers, so proud of what we were purchasing, remember?

When synthetic fiber hit the market for the first time — god only knows what was so wonderful about lousy synthetic blankets — we pooled our money in a savings club and managed to buy two blankets, one for each household. Now that I think of it, I'm still using that dresser inlaid with mother-of-pearl that I bought through the savings club. I used to be so delighted when at last I got some possession I'd been longing to buy, but now all those things have become burdens to me. "Why is that standing there?" I ask myself, feeling awkward in the presence of things I've dusted and polished for over twenty years. They seem foreign to me. Do you know what I usually do when I can't get to sleep at night? I rummage like crazy through dressers and kitchen cabinets looking for things to throw away, that's what I do. They're full of things to toss, you know.

People complain they're weighted down with things not good enough to keep but too good to throw away, but there's not a single thing I feel attached to. I just can't throw them all out at once, fearing what my daughters might think. Besides, I don't know how to get rid of something big like a dresser. I guess I should either give it away to someone or call a used furniture store, but that too is a nuisance. The thought that it was standing in a used furniture store or in someone else's house would get on my nerves. If it's a feeling of responsibility for the objects you've handled so long, well, I suppose that's also a kind of possessiveness or greed. Anyway, even with nothing precious to me left in this world, I still find it hard to throw things away. It's because I want them not just to disappear out of my sight, but to vanish altogether for good.

Sometimes I wish our house had an old-style wood stove in the kitchen, so I could chop up the furniture for firewood. Then again, that, too, may not be such a good idea, for the things manufactured these days don't easily turn to ash, you know? In a world where a robust, healthy life could vanish overnight into thin air, why is it that things are so tough and durable? Perhaps I hate things because of their toughness. The very thought of it is suffocating, as if I'm being crushed to death by things that refuse to burn or rot. I'm not at all scared of dying, but for some reason I really hate the feeling of death creeping up.

I hate things, so I never give things as presents to others. Of course, it's a newly acquired habit since losing my Chang-hwan. In the old days, as you know very well, with the approach of every gift-giving occasion, from birthdays in my own family as well as my husband's down to weddings of nieces and nephews and hundred-day parties for their babies, it was always a delightful problem to decide what sort of present to buy. I rarely gave money to the relatives or to my friends, not just because I could spend less on a present, but mainly because I wanted them to cherish my gifts for a long, long time. When I couldn't hit upon a suitable gift, I made the present myself, sewing a dress or some little thing on my machine. You used to pick on me for being too tight-fisted with money, remember? All the same, you secretly envied my skill as a seamstress. But the truth is, you need more than skilled hands to make such things. You have to have both creativity and love for the person. I no longer do such things. I take care of most of them with money. When it's absolutely necessary to bring something, I buy things to eat. If that won't work, I clear the matter by taking them out to dinner. I don't want objects to cause others to be reminded of me, not anymore. I resent it because I don't want to feel as though I'm oppressing others with such reminders. But that doesn't mean I don't like to be generous to people. If a young couple, finally married after a long, amiable courtship, stops by to see me, or if an old friend is emigrating to join her son in America, I do want to give them something. Still, not things. So I treat them to a fancy meal. Pleasant memories have fewer consequences than objects.

Even when it wasn't a special occasion, it used to be important to spend money in the ways that would do me most credit, but no longer. Spending ineffectually and to no purpose has become much more important. What is "spending to do yourself credit," anyway? Doesn't it mean giving others a certain burden of obligation heavy enough to keep them from forgetting about you? I resent that. To pick up the check after a cup of tea at a cafe with your friends, or to pay a taxi fare for a joint ride, those are perfect instances of spending money pointlessly, for you're likely to appear a fool and nobody will appreciate it. But I hate that brief moment after the tea is finished when everyone sizes up each other. I feel as if I could hear the wheels of banal routine squeaking. To spend money to no purpose means nothing more than to oil those wheels. I find it hard enough as it is to live through a single day. If there's a way to make it less hard, however slight, why not take it? Lubricating the wheels of daily routine makes no dent whatever, so people think it a waste. For me, however, it's an awfully important way to spend money, and, of course, I'm not stingy about it, not a bit. My daughters, Chang-sook and Chang-hee, are anything but pleased about my being that way. They think I'm a spendthrift, I suppose. Probably they think I'd throw away all we have down to the last penny if they let me, for they no longer let me have any of their earnings. Instead, they put it all in the bank, so I bet they've saved up tidy sums by now. Sure, they pay for what they eat, they aren't the kind who'd hoard money without even paying for their meals. I know you look down on professions like scriptwriting and fashion designing, but they make good money, I tell you. I can survive on the money the girls hand over to me for food. The pension is enough for my pointless spending.

You think you have some right to disapprove, clicking your tongue like that? But then, you wouldn't know, would you, that living out a single day can be like pulling a heavy wagon. Before I lost Chang-hwan, living was effortless for me, too, something that went smoothly and naturally of its own accord. Time flew by like running water. Since I never focused fully on the growing child, and never really looked at the calendar, there was never a spare moment to pause and ponder how fleetingly time was passing, you know. Perhaps it rushed by too fast and that was why I wanted to oppose it. The nicest thing anybody could say was to tell me how young I looked. Not any more. When people say I look young or I look good, it sounds like a curse to me. Then again, it's not like I want them to say I look old or haggard. I feel bad to hear such things, it makes me feel that my daily pain and suffering have been uncovered. It's a mystery to me why we Koreans are so inclined to comment on the other's physical condition when we meet: "How young you look!," "Have you been ill?," "You look spent!," and on and on.

What else was important once, but no longer, you ask? Well, you're the one who's doing things you used not to, don't you think? I mean, you show interest in the kind of story you never would sit still for years ago. Anyway, back then I used to think only tangible things, what I could see with my eyes, were important, but that's not so now. Now I find myself chasing after something invisible all day long. No, sister. This isn't a question of body and soul. That's too grandiose a subject for me. It's more a question of roses and fragrance. The roses are over there, but their fragrance is all over the room. In what form do fragrances exist, I wonder? That's about as far as I go. This year one of my house plants bloomed. Its blossoms were so shabby and dull I didn't even notice. Then, one day I walked in the house to find the whole place filled with the odor. It almost made me dizzy, and it dawned on me that people actually might be suffocated by the fragrance of flowers. I'm not saying I like that particular scent. For days I was perplexed that a thing, unquestionably a single entity, exists in two distinct ways. Once the flower is gone, so is the fragrance, of course I know that, but why do you say it in such a heartless voice?

The other day, Chang-sook brought home a big hunk of oxtail. She told me to cut it into several pieces and make soup. God only knows what she was thinking, for she knew very well that I can't stand meaty dishes. And my younger girl, Chang-hee, chimed in with her sister, lecturing me about how I was embarrassing them because I didn't eat enough, I was just skin and bones and looked ready to collapse at any moment. What worthless pieces of crap they are! Ordering me, their frigging mother, to fatten up so they don't lose face, huh? I didn't even bother to reproach them. Just as I was told, I dumped the stuff in a big stainless steel pot and started to boil it. I poured in plenty of water and the pot supposedly has a double or triple layered bottom, anyway I had no reason to doubt it was a first quality pot, specially treated steel, or whatever, so I let it boil all day long. It ended up thoroughly burned, and the bottom of the pot was ruined. You say I burned it because my heart wasn't in it? Well, you're right. Where in the world will you find a mother who pours her heart into something solely for her own body's well-being? Only when the house filled up with reeking smoke did I realize I'd left something on the fire in the kitchen. That damned oxtail was like charcoal, all black and shrunken, but the stench was so bad I couldn't conceal from the girls that I'd burned it. The tail didn't shrink, in fact it expanded, you know, because of the smell. I got rid of the

charred meat easily enough, but the stink lingered for more than a
month. There wasn't a corner in the house free of that smell. Even now
when I roll over in bed I sometimes catch a whiff of that smell. I guess
the stench lodged itself in the creases of the pillowcases, too. I asked
myself, just what did that lousy oxtail think it was, still hanging around
in another form after the charcoal was gone? Sister, I'm not a bit sorry
that I burned and wasted the oxtail, but I can't stop wondering about
the change it underwent that made its presence linger for so long. It's
more than curiosity. For me, it's become an obsession.

Sister, please, don't jump to the conclusion that I'm searching for
something akin to a human soul in trivial objects like flowers or ox-
tails. It's just a kind of habit. When I come back home after an outing,
there are times I have to unlock the door myself and times when
Chang-sook or Chang-hee opens the door from inside, right? That you
like it better when someone's there to greet you than when nobody's
there is just human nature, I guess. But for me, it's the reverse. When
the girls greet me I feel Chang-hwan's absence so much more, I miss
him so much that in spite of myself I drop the brave face I put on while
out and fall to pieces. But when I unlock the door with my key and
walk alone into an empty house, it's utterly different. As I head in, I
call out brightly, "Chang-hwan, Mom's home!" Tossing down my
handbag, changing my dress, getting a cold drink of water from the
refrigerator, and gulping it down, I keep on talking to him the whole
time. At those moments the entire house, every nook and cranny, is
filled with Chang-hwan's presence. I actually experience that I am in
him. I'm not sure which one of me is real. That one day he, my sound
and healthy son, suddenly disappeared, how on earth can I believe
that? Sister, I can't help thinking that we survived in such a cruel
world. Is it actually possible that there was such a ruthless and heartless world once? But then, sister, do you think we've lived through to
the end of that cruel world?

What's this weakling attitude all about? You say you thought I'd
gotten past all that by now, judging from my brave gestures and stately
demeanor up to now? So, even in your eyes I appeared fine and normal, didn't I? I bet it never occurred to you what heartrending effort it
takes for one who's feeling far from fine to appear to be fine, did it?
Probably you've never thought about the word "galaxy," either. When
it comes to a galaxy's scale, to the number of galaxies in the universe
besides the one to which our solar system belongs, or the fact that

more galaxies will continue to be discovered, I bet you don't know half as much as I do. Maybe that seems like an insult to you, you who are so proud of your admission to a high school in the Japanese colonial period, always saying that was more prestigious than being admitted to Seoul National University is today. So why "galaxy" out of the blue? I'll tell you why. The spell I chant whenever living becomes too much to bear begins with none other than this galaxy.

The galaxy consists of innumerable stars including the sun of our solar system. The distance between the focal point of the solar system, the sun, and the earth is about 500 light-seconds, and Pluto, which has the outermost orbit in the solar system, is about 5.5 light-hours from the sun. The diameter of the galaxy is about 100,000 light-years, and our sun is merely a small, peripheral star 30,000 light-years from the galaxy's center. One light-year is a unit of distance, the distance traveled by a ray of light constantly moving at 300,000 kilometers per second for one year. But the galaxy is not infinite. For there are plenty of other galaxies besides our own in the universe. The distance between our galaxy and the one next closest to it is about one million light-years. There exist galaxies one billion light-years away from us, but they're accelerating and going even farther away from us, because the infinite realm we call "the universe" is infinitely expanding. One light-year is a unit of distance, the distance covered by a ray of light traveling for one year without stopping, nine trillion four thousand six hundred and seventy kilometers.

That is more or less the essence of my spell. Where did I pick up all of that? I read it in a book that was lying around the house, *Astronomy for Boys* or some such title. It's an old, tattered book my children read when they were young, so the information may not be accurate. And there may be some parts I memorized incorrectly. Even if I make mistakes, it's no big deal, you know. Whether it's a trillion light-years or two million light-years, either way the numbers are beyond the reach of my imagination. Accuracy is not the point here. The point is that nothing is as effective as such an astronomical unit to reduce the earth, the place we live, to less than the size of a grain of sand on the beach of a wide, wide sea. Accordingly, things such as the destiny, the life or death, of human beings living on that speck of sand become utterly trivial. Now, do you see why it works as a spell for me? If only for the moment, the massive sorrow that feels like a mountain to me becomes, like that speck, so tiny and senseless. It's no longer necessary to think about what it all means. The degree of accuracy in what I'm repeating is just as pointless. Once I rattle it off in one breath, like a reflex, I feel sleepily enshrouded in a sweet emptiness. Sister, that's how I've been living all along. If the spell had continued to work, I wouldn't have told you about it now. You see, there were times when even that spell was no help to me. Now that the spell has become useless, that's why I'm telling you about it.

About ten days ago, I think it was, Myung-ae, my closest friend from high school — I mean the one I mentioned to you a while ago — well, Myung-ae said she'd like to take me someplace to pay a visit to a sick person. After hearing more, I was reluctant to go because I didn't think it was a thing I had any obligation to do. The woman was from the same high school, but we had never been good friends. Since graduation I hadn't seen her, not even a chance encounter. Besides, the sick person wasn't her, but her son, so why should I pop up all of a sudden, I thought? When I refused to go, Myung-ae said the son had been a friend of Chang-hwan and had come to my son's funeral. That was her bait to lure me along. My Chang-hwan, I told myself, departed with the entire nation in mourning, and if this friend was just one of so many people in this country who mourned Chang-hwan, there was nothing so special about him. All the same, my heart was giving in.

So, without even asking about the boy's condition, where and how he fell ill and so on, I just went along with Myung-ae. Wait, I did ask if the illness was the fatal kind. Myung-ae's reply was strange, somehow. "If so, what more could you ask?" That's what she said, you know. Then and there I should have inquired in more detail, but hearing her say such a thing, so callous about the life of another woman's son, made me choke down a sudden disgust for Myung-ae, and I clammed up. The house was in Seoul all right, but far enough away to take most of the day to get there. It made me think Myung-ae was a real busy-body to search out a friend with an invalid in the family and to pay a visit so far away. You know, my home is in the far east on the south side of the Han river. That house is located on the western outskirts north of the river. When we finally got to the neighborhood, a labyrinth of narrow and winding alleys, it seemed very old and rundown. It surprised me that such an area still stood so unchanged — time had passed it by. Myung-ae had been there before, but she made several wrong turns before we finally found the right house.

The friend is living alone with her sick son. I was told that the sick one is the youngest, and his elder brother and sister are married, enjoying health and prosperity. The illness is not just any illness. A few years ago the boy was in a car accident, and his brain and spinal column were injured. Ever since, he has been paralyzed from the waist down, and, to make matters worse, he is suffering from dementia. He'd lain helpless for quite a while after being struck by a hit-and-run driver, but apparently there was still life in him when he was found. I suppose that after the family was informed of the accident they did what they could to provide the best treatment for him. It was then, I later heard, that the family's wealth went down the drain. The mother has been caring for her sick son for just three years, but she's turned into such an old hag I could barely believe she really was one of our classmates from high school. Especially since I was never a close friend, I couldn't recover her old face from the face of that old woman. The first thing that came into my mind was that I shouldn't have come. She didn't seem pleased or shocked to see us. She treated us as if we were her neighbors who were coming in and out of the house all the time. I couldn't begin to guess her son's age, either. From his bone structure, the young man in the bed seemed stocky and strong, but he was on the fat side and his face, apart from occasional muscle twitches, showed no expression, nothing resembling joy, anger, sorrow, or pleasure. I felt too awkward to look him in the face.

Instead of calling her son by his name, she referred to him hatefully as her "foe" or her "arch enemy." Every sentence out of her mouth ended with a string of curses. What despair, what desolate panic she must have endured to reach such a state, I told myself. If that wasn't hell, I don't know what is. Even as she stuffed her son's mouth with the canned pineapple we'd brought, she'd say, "Scarf this up, my enemy, and croak." After treating me casually, as if I were her next-door neighbor, suddenly she gave me a knowing look and blurted out, "Phew, so you've come to ogle at this spectacle, something worse than dying!" I tell you, sister, that's what she said.

I was choking with humiliation, but I couldn't say a word in response. She looked so horribly desolate she seemed entitled to say even worse things than that. Besides I felt more resentment toward Myung-ae than toward her. As soon as I went into the house I had a vague idea why Myung-ae had dragged me all that way, but now it had become crystal clear. Myung-ae and her ilk always hushed it up when celebrating their sons' special occasions, reluctant to invite me lest I envy them. Now, she was trying for the opposite reason to show me the wretched sight of this mother and her son. Witness a tragedy worse than death and be consoled! That was her aim, I guess. Lower than low, that was, and abusing human nature at its most vulnerable point. I wanted to conceal that vulnerability at all costs. That was why I'd shielded myself by never envying others' sons, no matter who they might be. It made me miserable that my best friend, none other than Myung-ae, had treated me like that. Still, things might have been different if we'd left the house after that. I might have begun consoling myself by picturing that woman's paralyzed son instead of using my chant about galaxies, who knows?

After feeding her son three big rings of pineapple, right in front of us she casually rolled him over on his bed. It was a real feat, I tell you. I couldn't believe it. She does it several times a day to keep the son from getting bedsores. First she lays him on his stomach, then rolls him onto his back, then turns him on his side. She rolled that massive frame of her son's around at will, all the while massaging the parts of him that had been in contact with the bed, and keeping up an incessant chatter.

"Lord, this blob of an enemy is so damned heavy! He weighs a ton, a ton, I tell you. No worries, not a trouble in the world, eats well, good digestion, never fails to shit up a storm, no wonder he's so big! Thanks to this blob, this foe of mine, I won't live to a ripe old age, not a chance. What if I drop dead and leave you behind, what if I just shut my eyes, uh? How can I close my eyes with you here, what would become of you? You and those worthless limbs of yours, can't even drag yourself around to beg. Poor me, dear God, what've I done to deserve this?"

Meanwhile she kept on rolling and massaging the invalid this way and that. God knows where that wizened hag found the strength, and she was handling her son as if he were light as a feather, I'm not lying. Like the kids say, it was "awesome." Myung-ae and I were so stunned we forgot ourselves and just stared for a while. Then Myung-ae, muttering "My, my," reached out to lend a helping hand. I, too, stretched out my hand to help turn the patient around. But, lo and behold! The instant our hands touched him, the patient let out a hideous shriek. His eyes, cloudy and vacant till then, became wild like the eyes of an enraged beast. You have no idea how startled I was. I felt like my fingertips were incinerated. You see, that wildness in his eyes showed his deep trust and contentment. Only then did I decipher the vivid and tender love in his mother's expression, which I'd thought was deformed by endless curses.

"Dear me, this blob of an enemy is mimicking a dutiful son again," she said.

Judging by this remark, it obviously wasn't the first time he'd refused to let a stranger touch him instead of his mother.

Suddenly I was so smitten with jealousy that I was totally at a loss. I was the one who had never envied the son of another no matter how wonderful or successful he might be. In this case it wasn't good looks, success, health — nothing I could see, feel, or touch. That's why the jealousy was so agonizing. How could such a jealousy, so strong, so insufferably strong, exist in this world? I felt like my heart had been pierced through. Such agony, such bitterness, I was on the verge of crying aloud. No, not here, shouldn't cry here, I told myself, trying hastily to chant my galaxy spell. It was no use. I found nothing there, I mean nothing in the galaxy chant. Nothing. Finally I let go and wept. Sister, I didn't know I'd been holding back so many tears. My weeping was uncontrollable; a louder wail there never was. Once the tears started to flow, my galaxy chant drifted off like a dry reed. Whether that galaxy was the infinite or a dry reed, it has its place only in our minds, and without us, whether or not it actually exists makes no difference at all, don't you think? As I let out that wail, my friend, Myung-ae, was at a loss. I'm afraid the mother thought I was overcome by pity. She got upset and angrily told me I had no cause to feel so sorry for her. But Myung-ae was different. She seemed to have divined my mind somewhat. After all, we were old friends. She apologized, saying she'd wronged me. Not just then, but for days afterward, she kept saying she was sorry. But she'd done nothing wrong.

That outburst of crying liberated me, I felt. It was as if I'd finally freed myself from the stranger I'd forced myself to become with a frightful effort. Ever since, I've been living for the joy of crying when I feel like crying. That's probably why the date of the great-grandmother's ceremony slipped my mind. Even the galaxy has drifted off, so you can't expect a date for remembering some dead in-law I never once set eyes on to stay with me, can you? From now on, I'll cry whenever I like, that's how I'm going to live. Whatever drifts away from me, well, let it. From now on, I'm not going to try to pretend everything is fine. One day my sound and healthy son suddenly disappeared from this world. Thanks to that, all at once I was a glorious mother. How could that be just fine? Sister, how could such a cruel world actually exist? But then, do you think we've lived through the end of that cruel world? Are we done with it? You've never wondered, have you, if by any chance a tip of the tail of that monster has survived and is lurking somewhere even now? Sister, say something, please, anything. Why, you're crying now, aren't you, dear? Sister, how am I to go on living this life if you cry? You must go on being like a cliff till the end. You've always been the cliff where I wail. Even when I cried silently, I needed this cliff of wailing. No cliff of wailing is itself allowed to cry, not in this world, my dear.

translated by Chun Kyung-Ja

Chun Kyung-Ja holds a Ph.D. from the University of Texas at Austin and is a professor of English at the Catholic University of Korea, currently teaching Korean at Harvard University. She has published many translations of modern Korean prose and poetry, including such novels as *Peace Under Heaven* by Ch'ae Man-Sik (1991) and *The Shadow of Arms* by Hwang Suk-Young (1994).

In 1995, for her translation of *Peace Under Heaven*, Professor Chun won the Korean Cultural and Art Foundation grand prize for Korean literature translation.

The Translators:

Steven Epstein is a professor of classics at the Victoria University in Wellington, New Zealand.

John Frankl is a graduate student in the department of East Asian Languages and Civilizations at Harvard University.

Ryu Suk-Hee is a novelist residing in Seattle.

Ryu Young-Joo is a graduate student in the department of East Asian Languages and Cultures at UCLA.